Writing in an
Alien World

Writing in an Alien World

Basic Writing and the Struggle for Equality in Higher Education

Deborah Mutnick

Boynton/Cook Publishers
HEINEMANN
Portsmouth, NH

Boynton/Cook Publishers, Inc.
A subsidiary of Reed Elsevier Inc.
361 Hanover Street
Portsmouth NH 03801-3912

Offices and agents throughout the world

Every effort has been made to contact the copyright holders for permission to reprint borrowed material where necessary. We regret any oversights that may have occurred and would be pleased to rectify them in future printings of this work.

Excerpts from "Teaching Language in Open Admissions: A Look at the Context" by Adrienne Rich. From *Harvard English Studies* (vol. 4, 1973). Reprinted by permission of the publisher, Harvard University Department of English and American Literature and Language.

Library of Congress Cataloging-in-Publication Data
CIP is on file with the Library of Congress.
0-86709-371-4

Editor: Peter R. Stillman
Production: Melissa L. Inglis
Cover design: Jenny Jensen Greenleaf

99 98 97 96 95 DA 1 2 3 4 5 6 7 8 9
Printed in the United States of America on acid-free paper

Contents

Acknowledgments

This book grew out of a convergence between my doctoral dissertation and my involvement in revising a basic reading and writing curriculum. It reflects what I have learned from teachers, colleagues, and particularly students. As is always the case, it would be impossible to acknowledge all those who influenced me and contributed to this project. A partial list, however, must include thanks to the members of my dissertation committee, John Mayher, Berenice Fisher, and Keith Gilyard; and my dissertation support group, Harriet Malinowitz, Sue Ruskin, Joyce Harte, and Nancy Biederman.

I also thank my colleagues at Long Island University, especially Seymour Kleinberg, Barbara Henning, Esther Hyneman, Naomi Rand, and my former colleague, now at the University of Pittsburgh, Jim Seitz. I thank Provost Gale Haynes, whose type of leadership makes possible the reforms I believe are needed in higher education; and I pay tribute to Barbara Witenko, whose work with students in the Higher Education Opportunities Program will inspire many generations to come. Thanks also to Peter Stillman and Melissa Inglis at Heinemann-Boynton/Cook for their support for this project.

To the students and teachers who participated in the study, I give special credit and thanks. Their life stories, insights, and "conflict and struggle" on the academic border inspired my research and taught me a great deal about basic reading and writing.

On a more personal note, I thank John Sandman, Barbara Mutnick, Ilse Lind Polskin, Barbara Danish, and Mady Schutzman.

Above all, I thank my parents, George and Margaret Mutnick, to whom I dedicate this book. Although I am sad they will never read it, I take comfort in the fact that their spirits infused the whole project. My mother, who was an English teacher, would have been deeply interested in my teaching and research. My father did live to see the beginning of the dissertation, and I thank him for the conversations we had, especially at Schroon Lake, about Bakhtin, Marx, and everything else under the sun.

Introduction

*. . . The ideological becoming of a human being . . . is
the process of selectively assimilating the words of others. (1981, p. 341)*

Mikhail Bakhtin

*. . . To suggest that not only dead white men have writ-
ten (and will always write) the crucial text is to threaten
the entire notion of knowledge as something timeless,
universal, and therefore, on another plane above the historical and intimate concreteness and specificity of
"racism" and "sexism". . .*

*It's not just a matter of white people at the top and
people of color at the bottom (although that's often the
way it turns out), it's about the notion of order as an
arrangement in which some people are always better off
than others because it helps foster the inexorable self-
loathing that keeps everybody in their place, paying
taxes for cops and robbers shenanigans and awaiting the
inevitable expose at the televised hearings. (1988, p. 166)*

Michele Wallace

When I teach Michele Wallace's essay "Invisibility Blues" in my basic
reading and writing course, students often have difficulty understanding it. They struggle with what Wallace means by "the historical and
intimate concreteness and specificity of 'racism' and 'sexism'. . . ,"
unsure what a "historical context" is or how specific knowledge or
experience differs from that which is represented as timeless and universal. Together we unpack the language and discuss issues of inclusion and exclusion, mainstream and marginal voices, and what sort of
social arrangement might replace one in which a "top" and a "bottom"
are givens. The theme of the course is "identity," and our work focuses
on how the self is constructed in and through history, language, and
literature. We read published and student texts that emanate from various sociocultural locations in an attempt to theorize about ourselves
in relation to others in our multiple roles.

Through our investigation, which necessitates close reading, interpreting, criticizing, intertextual analysis, arguing, writing, rethinking, revising, and editing, students learn academic skills that hopefully enable them to participate more forcefully in public discourse of all kinds, inside and outside the university. Typically, at the beginning of the session devoted to Wallace's essay, the students complain they are baffled and frustrated. In an evening class I taught in the spring of 1994, composed mainly of older working students, I remember a roomful of strained, weary faces as we launched our discussion. Esmie, a woman from Jamaica in her forties, sat tensely on the edge of her chair, her mouth slightly parted, as if she needed more air to survive the distress she experienced in her effort to comprehend the essay. We proceeded slowly, looking at the examples Wallace gives of the invisibility of people of color in the news media, such as the TV cameras' focus on white male runners-up in the New York City Marathon, rather than the black winner from Kenya.

When we got to the passage about knowledge as timeless and universal or historically concrete and specific, Esmie looked at me nervously and confessed in a small voice, "Professor, I'm lost; I don't know what she means here." Other students, who both sympathized and identified with her, echoed her bewilderment as mature adults who genuinely wanted to understand the enigmatic words on the page and the historical contexts that gave them meaning. Sentence by sentence, we read the passage together, discussing the traditional canon and why it has been challenged, imagining what "the crucial text" might be, and distinguishing between universal and specific, timeless and historical. By the end of the session, most of the students grasped Wallace's thesis and could begin to use the terms of her argument in their own attempts to make sense of the theme of identity. As she left the room, Esmie assured me that she understood the essay better than she had before class but was still perplexed. "I try so hard, Professor," she sighed. "Really I do."

Basic Writing's Future:
Utopian Fantasy or "Remedial Underworld"?

I begin with the epigraph from Wallace's essay and a description of the classroom in order to summon two images: one is a vision of how universities themselves might be reconfigured to transform hierarchical structures into more egalitarian places for learning; the other is of the basic writing class as a site of cultural hybridity, intel-

lectual discipline, and collaborative spirit. Although this picture of
the academy may seem like a utopian fantasy, in some ways it has
already begun to materialize. For one, throughout the twentieth century, American universities and colleges have become steadily more
diverse in terms of gender, race, and class, a transformation in
which basic writing plays a small but important part. The phenomenon that gave rise to the current notion of basic writing was the
struggle for open admissions in the late 1960s and early '70s; but
other factors had already opened the academy's doors, from the creation of the meritocratic "new university" of the late nineteenth
century to G.I. Bill of Rights subsidies for college-bound World War
II veterans, the post-Sputnik expansion of higher education, and the
scientific-technological revolution in industry and commerce.

The democratization of higher education—far from wholly
achieved—is in the mid-1990s severely threatened by state and federal budget cuts, attacks on open admissions and affirmative action
policies, persistent racial and class inequality in the schools, and
structural changes like post-secondary education's increasing
reliance on part-time labor. At schools like mine, in which over
half the freshman class places into basic writing and the majority
of students are bound for professional programs, the future—insofar as education is a vehicle for democracy—seems to be written on
the wall with invisible ink. That is, if such universities continue to
expand and provide a liberal arts education to students entering
the technical and service job market, the priority should be to cultivate what Paulo Freire calls *conscientizacao*—critical consciousness—through reading and writing, enabling students to understand and help shape rapidly changing global realities. But what
seems obvious to some is not yet perceptible—or palatable—to
those nostalgic for a more homogeneous past, hostile to the aspirations of the dispossessed, or bitter about their own attainments and
prospects.

In his recent book on what he sees as the failure of open admissions at City College, James Traub (1994) presents a dismal picture
of a "remedial underworld" jeopardizing City's "glorious past." He
argues that "it is the students, and not the institution, that must
change," and that high standards are incompatible with educating
"large numbers of deeply disadvantaged students" (p. 204). Often
framed by the question of whether colleges should be in the "business of remediation," the issues Traub raises reflect widespread, if
frequently ill-defined and misinformed, concerns about literacy that
blur the distinction between linguistic etiquette and syntactic and
semantic coherence. In the absence of a public dialogue on literacy
and standards, the gap between popular and professional concep-

tions of writing instruction will widen, and these distinctions will elude most people as compositionists revise the writing curriculum in a vacuum.

Thus, while critics like Traub decry open admissions in fora like *The New Yorker*, and call for more stringent standards, many composition scholars advocate a pedagogy devoted to "reading the word and the world" that few people outside—not to mention within—the academy understand and/or support. According to this view, broadly stated, the point of composition instruction, including basic writing, is to equip students with literacy skills along with a critical-historical perspective on reading and writing in school, work, and everyday life. As the attack on open admissions escalates with deep budget cuts and, in some cases, total elimination of entitlement programs, composition teachers will need to explain this theory and method of writing instruction to a broader constituency. Such a public debate would both insert writing pedagogy into the battle for educational equality and underscore the effects on higher education of global economic trends like flexible, temporary labor; corporate downsizing; and technological changes, including distance learning and computerized classrooms.

Marginal Voices:
The Complex Role of Basic Writing in the Academy

The scope and intent of writing instruction may be construed as narrowly as dotting "i's" and crossing "t's" and as broadly as cultural or discourse studies. Writing and rhetoric have either been viewed as tangential to the construction of knowledge, as Plato insisted, or as central to its production, reception, and transformation. Within English departments, literature still often remains the elite discourse, while composition is accorded low status, driven by surface correctness; at the same time, aided by renewed interest in rhetoric and the "linguistic turn" in postmodern theory, the teaching of writing has come to be viewed, at least in some quarters, as central to English studies, if not the entire liberal arts curriculum. These competing visions of the role of composition in English departments are directly related to the emergence this century of mass post-secondary education, which has both foregrounded the teaching of writing and posed a "multicultural" challenge to traditional literary studies and canons.

The rapid influx of students into colleges and universities, particularly in the wake of open admissions, accentuated a perceived need for writing instruction and influenced research and curriculum reform in English and across the disciplines. In one sense, students on the academic margin helped transform universities into more democratic institutions by their sheer presence, diversifying formerly all-white campuses, and by the ramifications of that diversity on the canon, the curriculum, and the professoriate. On the other hand, educational reforms like open admissions, though spurred by grassroots political demands, also reflect economic and demographic trends as universities expand to new populations to meet both the growing demand for college degrees and the needs of a new technocratic class. While these structural changes revitalized the theory and practice of teaching writing, they also reinforced already existing social divisions through the creation of "basic writing" to accommodate "underprepared" students and the hiring of a part-time adjunct work force to teach them. Especially in urban universities with large inner-city and immigrant populations, increases in basic writing courses and part-time staff together produced an academic margin rife with contradictions.

When I first embarked in 1991 on the doctoral research project that forms the basis of this book, I set out to examine the "social construction of basic writing" and understand how student and teacher perceptions of themselves and each other interact with the existing social and discursive structures they encounter in basic writing courses. I theorized that the basic writer is constructed as "other," situated on the academic margin, and that, underlying the apparent linguistic codes that signified "basic writing," I would find less visible racial, gender, and class codes. In other words, I viewed the construction and institutionalization of basic writing as sociohistorical, economic, and political; hence, I speculated that its linguistic form, while often identifiable as a type of dialect or language interference, weak sentence boundaries, convoluted syntax, or gross misspellings, would merely reflect the far more intractable socioeconomic roots of class and racial oppression in the U.S. that give rise to what Michael Harrington (1962) called the "other America" or what Jonathan Kozol (1991) more recently termed "savage inequalities."

Within the university, the basic writing course has enabled socially marginal students to attend college and, at least to some degree, compete for jobs in a period of economic decline. Basic writing has also influenced composition theory and pedagogy by providing a rich terrain for research on the writing process, the relation of error to meaning, and the appropriation of often conflicting discourses. From Mina Shaughnessy to Min-Zhan Lu, an impressive array of composition scholars has transformed basic writing from its initial ghettoization as a skills-driven course to a model of composition instruction more akin to a graduate seminar. However, basic writing's position on the periphery of the university, often depicted as a revolving door, has created a subordinate class that reproduces the tracking system long viewed as problematic in high schools. On the one hand, conservative and, increasingly, liberal critics like James Traub deplore what they see as diminished standards and a conversion of the college curriculum to remedial instruction; on the other hand, composition theorists themselves have begun to question the validity of a two-track system in which some students, often arbitrarily, are remanded to basic writing while others take freshman composition.

It is unfortunate that these criticisms of basic writing coincide with one another, insofar as the pedagogical argument to dismantle an inegalitarian system may fuel the neoconservative agenda to tighten standards and deny admission altogether to students deemed unqualified. Those who favor a pedagogy of the contact zone (Pratt, 1995), as David Bartholomae (1993) has articulated it, would not exclude students now labeled "basic writers" from the university, but rather rethink the "institutional position" of the basic writing course in order to recapture its lost "strategic value" (pp. 20–21). However, the strategic value of basic writing today, in light of escalating conservative attacks on social services, the humanities, and education, is perhaps precisely its established place—clearly already a contact zone—within the academy, particularly if it is reconceived as a location in which alliances between teachers and students could subvert the margin-center hierarchy.

Contrary to the neoconservative view of basic writing, the majority of students are capable of academic studies. Only a fraction of individuals are admitted, despite evidence like unreadable placement exams, who seem doomed to fail due to disabilities of various, often interrelated kinds. Another, much larger, group are indeed weak readers and writers who need strong support to succeed academically. If basic writers' places in universities and colleges were assured, with sufficient resources and support services, the critique of basic writing as a liberal project, reinforcing the very inequalities it sought to redress, would be overdue. Presently, however, as attacks on open admissions intensify and the demand increases for a college education, such arguments, as Bartholomae acknowledges, may justify institutional reversals of the gains made in the 1960s and '70s, returning not only to a more traditional curriculum of "bonehead" English, but to a more traditional student body as well. Nor is it only the conservative agenda that makes the idea of getting rid of basic writing problematic. Regardless of political perspective, faculty across the disciplines reflect public concerns about illiteracy and often doubt or actively resist the goals and methods of recent trends in writing instruction, expecting basic writing students to accomplish in four years, if not fourteen weeks, what most middle class students start to learn as preverbal toddlers.

The other group situated on the academic margin, which according to some predictions will constitute sixty percent of college faculty nationwide by the year 2000, is part-time adjuncts. Of their growing ranks, a large proportion of adjunct faculty teach writing—often basic writing—courses. Like their students, they are constructed by the sociocultural structures and practices that define academic communities: if they do not hold doctorates, they are often considered less qualified than their full-time colleagues; if they do and have not yet found full-time jobs, they are suspect and therefore less employable. The widespread promise of academic jobs in the 1990s, as senior faculty retired, has of course not come true. The increasing national reliance on adjunct instructors, nowhere more evident than in English departments, constitutes a microcosm of the global effects of post-cold war capitalism: deregulation, the dispersion of cheap surplus labor, and the use of flexible, temporary, and part-time workers in a system marked by "the shrinking labor market core and the expanding periphery" (Ohmann, 1993, p. 44).

To offer basic writing—or any writing—courses in sufficient quantity and quality to support open admissions and other nonexclusive policies would require major reform in higher education. Either universities will have to reallocate resources to support student need and hire more trained, full-time faculty, or discard the very concept of a liberal arts curriculum. As Paul Lauter (1991) has pointed out, a two-tiered system of higher education has already emerged, in which more privileged students attend elite schools staffed predominantly by full-time professors, while nonelite, working students attend technical and service schools staffed mainly by part-time faculty. To hire adjuncts—at least those who staff writing courses and whose livelihood is teaching—in such large numbers is to exploit them; they truly become a reserve army of the unemployed. And although individually they no doubt rank among the best teachers, institutionally their transience cannot help but limit their commitment to teaching and diminish the quality of education.

Along with basic writing students and part-time writing teachers, full-time composition specialists and program administrators in most institutions remain marginalized, if for no other reason than that the rest of the university, including English faculty, hold them accountable for a "literacy crisis" rooted in socioeconomic problems outside the schools. In addition, until recently, composition research and scholarship were not viewed as legitimate academic pursuits that counted toward hiring, promotion, and tenure. To some extent, writing-across-the-curriculum initiatives have challenged assumptions about language learning, but academics frequently harbor as many commonsense notions about writing as anyone else, putting correctness before meaning and tapping into their own deepseated insecurities about writing. In light of these persistent tensions, it will be interesting to see what happens to the generation of Ph.D.s in composition and rhetoric recently hired or searching for full-time positions.

According to critics like Susan Miller (1991), the schism between literature and composition in English departments is far from mended, and while calls for "reading and writing" programs from freshman courses to the graduate level have been made, there appears to be no rush to implement them. A key tension persists between those who defend the canon on the basis of literary value and those who promote the production of texts in their classrooms in order to give student writing value; put another way, the traditionalists who defend the canon in its various formations, including, more and more, the "multicultural" canons, recycle a view of English literature as "a moral ideology for the modern age" (Eagleton, 1983, p. 27), while those, myself included, who would "read the world," subjecting a wide range of discourses to critical analysis, might be said to be practicing cultural studies.

How did I arrive at this juncture, what social and historical forces shaped me, and what ideological perspectives form the interpretive lens through which I see my research on basic writing?

My "Ideological Becoming"

My research, though completed prior to the current debate on basic writing, hopefully speaks to the complexity of these problems. I studied a basic reading and writing (BRW) program at Downtown University (DTU)[1], an urban, medium-sized, four-year, private school, where I got my first job as an adjunct composition instructor from 1986 to 1987. I had never taken a composition course, let alone taught one—a consequence, I now realize, of the widespread elimination of the college composition requirement in the early 1970s. Although I quickly eschewed the life of an adjunct, supplementing my income by the more lucrative if infinitely more boring job of

---

1. Unless otherwise indicated, all names of participants and places in the study are pseudonyms.

word processing, I was thrilled to find work that, as my father put it, could be an avocation as well as a vocation. I left DTU to enter a nearby doctoral program in composition and rhetoric, and, much to my own surprise, returned two years later to direct the Writing Center. In 1989, I helped develop the BRW program, implemented in 1990, and then went on in 1992 to direct the DTU Writing Program. I was thus immersed in basic writing pedagogy as I decided to focus my dissertation on the theory and practice of basic writing. Inspired by Mikhail Bakhtin's essay "Discourse in the Novel" in *The Dialogue Imagination* (1981) I could see that "basic writing" embodied the sort of *heteroglossia* that Bakhtin described as multiple social discourses that coexist and compete with one another.

These discourses, according to Bakhtin, are inherently ideological; thus, one's "ideological becoming" is "the process of selectively assimilating the words of others" (p. 341). As a "red diaper baby" (a child of former members of the Young Communist League, the youth group of the Communist Party), I grew up in a deeply politicized household that resonated with the words of my parents and other leftists. In the 1960s, my teenage years, their words competed with other voices, such as the Republican views of some friends' conservative parents, the audacious politics of the New Left, and the irreverent antics of the counterculture. My parents' lives had been transformed in the 1930s, when they became radicalized as college students, escaping the provincial, bigoted worlds of their families into an intellectual milieu that, whatever its limitations, imbued them with a consciousness of history, what Simone de Beauvoir called "the force of circumstance." It was their awareness of themselves as historical subjects, agents—at least to some extent—of their own destinies that impressed me as I was growing up.

My own identity has been shaped, in turn, by the political struggles and historical events I lived through: the civil rights movement, racial conflict in my town and high school, the war in Vietnam, the revolutionary movements in Africa and Latin America, feminism, the anti-nuclear movement, and more recently, the struggle for gay and lesbian rights. Awareness of the gross inequities and injustices in the United States and abroad has guided my work as a teacher with students whose educational experiences are often jeopardized by their social locations; it has also clearly influenced the type of research project I undertook, my interest in poststructuralism, especially its connection to Marxist thought, and my attraction to social and dialogic theories of language.

While I feel fortunate to have been exposed early on to progressive values that have given my life meaning in ways, admittedly, that seem almost religious at times, the assimilation of others' words has not been easy. One of the hardest realizations for me was the discovery, in my twenties, that the feminist ideals I had claimed as a teenager did not make me immune to the oppression of women. Nor was I prepared to deal with the class differences I confronted as a college freshman at a small midwestern liberal arts school when my insecurities, inherited from my parents along with their politics, left me feeling invisible. I suffered from a typical dilemma experienced by bright, middle-class, white females who assume a privileged position in the world only to find it is denied them. Although I had enough confidence as a high school student to perform music, speak in public against the war in Vietnam, and "find myself" through writing and other art forms, I was extremely shy in college, driven to silence, frightened.

In retrospect, I believe I felt overwhelmed by the college community because of a disparity between my assumption of entitlement as a middle-class person and my discovery that I was ignorant of social codes that other, more privileged, freshmen seemed to know intimately. I was often terrified of failure. This panic was accentuated by my realization that my repudiation of middle-class values as a teenager had not made me immune to them. I was a harsh social critic who fervently wanted social acceptance. The radical discourse of my childhood competed with that of middle-class, mainstream life, internally and externally, often leaving me mystified and distressed. That language eluded me, words failing me as I sat with sweaty palms listening to others speak, was for many years a mark of the impact on my life of this ideological quandary; I was engaged in what Bakhtin describes as a process of conflict and struggle in which external authoritative discourse becomes internally persuasive.

This brief account of my own ideological development parallels those of the participating students and teachers, of whom I asked questions like, "How would you describe your family's values?" and "As a child, what did you want to be when you grew up?" Such questions are crucial to a study of basic writing, insofar as we learn outside as well as inside schools, and all texts are embedded in surrounding discourses. My parents were literate, nonreligious, politically left, feminist, anti-racist, and anti-war. They took me to see foreign films as a child; they read to me and gave me books to read; and they supported my artistic, musical, and literary endeavors. Despite their radical politics, they were part of the post-war, upwardly mobile middle class, anxious about money, status, appearances; their chief contradiction was between their yearning for a meaningful intellectual and political life and their obeisance to middle class mores and financial pressures, a contradiction I too experience.

Thus I find myself teaching writing at an urban university,

obtaining the proper credentials, criticizing the very social phenomenon—the basic writing class—that has given me my job and formed a part of my social identity as an adult. My history has informed my research on basic writers and their teachers, and has led me to focus on particular social and discursive structures and practices that construct their identities through a complex process of accommodation and resistance.

Case Studies of the Social Construction of Basic Writers and Their Teachers

I conducted my research at DTU, a campus that has historically served a diverse, largely working-class student population now predominantly African American and Latino, female, and slightly older than average. In addition, there has recently been a large influx of Russian Jewish immigrants. In the late 1980s, faculty across the disciplines expressed growing concern about students' poor reading and writing skills. To address this problem, the campus curriculum committee charged members of the English Department with developing a proposal for a new basic writing course. The existing reading courses, under the auspices of the Developmental Skills Program, required students to skim for the main idea and identify topic sentences. In addition to pointing out the inadequacy of this pedagogy, we argued that separate reading and composition courses unnecessarily fragmented reading and writing, content and skills, in contradiction with the university's aim for its students to become inquiring learners. Compared to the reading program, theoretically dated and widely viewed as ineffective, the basic writing courses tended to be better taught but reflected no coherent theory or practice. Students routinely passed through the composition sequence and the reading program without learning to write or read (a complaint, by the way, that did not cease with the implementation of the BRW program); and the drop-out rate soared. It was this latter problem of student retention that pushed administrators and faculty to reconsider the basic reading and writing courses.

In 1990, the faculty senate approved a proposal, based on the program at the University of Pittsburgh described by David Bartholomae and Anthony Petrosky in *Facts, Artifacts, and Counterfacts* (1986), to reunite reading and writing under the aegis of the English Department. Premised on the belief that there is no prerequisite to reading and writing, to intellectual engagement, to academic discourse other than to begin—to read, write, talk, listen, reflect—the program invites students to read challenging books, theorize about the course themes, and write meaningful essays. This major revision of DTU's freshman curriculum combined developmental reading and basic writing courses to create two semesters of a holistic, twelve-credit, basic reading and writing program (BRW-1 and BRW-2), revolving around themes, whole books, and a seminar-style classroom. Together with two colleagues, I worked on developing a theme and description for a pilot program for the fall, as well as a plan for intensive staff development to prepare teachers—both full-timers and adjuncts—to teach the new courses.

DTU's first course in the two-semester sequence, BRW-1, "Different Voices in History,"[2] raised questions about whose "voices" enter the historical record and emphasized the social dimension of any written composition. The second course, BRW-2, "Environmental Crises," aimed to introduce students to science writing as well as invite them to become active participants in public discourse. A significant difference in DTU's adaptation of the Pittsburgh model was the expansion of the program from a six-credit course for a small percentage of students to a twelve-credit sequence that over half of DTU students pass through. In addition to the impact the DTU basic reading and writing program had on the English Department, it required a substantial commitment from the administration, one that remains controversial.

The majority of DTU students are enrolled in the university's professional schools, primarily studying pharmacy and nursing; more than half the freshman class places into the BRW program. Notwithstanding anecdotal reports of the program's success, there continues to be widespread faculty concern about students' poor reading, writing, and critical thinking skills, raising thorny questions about the program's effectiveness, particularly in relation to standards and evaluative measures. Despite attempts to acquaint faculty across the disciplines with the methods and goals of the program, their complaints still center mainly on students' error-ridden papers, echoing periodic media outcries about the "literacy crisis," and conflicting with the perception of BRW faculty (although the form/content schism can be seen among these teachers, too) that basic writing has been a site at which problems of form and content have been continually addressed.

These conflicting views of the BRW program helped me formulate my project as a lens through which to examine how the fear of low standards reinforces basic writing as an academic margin in opposition to the center. While basic writing may be a favorite

2. The original BRW-1 title, "Different Voices in History," was changed first to "Composing Ourselves and Others" and later to "Discovering Identity." The name changes indicate the controversial nature of the course, which was initially perceived by senior faculty as overly "political."

scapegoat, it serves to reassure its harshest critics by opposing the prepared to the underprepared, the normal to the remedial. Using a case study approach based on student texts, teacher commentary, and autobiographical interviews, I examined how the students perceived themselves and in turn were perceived by their teachers. Participants were enlisted through a letter to teachers in DTU's Writing Program, asking them to take part in my study and distribute a similar letter to students in their classes. I explained in the letters that the purpose of my research was to improve the quality of DTU's basic reading and writing courses. In collecting the data, I followed the guidelines for qualitative research delineated by Bogdan and Biklen (1982) insofar as my approach was: descriptive; concerned with process as much as products; inductive, grounded in interconnected if disparate evidence; and reliant on "meaning" elicited from the participants as they explored their own experiences, beliefs, and perceptions. Based on the response to my initial query, I interviewed eight BRW students and nine teachers from different sections of Basic Reading and Writing 1 (BRW-1) and Basic Reading and Writing 2 (BRW-2) in the fall of 1991.

Both student and teacher interviews consisted of a series of open-ended biographical questions that focused on three areas: educational and family history, attitude toward and experience with reading and writing, and personal goals. Additionally, the teachers were asked a set of questions about writing pedagogy (see Appendixes A and B). A key element of the interviews is what I called an "intertextual dialogue," in which participants were asked to comment on the student papers as they read aloud, creating a dialogue between the written texts and the "metacommentary." It is important to point out here that the focus of the study is on the student writing, the interview transcripts, and the semiotic process by which we construct the category of basic writer, *not* on the psychosocial or intellectual status of actual participants. In other words, I do not intend to analyze the participating individuals or make claims about their lives per se, which are obviously far more complex than my brief encounters with them represent. Rather, I want to show how, through a process of semiosis (in which both I and the participants "read" the data), we participate in constructing knowledge, in this case, through and about basic writing.

Data Analysis: Case Studies and Semiotics

The three case studies that form the core of the analysis illuminate the social construction of basic writing as a fluid, unstable border in which students *and* teachers cross boundaries and resist, contest, or confirm institutional and self-definitions. I used two primary analytical tools, one derived from traditional case study methods, the other a semiotic interpretation of student texts and interview transcripts rooted in Bakhtinian dialogic and other semiotic theories.

The semiotic analysis I use is based on theories of signification that posit linguistic and other symbolic signs as inherently rhetorical, that is, mediated by context, code, speaker, and listener. Ferdinand de Saussure's theory of linguistics is limited in that he sees the sign as a binary opposition between signifier (symbol) and signified (meaning), omits human agency, and by extension history, or the diachronic axis. It is this structural, or formalistic, tendency that postmodernists, as well as Bakhtin and C. S. Peirce, somewhat precociously, attempted to overturn by reintroducing the historical, active, living component to the rhetorical triangle—what Roland Barthes (1972) defines as signifier, signified, and sign—the third term that "is nothing but the association of the first two" (p. 121). Fundamentally, the sign is relational, its status fluid, and its meanings contested; verbal language is the paradigmatic sign system but not the only one, so that "text" can be image, sound, figure, etc., as well as the paradigmatic written word, and functions necessarily as a *trace* of discourses. As Hodge and Kress (1988) put it:

> The notion of text needs to be retained and contrasted to the notion of discourse as a process, precisely because a text is so limited and partial an object of analysis. Text is only a trace of discourses, frozen and preserved, more or less reliable or misleading. Yet discourse disappears too rapidly, surrounding a flow of texts. Analysis needs to be able to take account of both. (p. 12)

Feminist and critical pedagogies and theories have gravitated toward semiotics because of its concern with agency, subjectivity, and historical context. Thus, for example, deconstructing the sign "woman" has enabled feminist theorists to illuminate the social construction of gender by separating the referent—an actual human being—from the signifier and its signifieds.

Finally, it is to Bakhtin that I turn for the primary terms of analysis I use to discern what he calls the "interanimation" of social voices in the student papers and transcribed interviews that form the nucleus of the study. In particular, I rely on his explanation of the hybridity of language, that is, how indirect and quasi-direct discourse is quoted as reported speech, what Volosinov (1986) describes as "the 'contrived' word. All verbal activity . . . amounts to piecing together 'other persons' words' and 'words seemingly from other persons'" (p. 159). I also rely on Bakhtin's extensive explanation of dialogism, in particular, the function of centrifugal (decentralizing) and centripetal (centralizing) sociolinguistic forces. Centrifugal forces tend toward a recognition of multiple social voices and difference, while centripetal forces tend toward nationalistic and monologic discourse. One sees these trends today, for example, in the contest between bilingual education and the English Only movement, or in the often acrimonious debates on multicultural education.

The most important Bakhtinian concept in my analysis of the data flows from his discussion of externally authoritative and internally persuasive discourse. It is Bakhtin's cogent articulation of the permeable border between self and other, and the ideological accent of the word as we struggle to make what is inevitably somebody else's word our own, that transformed my own thinking about language and culture, and motivated and guided me throughout this study.

My central question is how semiotic processes of interpretation and identification, including my own, construct basic writing students *and* teachers, as well as the field of basic writing instruction, and to what extent such processes situate students and teachers to become agents or passive recipients of their educational experiences. My research hinges on problems of representation—who speaks for whom, how one renders the world through language, and what the consequences of that are. In this endeavor, I echo Linda Hutcheon's (1989) description of postmodern theory as "a strange kind of critique, one bound up, too, with its own *complicity* with power and domination, one that acknowledges that it cannot escape implication in that which it nevertheless still wants to analyze and maybe even undermine" (p. 4). In other words, as a teacher-researcher who ultimately speaks for the students and teachers in this study, I need to question my relatively privileged position at the same time that I use it to "analyze and maybe undermine" the category of basic writing.

An Overview of the Study

This study of the social construction of basic writers and their teachers developed in tandem with DTU's basic reading and writing program. Ironically, in light of the recent theoretical critiques of basic writing, the concrete realities of the program enabled me to rethink my initial questions about the political and pedagogical effects of 1) creating a separate instructional category of basic writing, and 2) assigning the "basic writing" label to students, teachers, and courses. Although these questions continued to guide the research, my focus shifted from an abstract critique of the category of basic writing to a more ethnographic exploration of how it was sociohistorically constructed, how students and teachers defined themselves within already existing structures, and how their perceptions of their experiences affected their further development. Thus the study became in part a story about DTU, the impact of the new curriculum on students and teachers, and the prospects for urban, multicultural education.

Specifically, the study has helped to assess the effectiveness of the Pittsburgh model in an urban, multicultural setting. As Pittsburgh proceeds to reassess its basic reading and writing program, it will be interesting to see how programs like DTU's respond. One answer might be to reform the rest of the English department in line with the BRW program rather than reabsorb basic writing into the mainstream. In other words, rather than ask students to "invent the university" through their appropriation of academic language, we might think of reconfiguring the academy itself, bearing in mind Michele Wallace's criticism of hierarchical thinking that presupposes a top and a bottom, a center and a margin.

The study was also inspired by my classroom experience, my theoretical interest in the dialectic between individual consciousness and social systems in arenas like language and culture, and my commitment to democratizing higher education. I am interested in how inexperienced adult readers and writers develop intellectual abilities along the lines suggested by Antonio Gramsci's (1971) notion of the "organic intellectual": how formal aspects of language become internalized; how form, function, context, and content relate; how ideology suffuses them; and what sort of pedagogical interventions make sense. However, I also remain interested in basic writing from a more structuralist perspective, as a social site that serves numerous, often contradictory purposes—namely, its dual role as a border crossing into universities (and sometimes the job market) and a border patrol denying entry. Underlying this view is a sense of the interplay between these two dimensions of basic writing—the process by which students develop as readers and writers and the social context in which that happens.

When I started this research project, I questioned basic writing's construction of the student as "other." As in other types of oppression—sexism, for example—the basic writing student is often viewed as alien and inferior, the "body" of his or her texts regarded contemptuously. Of course, many basic writing students happen also to be women and/or people of color and/or working-class, so the objectification is compounded. However, as I pored over participants' transcripts and texts, a complex picture emerged that depicted both an appreciation for the course, free of stigma, and a far less clearcut dichotomy between students and teachers, basic and mainstream writers. The individuals who talked and shared their writing with me do not fit neatly into preconceived categories; rather, as a random, self-selecting group, they cross categories and assume a range of context-dependent roles, their subject positions constantly shifting in relation to others and through time. Although I did not set out to defend basic writing, in light of these findings and the current debate about its status I would now firmly advocate not the category itself, but the pedagogy it has given rise to at places like the University of Pittsburgh and DTU.

Chapter 1, "Voices from the Academic Margin," introduces the students and teachers who participated in the study in the context of my analysis of the rhetorics of basic writing and the evolution of DTU's basic reading and writing program. In Chapter 2, "Constructing the Margin: Theories of Basic Writing," I describe the location of basic writing—the academic border—from an historical perspective, which I then suggest might be reconstrued as a site of resistance and transformation rather than deprivation.

Chapters 3, 4, and 5 are narratives of student and teacher experiences that emerged from the student texts, the responses of both students and teachers to those texts, and the interview transcripts. I found it necessary to revise my method as specific, unanticipated questions arose; similarly, as I analyzed the data, it became clear that each case study encompassed a different set of pedagogical issues. What links the case studies together is a semiotic method of reading texts in relation to discourses.

In Chapter 3, "Surface Errors and the Female Body: Basic Writers Who Make Mistakes," I tell the story of a young Puerto Rican woman who survived sexual and emotional abuse and came to view writing as a means of making sense of her life. The chapter focuses on the dynamics between Inez Moreno and her teacher, Anna Tremont, and suggests a correlation between our cultural fixation on the female body—perfected in media images, deeply imperfect in life—and surface errors in writing.

Chapter 4, "Writing in an Alien World: Basic Writers and the University," is about the possibilities for resistance to and transformation of oppressive personal and social realities. In an essay on the exclusion of blacks from science fiction, Joe Baxter asks how any author can envision a world that excludes entire groups, such as blacks, women, or the disabled. His protest about science fiction suggests a metaphor for higher education, while his description of reading and writing as activities that sustain him sharply contrasts with the apathy and despair of his peers whose credo is "Tomorrow's not promised to you." Responses to Joe's writing from both his teacher, Sandra Bennett, and another faculty member, Thomas Riley, confirmed my own sense of Joe as a talented writer. A critical question, given his talent, is why he was labeled a basic writer.

Chapter 5, "Multiple Teacher Responses: Authorizing Words and the Discipline of Writing," revolves around Ethel Martin, a student from rural Guyana, and Rivka Minsky, a Russian Jewish immigrant. The central text is Ethel's paper on skin color, "Complexion," written in response to Richard Rodriguez's *Hunger of Memory* (1983). Read by her own teacher, Karen Stein, and several other instructors, including a Guyanese man who now teaches basic writing but was once a basic writing student himself, the paper elicited a wide range of responses. A perplexing set of questions arose as a result both of Ethel's elusiveness—she literally disappeared during the course of my research—and the contrast between Karen's overt rejection of Ethel's writing and her close identification with Rivka's. The combination of Ethel's self-effacement and Karen's bewildered attitude toward her prompted me to elicit other teacher interpretations; thus in Chapter 5 the emphasis is on cultural identity, teacher response to student writing, and the process of authorization that gives voice to people or silences them.

In Chapter 6, "A Two-Way Flow: Social Construction Theory and Critical Pedagogy," and Chapter 7, "A Multiplicity of Voices: Postmodern and Feminist Pedagogies," I draw conclusions from the case studies and discuss the tendency in composition to adopt a pedagogy that emphasizes *either* the student *or* the text, a subjective or objective rhetoric, essential or constructed categories, rather than a dialectical approach that understands them as always interrelated. I explore why the concept of transactional rhetoric—what I will later call *dialogics*—has been difficult to sustain in composition pedagogy, especially in basic writing. I then discuss and begin to synthesize four pedagogical perspectives—social constructionist, critical, postmodernist, and feminist—all of which have deeply influenced the field of composition and given me several theoretical lenses through which to analyze my research data. These perspectives allow a critique of the dominant culture and an analysis of how we are constituted in and through discourse. Together, they present a view of social realities as constructed, dynamic, and subject to change; as such, they provide hope that education can give rise to what Stanley Aronowitz and Henry Giroux (1985) have called "a language of possibility," to social resistance and even transformation.

Finally, in Chapter 8, "Basic Writing and the Politics of Articulation," I draw conclusions about the implications of this study for the potential of the basic writing class to generate "a politics of articulation" that validates students as intellectual agents and gives voice and visibility to their perceptions of the world as we move toward the twenty-first century.

Part One

Constructing the Margin

Chapter One

Voices from the Academic Margin

Educate the uneducated so they have some type of skills to look for work so in the future they can help themselves. Education is what is needed . . . If we don't educate we might as well start spending money on more jails and burying more people.

Inez Moreno

Until other writers share the same vision of [Gene] Roddenberry and [Octavia] Butler that all races of humans can be explorers of time and space and can deal with the unknown, blacks and other ethnic groups will be invisible in science fiction.

Joe Baxter

When I came to America to live the only problem I had was understanding what the American was saying because it seemed as though everyone was speaking very fast. I can remember listening and could not understand anything but I just said yes to make to person think I understand.

Ethel Martin

Everything has to be in order. Everybody wants to live well, in peace. Who has to make this order, who is making the rules? . . . I am not offering principles of Communism, I had enough of it. But simply we have to be aware that we are surrounded by other people, who could have other opinions. There has to be some middle ground . . . in which everybody could live and to be happy. I do not know how to do it. This is why I felt I have to study, in order to do my part in life well.

Rivka Minsky

A basic writing student at one of DTU's three neighborhood branch campuses, Inez Moreno describes life on the margins of society in the 1990s in a paper ostensibly on prostitution. In addition, she writes about unemployment, federal and state budget cuts, mental illness, drug addiction, AIDS, and inadequate educational opportunities. Unable to unravel the complex web of problems she sees in her neighborhood, she wrestled in revising the paper with what her teacher said was lack of focus. As we sat talking in a drafty room of the community center in which the branch campus is housed, I made a mental note that she looked and sounded depressed. As it turned out, she spent a large portion of the interview relating a series of tragedies in her life, including sexual abuse and physical injury, that seemed very close to the surface. Even when she felt discouraged by her slow progress in school, she said, these tragedies had motivated her to write. Despite them, she is a fully functioning, responsible parent with strong views on how to remedy the social problems, if not the personal ones, that concern her. Her plea to "educate the uneducated" seems especially poignant as she and her classmates seek to improve their personal circumstances in a time of global economic recession and social flux.

Inez and the three other students who participated in the study and whose voices open this chapter are representative of DTU's diverse, working-class student population: Latino American, African American, African Caribbean, and, most recently, Russian. In striving to get a college education, they give testimony to conditions of life in late twentieth-century urban America that I believe needs to be heard by people other than their classmates and teachers. As Eduardo Galeano (1988) puts it, "The testimonies of the people as they express in a thousand ways their tribulations and their hopes are more eloquent and beautiful than the books written 'in the name of the people'" (p. 121). Thus it seems important both to present these students and their teachers in a broader sociohistorical context—as they grapple with the global effects of advanced capitalism that affect local life, such as massive immigration to the U.S.—and to let them speak through their own writing and oral histories.

First Impressions: Meeting the Students and Teachers

A young Puerto Rican mother of five, Inez told me she was attending school at night so she could get a degree in business and earn enough money to pay for more than childcare; otherwise, it made no sense for her to return to work. Although her writing skills were weak, she was a disciplined student who said she wrote for herself as a way to understand her experience. Her teacher, Anna Tremont, a white poet with a working-class background, had been teaching at DTU since the mid-1980s. An experienced teacher who empathized with DTU students, Anna described Inez as a "C" student who seemed intellectually "blocked." Several issues emerge: Inez's preoccupation with surface errors in her writing seems to parallel concerns about her physical appearance, which like her prose is disfigured by an "error" of judgment; at the same time, her experience of writing as therapy seems to "unblock" disturbing memories of sexual abuse. Although Anna says she wants Inez to think more deeply, her written comments and recollections of interactions with her stress issues of error, focus, and detail rather than analysis, suggesting the need for a pedagogical "bridge" she describes in her own life as having helped her link postmodern theory to everyday life and art.

Joe Baxter, an African American man in his early twenties, was a branch campus student in a different neighborhood. I first met him when he came to the main campus for an interview with me. Once I explained that I wanted him to read his essays aloud and comment on them, he proceeded to talk eloquently and virtually unprompted for over an hour, analyzing both his own development as a reader and writer—he had started reading early, and became a science fiction fan as a kindergartner inspired by "Star Trek"—and his peers' self-destructive embrace of nihilism. Joe's teacher, Sandra Bennett, a young, middle-class, African American writer, had been teaching as an adjunct in the department for several years. In addition to recognizing Joe's verbal abilities, she shared his love of science fiction. Because Sandra and I were both so impressed by Joe's papers, I asked Thomas Riley, a white senior faculty member, to read them as well. I was curious to see how Tom, an older teacher with a reputation for being gruff and intolerant but also strongly committed to teaching and interested in science fiction, would respond to Joe's writing.

The final case study focuses on two students on the main campus in the same evening class: Ethel Martin, an African Caribbean woman from Guyana, and Rivka Minsky, a Russian Jewish immigrant from the former Soviet Union. I met with Ethel, a slight, shy woman with a soft voice that sometimes disappears on the audiotaped interview, in the English Department. She seemed frightened, repeatedly voicing concern that she had responded poorly or incorrectly to my questions. Rivka, on the other hand, was poised, funny, mildly self-deprecating, and very warm, eager to tell me about her childhood, her experience as a reader and writer, and her perceptions of DTU. It was easy to understand how their teacher, Karen Stein, would thoroughly enjoy Rivka as a student and feel perplexed by Ethel. However, I was unprepared for her inability to read

Ethel's writing as anything but "alien" or to imagine how to respond as a teacher to her.

The contrast between Karen's embrace of Rivka and her rejection of Ethel led me to wonder how other teachers would read Ethel's writing. Three other teachers, John Ross, Miriam Goodman, and Clinton Crawford[3], responded sympathetically to Ethel's paper, "Complexion," confirming my sense that there was something curious about Karen's utter mystification by Ethel. A Jewish American woman in her late forties, Karen had only started teaching writing several years previously, but her background in meditation and sensory awareness work seemed to have predisposed her to a process approach to teaching writing and a sympathetic response to students. Her difficulty relating to Ethel seemed anomalous. The other three teachers who read Ethel's writing ranged from a second-generation New York Jew in his mid-forties, then completing his doctorate in psychology, to a Guyanese man who, once a basic writer himself, was in a doctoral program in art history, writing his dissertation on ancient Egyptian art.

Teachers and Students as Writers

In each case study, but particularly the last, a striking pattern emerged: those individuals who identified as writers, whether students or teachers—and, of course, the teachers recalled experiences as children or students—were better able to withstand the force of others' words, actions, and expectations by internalizing and transforming them, by making them their own. By definition, writers have something to say, a point of view, a narrative voice. Once these individuals had claimed the identity of "writer," often through painful struggle, they were able at least to some degree to narrate the stories of their own lives; those who had submitted to discipline—punitive or not—meted out by parents, teachers, or other authority figures often expressed feelings of inferiority, shame, and apathy, and tended to submit to others' authority rather than assert their own. As adults, they assumed the identities of their "oppressors," enforcing similar rules and punishments on their children or students. None of the participants demonstrated this tendency more clearly than Ethel, who said she "whacks" her son just as she was hit repeatedly by her teachers.

Writing here is a metaphor for authority as well as an instantiation of it. The "narration sickness" that Freire (1988) criticizes is

---

3. At his request, Clinton Crawford, a participant in the study, is referred to by his real name rather than a pseudonym.

imposed on us by external, authoritative voices—stories, for example, of colonial glory, compulsory heterosexuality, or the white suburban world portrayed in the "Dick and Jane" primers. These are powerful narratives that construct reality for millions of people. To resist them takes not only courage but access to alternative stories, media, news, and lifestyles that inform us of other perspectives, interpretations, and responses to experience. As Foucault (1979) tells us in *Discipline and Punish*,

> We must cease once and for all to describe the effects of power in negative terms: it 'excludes', it 'represses', it 'censors', it 'abstracts', it 'masks', it 'conceals'. In fact, power produces; it produces reality; it produces domains of objects and rituals of truth. The individual and the knowledge that may be gained of him belong to this production. (p. 194)

The interesting twist in the stories of the DTU teachers and students is that many of them gained or lost authority according to their identification as writers, as well as their social status or roles, blurring boundaries between teacher and student and confirming Freire's definition of the word as constituted by reflection and action: "Thus, to speak a true word is to transform the world" (1988, p. 75).

Rhetorics of Basic Writing

In the spring of 1990, I worked with several members of DTU's English Department to revise our basic writing course, based on the University of Pittsburgh's program. Our situation differed from Pittsburgh's primarily in that a majority—not a handful—of DTU students place into basic writing their freshman year. The politics of language and literacy thus raised for us more pressing questions than might arise in a more traditional college like Pittsburgh. For example, how do racism and class prejudice affect the dynamics of writing instruction—from required texts and assignments to teacher and peer response? How do our educational goals reflect our relationship to the dominant culture? Do we resist, accept, criticize, reproduce, or seek to change that culture, and what are the consequences of those positions for us as readers, writers, students, and teachers?

Historically, the basic writing course that emerged in the 1960s was a hotbed of social criticism and dissent. Students who enrolled in the SEEK Program—the program that preceded open admissions at the City University of New York—according to Adrienne Rich (1979), were "becoming . . . more lucidly conscious of the politics of their situation, the context within which their lives were being led" (p. 58). A SEEK teacher, Rich recalls student negotiations with the administration in 1969, after the Black and Puerto Rican Student Community seized the South Campus, to expand the SEEK Program into what became known as open admissions. Variants of writing remediation had been part of the college curriculum long before the advent of basic writing; what distinguished basic writing from other forms of remedial instruction was its specific orientation to students previously excluded from higher education, mainly poor and working-class whites, blacks, and Latinos. Race, in particular, figured significantly into the experience of open admissions.

To teachers like Mina Shaughnessy, who pioneered a philosophy and method of basic writing instruction, many open admissions students were "true outsiders," "strangers in academia," who "had grown up in one of New York's ethnic or racial enclaves" (1977, pp. 2–3). The problem Shaughnessy and others addressed was a linguistic one: how to induct these students, these outsiders, into the discourse of the university and, by extension, the dominant culture. Despite the democratic impulses that guided such efforts, the pedagogical focus on the standard language, particularly surface-level errors, as the key factor in academic success or failure both reinforced linguistic prejudices and masked the underlying problems of racism, class discrimination, and other forms of social inequality that had necessitated open admissions in the first place. From its inception, basic writing has served contradictory functions, giving students a chance to develop reading and writing abilities that is then often foreclosed by inferior instruction—skills-drills, rote exercises, an overemphasis on error.

On the margins of the university, the basic writing class has traditionally policed the academic borders, mirroring an unequal society that benefits some and harms others. However, it has also made the borders more permeable for those who might not go to college otherwise. Basic writing is thus a multidimensional site of instruction that has inspired advances in theory, practice, and research, but has reproduced enduring inequalities by inviting academic outsiders to enter and often exit a revolving door, and in either case, relegated them to the university's lowest status. For the poor and working-class students who arrive in a basic writing class, the academic border coincides with the geographical borders some cross into the U.S. and the sociocultural boundaries others negotiate to gain admission not only to college but to middle-class life. Thus the basic writing class quite literally becomes a frontier these students traverse to enter into a more privileged sphere of existence—or so they hope.

The apt metaphors of frontiers, borders, and border crossings have been appropriated by basic writing theorists to describe the process students undergo as they move from one social location to another. But the image of the border can invoke several routes for the basic writer to travel, which correspond roughly with what James Berlin (1987) calls "rhetorics of writing." In his study of twentieth-century composition, *Rhetoric and Reality*, Berlin posits objective, subjective, and transactional rhetorics. As he explains, these rhetorics emerge out of epistemological stances that locate reality in, respectively, the objective external world, the subjective internal world, and the dialectic between them. Along similar lines, Min-Zhan Lu (1992) has identified three positions in basic writing: "education as acculturation," "education as accommodation," and "education as repositioning." Lu points out that basic writing teachers who assume the role of gatekeeper share some assumptions about language learning with those who adopt acculturation and accommodation models—namely, that the essence of meaning precedes linguistic form, and that the academic discourse community is monologic, unified, and stable.

The rhetoric of acculturation, which Lu associates with Kenneth Bruffee (1984, 1986), stresses the student's initiation into academic discourse as legitimate and unavoidable; Shaughnessy (1988) discusses this position in terms of "converting the natives." The rhetoric of accommodation, which Shaughnessy espoused, reassures the student that academic instruction can accommodate, without weakening, ties to the home culture. The rhetoric of repositioning, which Lu advocates and illustrates with the writing of Gloria Anzaldúa, acknowledges conflict as an important element of development, particularly when education is viewed as a means of empowerment. But proponents of acculturation and accommodation share an assumption that conflict and struggle are negative, undesirable. Lu uses Anzaldúa's *Borderlands/La Frontera: The New Mestiza* as a model for writing that captures conflict and struggle— what I will call a dialectic—between inner and outer forces, producing a new consciousness that "enables a border resident to act on rather than merely react to the conditions of her or his life, turning awareness of the situation into 'inner changes' which in turn bring about 'changes in society'" (p. 888).

According to social constructionist theory and Lu's notion of education as repositioning, language mediates social reality and constructs our knowledge of the world and ourselves. The aim of writing instruction is thus to develop consciousness and control of rhetorical forms, not promote one speech variety over another or merely accommodate subcultures into a tradition that is viewed uncritically. Institutionally, as I have already suggested, basic writing reflects the geopolitical realities of today's world, as "minority" groups in this country and abroad struggle for socioeconomic equality against an historical backdrop of colonialism, racism, and class oppression. Especially because the basic writing class borders on multiple social realities and is a point of entry into a system of higher education that has historically excluded such groups, it requires a language pedagogy that places writing in a social context. Researchers and theorists influenced by social constructionism have argued that the troubled border or margin of basic writing lends itself particularly well to a pedagogy that treats language—including academic discourse—as conflicted and multivoiced.

The Politics of Marginalization and Basic Writing

While attention by activists, and more recently academics, to the politics of marginalization has promoted "cultural diversity" and revisions of both the canon and the curriculum, it has also diluted progressive critiques of education and exacerbated the problem of essentialism. Wahneema Lubiano (1992) makes the distinction between "strong" and "weak" multiculturalism in her essay on "negotiating politics and knowledge." Weak multiculturalism, "an intellectual and social smorgasbord," neutralizes challenges to "Eurocentric areas of knowledge" by creating simplistic dichotomies between cultures, silencing discussion of class and its relationship to gender and race and maintaining cultural dominance "in slicker, Benetton colors" (p. 13). Strong multiculturalism, on the other hand, contests and transforms dominant forms of knowledge while constructing new knowledges. In basic writing instruction, a smorgasbord approach to cultural diversity reproduces a notion of "difference" as stable, fixed, and essential, thus maintaining racial, national, and gender stereotypes rather than demystifying and historicizing them.

The difficulty of puncturing such stereotypes, as Dorothy Allison (1994) explains, is that "we internalize the myths of our society even as we resist them" (p. 24). Caught between the white, working-class, racist world of her childhood and the predominantly middle-class, lesbian, feminist world of her adult life, Allison felt that she "straddled cultures and belonged on neither side" (p. 26). Finally, through writing *Bastard out of Carolina*, she reclaimed her family's painful, impoverished history, and concludes:

> Most of all, I have tried to understand the politics of *they*, why human beings fear and stigmatize the different while secretly

dreading that they might be one of the different themselves. Class, race, sexuality, gender—and all the other categories by which we categorize and dismiss each other—need to be excavated from the inside. (p. 35)

Similarly, the dozens of multicultural readers currently promoted for use in basic writing courses are frequently organized along racial and ethnic lines: Native American, African American, Latino American, Asian American, and European American perspectives. Like Allison, basic writing students—often immigrants, inner-city people of color, and working-class whites—must negotiate complex identities in relation to textual representations of ethnic and racial selves that generally dilute or omit the politics of class. Rather than provide a critique of American society that might help students understand their marginality, these representations are intended mainly to enable students to identify with authors of their own race or ethnicity whose voices, like their own, have only recently been allowed into the academy.

This sort of identity politics is double-edged, in that it both reinforces essentialist views of complex human experience—reaffirming the very binary oppositions of male/female, white/black, and hetero/homo that have been oppressive to women, people of color, and gays and lesbians—and supports the aspirations of social groups that have been historically silenced. One problem with locating ourselves in essentialist categories is that we reduce complex realities to simple terms and encourage identification with those who are like us rather than those who may be different; another problem is that essentialist politics, in isolating groups from each other, may undermine efforts to build broad-based coalitions for social change. Yet groups who have been excluded from social discourses and institutions have little reason to believe in universal claims about the common interests of humanity, especially when pronounced by those who already enjoy social privileges.

The politics of marginalization, including the problem of essentialism, raised key questions for me in my research on basic writing about how I situate myself as a researcher and how students and teachers situate themselves in the classroom. As an alternative to essentialist views of identity that can nonetheless account for the sociohistorical effects of race, class, and gender, I borrow a phrase from Stuart Hall: "the process of identification." This notion captures both the particular consciousness produced by individual experience and the fluidity of social identity. It allows for identification with groups across and within class, color, and gender lines based on common interests and aspirations. At the same time, however, there may be a need for what Gayatri Spivak (1987) has called "strategic essentialism," in order to deal with the contradiction between a poststructuralist view of human identity as constructed and the actual historical legacy of racism, sexism, and class oppression, constructions that may require us to identify as a woman or a person of color, or to advocate on behalf of particular oppressed groups.

While I agree with Spivak that "we want the [subaltern] to disappear as a name so that we can all speak," cited in an epigraph to Bartholomae's (1993) recent critique of basic writing, abolishing basic writing will not reverse the historic inequalities in education that open admissions policies, which gave rise to basic writing in the first place, sought to redress. If "basic writer" disappears as a name, actual students may disappear as well. Thus, for the time being, it may be important to preserve the name "basic writing," despite its essentialist connotations, as a strategy to protect "underprepared" students from budget cuts, rising admissions standards, and linguistic and cultural chauvinism.

The Pittsburgh Basic Reading and Writing Course

Pittsburgh's BRW course synthesized composition theory and practice and reconceived basic writing instruction, replacing a traditional skills-based course with a sophisticated, thematically driven seminar in reading and writing. It is in this light that Bartholomae and Petrosky (1986) explain what they mean by the title of their book, *Facts, Artifacts, and Counterfacts*, in regard to the theory and method of BRW: *facts* are the conditions under which students function, their relationship to the university and the materials they encounter; *artifacts* are the student papers and performances that result from those facts; and *counterfacts* are pedagogical interventions that motivate students to revise their papers and "reject their apparent inevitability" (p. 8). With BRW, Bartholomae and Petrosky reclaimed "basic reading and writing" from skills-based approaches that reduce complex sociolinguistic activities to transparent processes of retrieving and transmitting information.

Influenced by the philosopher George Steiner and postmodern theorists like Jonathan Culler, the Pittsburgh faculty, as described in *Facts, Artifacts, and Counterfacts*, want their students to learn to compose a response to a reading as well as to compose a reading; rather than coach students on scanning a text, they advise them to write in the margins of their books, checking or starring what interests or perplexes them, so they can return to a record or memory of their reading instead of an unmarked page. Instead of testing for comprehension, they provide strategies for reading and writing, welcoming, not just acknowledging, the inevitability of different readings. They teach writing by teaching revision and editing; that is, they understand how the writer's struggle with her own material shapes her writing, and they believe the provision of ready-made forms for writing and reading discourages such encounters with thought and language from happening at all.

Bartholomae and Petrosky's most basic assumption perhaps is that reading *is* writing. Whether or not we write a response to a text, we must "compose" it; meaning is not given, but made, and reading requires us to construe meaning actively. However, it is only once this act of composition becomes stated, orally or in writing, that we really know what we have understood by our reading. Two assumptions closely linked to the interrelationship between reading and writing are that our ability to respond depends on how much authority we can claim for ourselves as makers of meaning, and that reading is *misreading* because the construal of meaning through language always requires us to displace the original text. Meaning, argue Bartholomae and Petrosky, "results when a reader or writer finds a language to make the presentation of meaning possible" (p. 11). Thus a writer must invent herself, imagine a reading, and adopt a role of authority within the academy, performing rather than possessing meaning.

DTU's Courses: "Different Voices in History" and "Environmental Studies"

The content of DTU's program differs from Pittsburgh's in two important respects: first, we chose themes and texts that make explicit the politics of race, class, and gender, situating our students in history in order to teach rhetorical analysis and strategies; and second, while we appreciate the metaphor of performance and the importance of the individual student's appropriation of academic discourse, we hoped to shift the emphasis of the courses to a more social, dialogic interaction between teacher and student, among students, and between readers and writers. As we designed our first semester of BRW-1, focusing on the relationship of stories to history, we reread Bartholomae and Petrosky's account of their choice of themes:

> . . . we have tried to identify subjects that would bring forward powerful and pressing themes from our students' experience. We

want students to see quickly that they have a stake in the transformations they can perform on the ways they see and, thereby, participate in the world. (p. 30)

At DTU, we had not so much a different set of objectives as a different social lens through which we saw them. Most DTU classes are a mix of recent high school graduates and older, returning students. Sixty-one percent of the undergraduates are over age twenty-two; racial and ethnic "minorities" compose seventy percent of the school's population. The "underprepared" students in BRW-1 and BRW-2—educationally and usually economically disadvantaged—are the majority, not marginal outsiders; we wanted to address the historical reasons for their difficulties with reading and writing and their systematic exclusion from full participation in society. Thus, while we share the goals of the Pittsburgh program—to promote a participatory stance that invites change—we wanted to politicize and historicize the course content, making explicit connections between individual and social change.

Thus, as we designed the course, we asked whether the texts and the themes would lend themselves to a static, timeless, universal definition of human experience, dislodged from history, or to a historically specific investigation of identity. In our first discussions, we agreed that we wanted to accentuate both the role of story in reading and writing and a more dynamic, multicultural perspective. Our discussions led us to ask: Which stories prevail? How do our stories become *his*tory? What socioeconomic and cultural forces determine that? What would happen if we used these questions, which are critical for students who continue to be excluded from the political process, to frame a course in reading and writing? We hoped that the theme of identity would not only motivate students but actually begin to challenge the conditions and practices by which they have been silenced.

By exploring how they and other individuals are historically situated, students in BRW-1 examine issues of exclusion, silencing, power, and inequality, while they reflect on their own place in society, the academy, and ultimately among other writers to whom they are beginning to "talk back." Students in BRW-2 explore environmental crises, bringing what they have learned about their own and other "voices in history" to bear on one of the most pressing sets of issues of the 1990s. In a sense, in BRW-2, we are asking them to exercise the authority, fragile as it often is, that they begin to develop in BRW-1. That the majority of our students are unable to find the *New York Times* in their New York City neighborhoods when we assign them to bring it to class is a telling indication of their "place" in society. Both BRW-1 and BRW-2 ask students to consider the possibility of transformation, not simply as an aspect of personal experience, but as a dialectic between individual and social realities.

At the time of the study, for example, the first unit of BRW-1 on reading newspapers included a critique of the television news program "Nightline" by Fairness and Accuracy in Reporting (FAIR). The FAIR report criticized "Nightline" for presenting news analysis through the eyes of guests who belong to the male, white establishment. Students watched and wrote about "Nightline" and other news programs, reflecting on their own experiences and observations and confirming or disconfirming FAIR's assertions. Other BRW-1 texts designed to foster awareness of how individuals shape and are shaped by social and historical forces included Harriet Wilson's autobiographical novel *Our Nig* and Henry Louis Gates' introduction to it; a novel about repression in Argentina by Lawrence Thornton called *Imagining Argentina*; David Malouf's fictional narrative of Ovid in *An Imaginary Life*; and James Baldwin's angry account of an Atlanta child murder case, *The Evidence of Things Not Seen*. This list has been revised for ESL classes, adding, for example, Richard Rodriguez's autobiography, *The Hunger of Memory*.[4]

More than the particular books, however, we found that the course worked best for those instructors who have understood and have been able to communicate to their students the historical basis of the themes. Viewing issues of exclusion and oppression from an historical perspective, rather than as brute facts of life, created a context in which learning felt purposeful, meaningful—an antidote to the rote exercises that define so many of our students' educational experiences. Some BRW-1 instructors reported in response to a questionnaire that their students reacted negatively to the theme. "A bit heavy," one adjunct described it. ". . . It has dampened enthusiasm and spirit." Corroborating this view, a full-time faculty member recalled that "all three teachers I observed said that their students complained, as mine did all semester, of endlessly reading about and discussing oppression."

One response to complaints like these is simply to foster discussion and debate about the course and allow for multiple interpretations and approaches to teaching it. But another, deeper response is to explore the resistance to the assigned books and the thematic content in both classroom and faculty discussions, and ask

---

4. Since 1990, the book lists have changed periodically; the themes of identity and the environment, however, have remained the same for BRW courses, with modifications of the titles and the option for anyone who has taught the standard syllabus at least once to propose changing the theme and/or texts.

questions such as: What accounts for negative reactions to the books? How do we see ourselves in relation to literature we read? What assumptions do we have about social class, conflict, hardship, and privilege? If one sees the course as mired in gloom, casting the oppressed as hapless victims of circumstance, it may indeed be a depressing experience for everyone; but if the course is about resistance—the historical struggle of those who have been silenced to enter political and cultural discourse—then it can both introduce students to discursive worlds inside and outside the academy, and give them concrete historical examples of how social change takes place. Nevertheless, the relevance of this perspective may be difficult to convey to students *and* teachers who are products of a culture of consumption and spectatorship and would like to transcend the struggles of everyday life rather than confront them in literature or politics.

DTU's approach to curriculum design aimed to invite students into a dialogue, to become active participants in history (the classroom as history) through their own talk, reading, and writing. Students in one BRW-1 section, for example, underscored their pride in joining in this larger conversation when they titled the anthology of their final papers—autobiographies in which they attempt to place their personal experience in a larger historical context—"These Are Our Voices." Indeed, the liberation of such voices seems to be what Bartholomae and Petrosky are talking about when they discuss writing and reading in terms of "'alternities,' the possibility of 'freedom,' and the assertion of personal and territorial rights" (p. 4). However, unless such claims are grounded in the sociohistorical realities that construct social differences and inequalities, they can be used to support the "bootstrap" individualism that underlies so much of the discourse of American culture. Freedom, I would argue, is always contingent on socioeconomic and cultural conditions; to suggest otherwise is to reinforce assumptions that individual merit rather than collective struggle will change oppressive social conditions. Despite its basically social and postmodern perspective, the rhetoric of the Pittsburgh program occasionally slips into what Berlin has termed "expressionist" rhetoric—the view that truth resides within us and that individual quests for meaning yield the most authentic testimony.

Clearly, Bartholomae and Petrosky recognize the importance of classroom dialogue. But they seem to reserve another sort of dialogue—what might be called "contentious" or "conflicted" dialogue—for the last portion of their BRW program, in which the students, who until then have been shielded from "the presence and pressure of the institution," are expected to make the transition from reading and writing as experiences of "self-possession" and making meanings of their own to an acknowledgement of the public nature of discourse. It is this social, or institutional, constraint that they suggest fosters for students

> . . . a way of seeing themselves at work within the institutional structures that make their work possible. What we are offering them is not an affirmation of a person, free and self-created, but an image of a person who is made possible through her work, work that takes place both within and against the languages that surround and define her. (p. 40)

I believe that this image of human existence is not a "*compromise* between idiosyncracy, a personal history, and the requirements of convention, the history of an institution" (p. 8, emphasis added), as Bartholomae and Petrosky argue, but a *condition* of human life. As Paulo Freire (1987) explains in *A Pedagogy for Liberation*—his "talking book" coauthored with Ira Shor—dialogue is neither a tactic nor a technique but

> part of our historical progress in becoming human beings. Dialogue is a moment where humans meet to reflect on their reality as they make and remake it . . . [I]n the process of knowing the reality which we transform, we communicate and know *socially* even though the process of communicating, knowing, changing, has an individual dimension. But, the individual aspect is not enough to explain the process. Knowing is a social event with nevertheless an individual dimension. What is dialogue in this moment of communication, knowing and social transformation? Dialogue *seals* the relationship between the cognitive subjects, the subjects who know, and who try to know. (pp. 98–9)

Like Freire, Mikhail Bakhtin (1981, 1984) has given us a theory of dialogue that is at once descriptive and utopian. Bakhtin describes a profusion of social languages, emanating from differences of class, region, age, profession, gender, and so on, as well as a dialogic process by which the authoritative language of the family, teacher, and others in positions of power becomes "internally persuasive" language in what he calls our "ideological becoming." Dialogue, he tells us, "is not a means for revealing, for bringing to the surface the already ready-made character of a person; no, in dialogue a person not only shows himself outwardly, but he becomes for the first time that which he is—and, we repeat, not only for others but for himself as well" (1984, p. 252). Neither Freire nor Bakhtin argues that dialogue is a given; rather, writes Freire, it is "part of our historical progress as human beings." Feminist theorists, sensitive to how dialogue excludes as well as includes, have further addressed the question of inequality of voice in ways that are relevant to our students' tenuous relationship to the authority of the university. As Dale Bauer (1988) notes in her attempt to theorize a feminist dialogics:

> My first reaction to Bakhtin was to become seduced by his theory of dialogism since it seemed to offer a utopian ground for all voices to flourish . . . Yet Bakhtin's blind spot is the battle. He does not work out the contradiction between the promise of utopia or community and the battle which always is waged for control. (p. 5)

Rather than see BRW-1 and BRW-2 in terms of a movement from the private vision of the individual student toward the language of the university (or any other public, collective discourse), I see an ongoing dialectic, indeed, sometimes a battle, between the student and the academic community in which we cannot shield students from institutional pressures. Such pressures—from the demands of parenthood to the workplace, as well as the university—pervade students' lives, as they do ours. Nor do I believe that universities necessarily hold the answers for students. Instead of a compromise, I see the relationship between the individual and society as both dialectical (an interaction of forces in which each term affects the other) and dialogical (an interaction between people, through face-to-face talk, or reading and writing or other technologies). I believe this dialectic between personal and social history, as well as between reading and writing, self and other, is the basis of what we and our students do as active learners, as makers of meaning. The dialogue that ensues both renders and, as part of the dialectical process, begins to change our myriad accounts of these interactions, including the establishment of our methods, goals, expectations, and standards.

The Impact of the Program on DTU

Although it is too soon to tell what the long-range effects of BRW-1 and BRW-2 will be on students, faculty, and the university as a whole, we can already document some changes and try to predict others. In the English Department, orientations and regular staff development meetings are held to train adjuncts as well as full-time faculty to teach the new courses. Senior faculty members who taught BRW-1 in the fall of 1990 reported that, as a result of their experience, they have changed their teaching methods. Adjunct and workshop instructors have enrolled in record numbers in graduate courses in the teaching of writing. The workshops attached to the course are more stimulating and better coordinated with the class, although there continue to be problems of authority and communication due to the hierarchy built into the course structure. Graduate assistants in the teaching practicum have begun to apply some of the theory and method of BRW-1/2 to the intermediate and advanced composition courses they teach. Fourteen new full-time faculty have been hired since 1990; two compositionists left, and of the remaining twelve, half are trained in composition and rhetoric.

As for students, we anticipate they will be better prepared for their other courses across the disciplines. In addition to being better readers and writers, they will know what it means to be a student, to participate in a dialogue, and to engage in inquiry of various kinds. We imagine that their expectations of what a university education should offer them will change as they become more active, responsible learners. We also anticipate that retention rates will improve and academic success stories will become more common. Concretely, behavior patterns seem to have changed: attendance—a real problem for DTU students, burdened with overwhelming financial, familial, and societal pressures—has improved, and BRW-1/2 instructors generally report that the quality of classroom discussion and written work is markedly better—students are more punctual, alert, engaged, and serious.

One of the most interesting experiences for our students is to return at the end of the semester to revise the first essay they wrote in class. The diagnostic essay, like the new placement exam, asks students to read a short passage from one of the course books and respond to it in a single essay, both interpreting what the author says and relating their own experience and observations to it. For BRW-1, in the fall of 1990, we gave students a passage from Baldwin's *The Evidence of Things Not Seen*, in which he writes about the hypocrisy of American leaders who show concern for poor communities only during political elections or times of crisis. By the end of the semester, the students had read, discussed, and written about this book in the context of our theme, "Different Voices in History." In revising that first in-class essay, many of them said that rereading it appalled them and made them feel they had truly changed as writers; most approached revision by discarding large portions of the early drafts and writing anew. One student, an avid reader, wrote a rather cursory response at the beginning of the semester, quoted in part:

> The message that Baldwin is trying to get across. Is that we can not change our race, we have to live with it. Not only do we have to live with it but we have to deal with it in the best way we know how.
>
> Sometimes we meaning monorities have to show violence not because that is expected of us, but because society pushes us in that direction. When it get to much for some of us to bare instead

of taking a deep breathe and trying to find out where we went wrong, we sell out to the other side. The more of us that sells out the worst it will get.

Despite the typical move of describing Baldwin as *trying* to get across his message, as if she has projected her own uncertainty onto him, she mistakes his anger as self- rather than outer-directed. This misreading reveals her tendency to blame the victim (her own community—"we meaning monorities"); although she recognizes that "society pushes us in that direction," ultimately, she argues, resorting to violence is a form of selling out. Instead, "we have to stick together to stop the disease before it spreads any further."

By the end of the semester, the student assumes a more authoritative voice, integrates other course readings, and becomes much more specific about the "disease" of urban crime and violence she wrote about so vaguely at first:

> Baldwin is saying that the minorities only exist during a crisis. To the majority we cause problems but on the same token minorities are the problem solvers. They seperate the minorities into groups so we have nothing to do but condition ourselves. From there we are put into a never ending cycle of crime & drug wars against one another and towards other people as well.
>
> The minorities are unrecognized or as Michelle Wallace said, "We are victims of invisibility blues." That is until we are needed for something. Whether it is to fight a war or election time: examples the only reason why slaves were freed was to fight a war that the majority wanted to win. Which ended up in a lot of blood shed and a high body count. The sad thing about it was they fought each other. . . .

More than the assurance she evinces in the second essay, the student has begun to enter into a genuine dialogue with the authors she has read, her implicit reader, and history itself. Traces of the first essay remain—"The sad thing about it was they fought each other"—but are now contextualized in a way that authorizes her to participate in a conversation that includes but extends beyond her own experience.

Inez Moreno, Joe Baxter, Ethel Martin, and Rivka Minsky all took BRW-1, "Different Voices in History," in the 1991–92 school year. Before continuing with their stories, however, it will be useful to examine the history of basic writing and the theoretical positions that shaped it. In the next chapter, I trace the construction on the academic margin of a basic writing course in which remedial skills-drills courses are reconceived as graduate seminars, and ask whether basic writing, as it is presently constituted, opens the academic borders, seals them off, or creates a permanent underclass within the university.

Chapter Two

1960s–1990s
Theories and Politics of Basic Writing

> . . . I want to note that I am not trying to romantically re-
> inscribe the notion of that space of marginality where the
> oppressed live apart from their oppressors as "pure." I
> want to say that these margins have been both sites of
> repression and sites of resistance. And since we are well
> able to name the nature of that repression we know better
> the margin as a site of deprivation. We are more silent
> when it comes to speaking of the margin as a site of resis-
> tance. We are more often silenced . . . (1990, p. 151)
>
> bell hooks

> After having taught basic writing at two large open-
> admissions schools, I tend to define it as that kind of stu-
> dent writing which disturbs, threatens, or causes despair
> in traditional English faculty members . . . Different
> teachers may react very differently to the feeling of dis-
> turbance, but if a piece of writing turns a harmless
> Shakespearian into either a Schweitzer or a Botha you
> can be pretty sure it's basic writing. (Enos 1987, p. vi)
>
> Robert Connors

The trope of marginality in recent accounts of basic writing has created a fictive borderland often described as a site of deprivation.
Lives on the Boundary, for example, Mike Rose's (1989) "hopeful
book about those who fail," is an educational rags to riches story that
shows "what happens as people who have failed begin to participate
in the educational system that has seemed so harsh and distant to
them" (p. xi). Rose proves his thesis, in this heartfelt narration of the

educational underclass, through his own experience: not only has he "worked for twenty years with children and adults deemed slow or remedial or underprepared," but he himself is a survivor:

> . . . at one time in my own educational life, I was so labeled. But I was lucky. I managed to *get redefined.* The people I've tutored and taught and the people whose lives I've studied—working-class children, poorly educated Vietnam veterans, underprepared college students, adults in a literacy program—they, for the most part, hadn't been so fortunate. They lived for many of their years in an educational underclass. (p. xi, emphasis added)

Rose is referring to a clerical error, a case of mistaken identity in which his I.Q. test scores were confused with those of another boy named Rose. He spent two years in a vocational track, until an observant sophomore biology teacher noticed 98s and 99s on his tests, checked the records, discovered the error, and recommended him for the college preparatory program in the fall, an incident of crossing tracks in high school that Rose calls "virtually impossible" (p. 30). Presumably, he means to say that his *status* is redefined, but he writes, "*I* managed to *get* redefined." Taken out of context—how lucky he was to escape the vocational track—the sentence illuminates the abject position in which even the most fortunate students on the academic margins are often placed. The "I," though passive, is capable of having "*managed*" to become the object of external redefinition.

Alternatively, bell hooks (1990) views marginality as including "both sites of repression and sites of resistance," a theoretical framework that assumes basic writers are agents who can redefine themselves. Her sense of the margin as more than a site of deprivation is rooted in her experience growing up in a small Southern town in which, typically, railroad tracks divided the black and white communities. But while white residents stayed for the most part on their side of town, ignorant of the black community, black residents who worked as maids, janitors, and delivery men went back and forth, developing what W. E. B. DuBois termed "double consciousness." They had a global view of the town that white people lacked; it is this perspective of the whole, gained in the white community, hooks explains, that gives black people "an oppositional worldview," which she hopes to cultivate in the academy.

Although the margin of basic writing is not identical to the margin that hooks describes, there is considerable overlap. As research on basic writing accumulates, the question arises, more insistently, of *who* is being taught and *why* they place into basic writing. Reports of basic writers cover the gamut of white, black, Latino and other ethnic groups, middle-class, working-class, and poor; moreover, placement and instruction vary, as most composition scholars and teachers would support, according to the specific contexts of different schools. However, social divisions along class and racial lines are evident both within and between institutions; and the majority of basic writers are from lower socioeconomic and racially oppressed groups.[5] To promote literacy as a force for liberation—as "critical literacy"—requires a political analysis of the specific ways in which race and class intersect with the teaching of reading and writing.

The narratives of liberal democracy and humanism often obscure class and racial conflict, as the following example shows. Asked to supply definitions of basic writing for the introduction to *A Sourcebook for Basic Writing Teachers* (1987), Robert Connors uses Schweitzer and Botha to symbolize the negative reactions of traditional faculty to basic writing, creating a subtext of race framed by the double reference to colonial Africa. Karen Greenberg takes issue with the term "basic" and suggests it be replaced by "inexperienced"; in a more overt political challenge to basic writing, Patricia Bizzell notes the close connection between "the cultural literacy required by the academy" and the discourse of "the dominant classes," and argues that the academy might expand and change its notion of literacy more easily than other social institutions. To these disparate perspectives on basic writing, Theresa Enos, the volume editor, rejoins: "These complementary definitions can help us recognize basic writing as the humanistic activity it is . . ." (p. vi).

Far from complementary, from a postmodern point of view that liberal humanism is founded on rational justifications of racism, colonialism, and sexism, the three brief statements can be read not as tributes but indictments of basic writing as yet another colonizing mission. Connors, in particular, points to an element of racism in basic writing instruction that I want to pursue further as a crucial factor, along with class, in constructing the marginal status of basic writers. It is from this critical perspective that I reexamine the sociohistorical contexts and theoretical assumptions of basic writing instruction as it has evolved since the 1960s.

Urban, Suburban, and Industrial Wastelands

Although accounts of basic writers across the country vary widely according to region, class, and race, many portray these students'

---

5. White middle-class basic writers, such as those described later in this chapter by Daniel Lazere, are by no means immune to the cultural forces that produce an ideology of anti-intellectual, passive consumerism, nor do new arrivals to the middle class enjoy the same privileges as established members.

lives as desperately bleak or vapid. Indeed, my own recollection of a class I taught in the fall of 1991 is full of despair and pain: a black student who described himself as the only one of his male friends who was in college rather than selling drugs, imprisoned, or dead; a young black woman, said to have suffered brain damage as a child, who failed the course three times; a talented writer from Trinidad in her late twenties who died the following semester, apparently from the cold—there was no heat in her apartment—but according to the autopsy report, as a result of undetected diabetes. That same fall of 1991 in a *College English* essay, Barbara Henning (1991) opens her discussion of basic writers by quoting student papers that describe lives of poverty, hunger, and dreams of escape.

Such students, Henning believes, either "struggle alone and prove themselves, believing in the strength and responsibility of the individual and thereby gaining respect and economic security," or remain "passive, depending heavily upon the benefits of traveling the *proper* road, hoping to earn 'placement' by the dominant social order into a better position" (p. 675).

Composition instructors, too, subscribe to "these two narratives of progress," which alienate students and result in high failure rates or a return "straight back into the world of poverty and ignorance." Later, Henning offers social criticism and understanding of history as the basis for an alternative writing pedagogy to those she criticizes as reductive—current traditional, cognitive, and expressivist. These rhetorics concentrate, respectively, on written error, psychological deficiencies, and the development of an inner view and voice. To illustrate her disagreement with them, Henning quotes an older female student forced to quit school for financial reasons who writes that she wants not a future as a welfare mother, but a career her children will respect. Rather than "find an inner voice" or "be trained in 'thinking,'" Henning argues, "This woman needs a paycheck and a babysitter, and in lieu of that at least an understanding of history and the rhetorics of consciousness and a recognition that the myth of progress along with the other myths perpetuated by the media and often the university, are indeed *only* myths" (p. 681).

Describing a very different basic writing population, Daniel Lazere (1992) states, "[I]t is not only minorities and the poor who are having difficulties in reading and writing at the college level, but many whites of the middle and upper-middle class who have never gone hungry or suffered other social or educational deprivation" (p. 11). Lazere questions whether the "back-to-basics" movement is "a force for oppression or liberation," concluding that radical critics who believe the "literacy crisis" is a hoax are mistaken; as evidence, he cites his poorly prepared white middle-class students. Radical educators who claim that standard English is "an instrument of domination" and refuse to impose it on their students, according to Lazere, may limit students' social and intellectual worlds by permanently excluding them from what Basil Bernstein calls an "elaborated" linguistic code. Lazere's students at the University of California and California State University systems, who use a restricted code marked by their class position, are often conservative, "indeed, potentially reactionary elements" (p. 9).

> The majority . . . come from families that are middle-class economically but lacking in what Pierre Bourdieu calls cultural capital—including proficiency in standard English, cultural literacy, and critical understanding of social forces . . . They are typically being tracked for skilled-labor or middle-managerial positions at best, in high-tech industry, or for careers like sales and accounting. (p. 18)

Although he asserts that these students' preparation in basic skills, including "cultural literacy," is "woefully inadequate," Lazere gives no examples of their writing, nor any sense of their thinking before or after they took his course. Instead, he describes his own liberation from "an uncritically conservative Middle American upbringing" into "the culture of critical discourse" and leftist politics to exemplify how middle- and working-class students can benefit from the academy as a liberating force. But in equating the "back-to-basics" movement to his own college education, Lazere implies a correspondence between his introduction to critical discourse and the narrow goals of a remedial skills course. Moreover, he assumes that his college experience was shaped more by classroom instruction than by the ethos of the 1960s and 1970s, the politically turbulent period in which he was a student.

Another basic writing population can be seen in J. Fogarty and S. Robins' (1990) description of their students at a community college in Saginaw, Michigan, "fondly known as the 'rust belt.'" Fogarty and Robins write:

> Most of our students would never have dreamed of going to college five or ten years ago. They would have left high school and worked for General Motors or Ford where they would have remained until they retired. With the decline of the automobile industry, these people now feel compelled to enter college in order to upgrade their skills or qualify themselves for work in fields other than those connected with the automobile industry. We have a number of middle-aged students whose lives have been disrupted by layoffs and who see college as a means to regain the security once afforded them by the automobile corporations. (pp. 5–6)

Rather than an "exciting new experience," as Fogarty and Robins assume college should be for first-generation students, these students "want it to be over with so that they can get on with the real task of making money and working at a steady, predictable job." Thus reading "is a slow, silent process that they perceive to be a non-activity. The text is more than mute for them. It is an inert insult to them" (p. 6).

This portrait of basic writing students across the country depicts a socially diverse population, including lower-middle-class whites, unemployed ethnic workers, and poor and working-class people of color burdened with double and triple (for women) oppressions. It paints a devastating picture of American life at the turn of the century, with social service cuts and unemployment, not illiteracy, tearing the country apart, and reveals the impact of the Reagan-Bush era on the country's morale. Given this level of social despair, resistance to oppressive conditions is understandably difficult, if not impossible; on the other hand, such conditions can change quickly, as the political tumult of the 1960s, in the wake of the quiescent preceding decade, demonstrates. Compare these scenes of an American wasteland to Adrienne Rich's exuberant account of teaching in the SEEK Program at the City University of New York (CUNY) in the late 1960s.

"We Learned from the Students"

Rich (1979) explains in "Teaching Language in Open Admissions" what it means to her to learn from the students: "our white liberal assumptions *were* shaken, our vision of both the city and the university changed, our relationship to language itself made both deeper and more painful" (p. 57). In tracing her own path from elite institutions like Swarthmore and Columbia to CUNY's City College, she describes her relationship, which she "can only call love," to the crisis-ridden city of the sixties:

> The city as object of love, a love not unmixed with horror and anger, the city as Baudelaire and Rilke had previsioned it, or William Blake for that matter, death in life, but a death emblematic of the death that is epidemic in modern society, and a life more edged, more costly, more charged with knowledge, than life elsewhere. (p. 54)

She admits that white liberal guilt in the wake of Martin Luther King's assassination and a political desire to work with "disadvantaged" students drove her to apply for a job at City College; but she was also fulfilling her need to get involved in the "real life of the city." The questions she confronted included: "What are the arguments for and against 'Black English'? The English of academic papers and theses? Is standard English simply a weapon of colonization?" (p. 56) Her students had "a capacity for tenacious struggle with language and syntax and difficult ideas, a growing capacity for political analysis which helped counter the low expectations their teachers had always had of them and which many had had of themselves; and more, their knowledge of the naked facts of society, which academia has always, even in its public urban form, managed to veil in ivy or fantasy" (p. 58).

Nor were her students only black and brown; two-thirds of basic writing students at CUNY were white students about whom Rich reflects:

> There is also a danger that, paradoxically, or not, the white middle-class teacher may find it easier to identify with the strongly motivated, obviously oppressed, politically conscious black student. . . . Perhaps a different set of prejudices exists: if you're white, why aren't you more hip, more achieving, why are you bored and alienated, why don't you *care* more? . . . In many ways the damage is more insidious because the white students have as yet no real political analysis going for them; only the knowledge that they have not been as successful in school as white students are supposed to be. (pp. 62–63)

A political analysis is precisely what many students and teachers, across color and class lines, had in the 1960s; the lack of a cogent analysis of today's socioeconomic problems is likewise a result of complex historical forces in the post-Cold War era.

Now, some twenty years after Rich described her experience teaching CUNY basic writers, there is a trend in the CUNY administration toward reversing the gains of open admissions and reallocating resources to predominantly white schools. As City College psychology professor William Crain argued in a December 1992 letter to the *New York Times*, the plan to reorganize the university would "have particularly negative consequences for people of color." As a result of the proposed consolidation of programs, "the colleges that stand to lose primarily serve students of color. The colleges that stand to gain are predominantly white." Furthermore, CUNY Chancellor Ann Reynolds suggests that "remediation" be remanded to the high schools, threatening the existence of developmental writing programs and echoing repeated calls to eliminate the composition requirement from the college curriculum. Indeed, as of the fall of 1995, a tighter admissions policy will go into effect at

CUNY'S four-year colleges, requiring students to complete all remedial courses within one year.

Evidence of this trend can be seen much earlier, according to
Rich, who looks back just seven years after the initial publication of
her essay in 1972 and calls open admissions a "profound if naively
optimistic experiment in education" in which

> white faculty at least, those of us even who were most committed
> to the students, vastly underestimated the psychic depth and eco-
> nomic function of racism in the city and the nation, the power of
> the political machinery that could be "permissive" for a handful of
> years only to retrench, break promises, and betray, pitting black
> youth against Puerto Rican and Asian, poor ethnic students against
> students of color, in an absurd and tragic competition for resources
> that should have been open to all. (pp. 51–52)

If CUNY basic writing programs survive the cutbacks, it will be
because students, faculty, and community members fight in the
courts and on the streets to save them. Both students and teachers
have been affected by the political anomie of the 1980s and the
recessionary budget cuts of the 1990s—an interesting contrast to the
zeitgeist of an earlier era that radicalized Lazere as a graduate student on the West Coast and Rich's basic writing students on the East
Coast; there was then, one could say, a degree of convergence
between resistant or subcultural discourses and what Geneva
Smitherman calls "the language of wider communication."

Given the growing polarization between rich and poor in this
country, including a disproportionate number of African Americans
among the poorest, it is not surprising that the gap has once again
widened between these discourses. Citing a study by William Labov
showing that Black English is diverging from standard English,
Smitherman (1987) points out that if the "language of wider communication" does not "provide entree to power and resources," there
is little impetus to learn it. To overcome this linguistic gap, she calls
for the inclusion of the mother tongue into the curriculum to serve
as a bridge to mainstream discourse. For Smitherman, "there is no
question, nor has there ever been any, about the need for linguistic
competence in this language" of wider communication. On the other
hand, she insists that educational reform is imperative, especially for
communities faced with economic and cultural devastation, and
proposes a national public policy on language that would mandate
tripartite instruction in the language of wider communication, the
mother tongue, and one or more foreign languages.

Another sociolinguistic perspective that sheds light on the
problems basic writers from different communities are likely to

experience can be found in Shirley Brice Heath's (1983) ethnographic study of three North Carolina communities. Focusing on two working-class communities—one black, one white—and one mainstream town community in North Carolina, Heath identified specific linguistic features in preschool children that predicted their performance in school. In the black working-class community, she found that the high value placed on orality, story-telling, and analogic problem solving, rather than on decontextualized reading and learning skills, led to early failure in school; in the white working-class community, conversely, children learned at home to perform well on primary grade tasks like discerning letters of the alphabet and to respond passively and obediently to adult directives, thus postponing failure in school until later grades when critical and imaginative thinking were rewarded.

Heath's research arose out of the transformation of the South caused by desegregation and the sudden intermingling of black and white communities. Specifically, she and the graduate students with whom she worked argued that "To categorize children and their families on the basis of either socioeconomic class or race and then to link these categories to discrete language differences was to ignore the realities of the communicative patterns of the region" (pp. 2–3).

These teachers, many of whom returned to graduate school as a direct result of public school desegregation, used the communication ethnographies they conducted in Heath's class to reexamine and change their teaching practice, a circumstance that profoundly, if temporarily, benefitted area schoolchildren from all three communities. But in the 1980s, decreased teacher autonomy, along with increased emphasis on testing and standards, "forced many of the teachers described here to choose either to leave the classroom or to revert to transmitting only mainstream language and culture patterns" (p. 368). In an epilogue that echoes Rich's description of the deterioration of open admissions at CUNY and gives a sense of the nation's shifting priorities, Heath concludes:

> . . . unless the boundaries between classrooms and communities can be broken, and the flow of cultural patterns between them encouraged, the schools will continue to legitimate and reproduce communities of townspeople who control and limit the potential progress of other communities and who themselves remain untouched by other values and ways of life. (p. 369)

This disempowerment of teachers has the same socioeconomic roots as the alienation and despair felt by many students. Marginalized teachers play an important role in any analysis of academic borders, especially low-status basic writing classes frequently staffed by part-time, temporary, and female faculty.

Teachers on the Boundary

The effects of part-time and temporary status on college teachers, writes Mary Kupiec Cayton (1991), "can be devastating. Many members of the academic proletariat suffer from diminished self-confidence, feelings of inadequacy . . . We become, as Paulo Freire suggests of all oppressed peoples, self-deprecating" (p. 649). The ratio of part-time and temporary faculty to full-timers in higher education is roughly one to three; but in disciplines like English, non-tenure-track lines constitute two-thirds of new full-time appointments (p. 647). As a temporary faculty member teaching composition from 1982 through 1988, Cayton—whose degree was in American cultural studies—was unable to revise her dissertation into book form because she suffered from writer's block emanating from her conviction that, despite "21 years of successful formal education," she "was incapable of speaking and being heard by those who counted" (p. 649). Her writing problems, she maintains, did not stem entirely from a lack of self-confidence, but rather from complex social factors that rendered her silent. Citing composition scholars like James Berlin and Patricia Bizzell, Cayton argues that

> [D]iscourse is the product of communities who use and shape it. It excludes as well as includes, and its exclusiveness has less to do with the intellect of the user than with her access to situations that enable her to master its conventions and syntax. (p. 650)

Cayton explains that shifts in academic writing from a more public lay audience to an all but exclusively professional one have produced a "private universe" that excludes and marginalizes part-time and temporary faculty along with students. She observes that the notion of teaching the outsider student to write by imagining herself as an academic insider, as Bartholomae suggests, creates a bind: "in order to write academically respectable prose, she must already be a member—and an equal member—of the community she seeks to enter. The task is virtually an impossible one." Moreover, the aim of such a pedagogy is ultimately to train students "to take their places in complex bureaucracies which will require them to use language in equally technical, recondite, and privatized ways" (p. 652).

By explicitly linking her own experience as a marginalized temporary teacher suffering from writer's block to the experience of student writers uninitiated into the conventions of academic prose, Cayton calls into question the "remediation" needed to gain insider status. In so doing, she enables us to view the concept of marginality as problematic and socially constructed, rather than given, a place that some of us just happen to occupy; hence, "to accept uncritically a particular form of discourse is to accept as well the social underpinnings that give rise to and perpetuate it—and which it perpetuates" (p. 653). Through questioning the social forces that legitimize and reproduce academic discourse, Cayton understands her marginality as a condition that "springs from contradictions in the academic system itself, rather than from inadequacies within ourselves" (p. 657). Refusing either to blame herself for remaining on the margins or to see herself as simply less fortunate than her colleagues, as Mike Rose saw his students, Cayton argues that "those who benefit by the systematic operation of power in their favor may be less likely to experience the problem as structural and more as an unfortunate circumstance involving a person whom they may or may not like, for whom they may or may not have sympathy" (p. 658).

In *Textual Carnivals*, Susan Miller (1991) considers composition's marginal status in the academy a self-perpetuated, negative myth. Like other marginalized groups, composition teachers assume an institutional identity that is culturally determined in both symbolic and actual terms. In a chapter titled "The Sad Women in the Basement," Miller theorizes the "blurred identity" of the composition teacher as apparent reforms leave intact the very oppositions that stigmatized writing instruction in the first place. Rather than simple polarities, Miller argues, literature and composition are interdependent entities that construct each other's "high" and "low" status, and together fulfill the important cultural function of regulating discourse. Says Miller:

> This labor allows an academic activity to domesticate otherwise "illegitimate" writing, not only by organizing academic values around it, but also by making this writing an emblem of related values throughout society. (p. 4)

In this account of the composition industry, teachers become surplus Ph.D.s who supply the academy with cheap labor; "mothers" and "servants" who both nurture and provide a service. This reserve army of potentially unemployed writing instructors is both deprived of institutional power and authorized to control unauthorized student texts. Underlying these conditions, Miller argues, are persistent structural inequalities in English departments, despite the "paradigm shift" from a current-traditional to a process approach. Although process pedagogy has been a "monumental achievement" that opened a space for theoretical work in composition, it has reinforced tradition rather than shifted the paradigm. She argues that the terms "process" and "paradigm" have seemingly contradictory purposes but function together to reproduce English, justifying the subjectivity of writing instruction and giving it scientific value. Thus,

> *Process* practices extend and preserve literary subjectivity, while their explanation in a *paradigm* theory extends and preserves the anxiety about status that has always been associated with English studies, both in regard to the perfection of elitist texts and as a professional concern about identity in relation to older, "harder" disciplines. (p. 140)

Both Miller and Cayton describe the situation of teachers on the margins of the academy in terms of social structures rather than individual failures; they also show how composition teachers have been complicit in maintaining the very structures that result in their marginalization and, worse, perpetuate the discursive practices and power relations that silence student (and teacher) writers or convert them into technocratic writing machines. Their critiques suggest a third position, following product and process paradigms, of social constructionism—what Berlin (1988) calls "epistemic rhetoric." A parallel can be seen in basic writing instruction in the shift from error analysis and a pedagogy of assimilation to the metaphors of dialogue and a "borderland" in which the writing class is viewed as productively conflicted and multivoiced.

Mina Shaughnessy's Guide Book

Since the publication nearly two decades ago of Mina Shaughnessy's (1977) influential book, *Errors and Expectations: A Guide for the Teacher of Basic Writing*, there has been a trend away from a focus on error toward a more sociocultural understanding of the problems faced by basic writers. Indeed, Shaughnessy initiated this trend. She wrote *Errors and Expectations* in the context of open admissions at City University of New York, intending to avoid the negative connotations of terms like "remedial" and to provide a guide to teachers disoriented by the needs of a new student population whose writing appeared to them garbled and inchoate. Sensitive to the anxiety teachers felt about the high level of error in these students' writing, Shaughnessy argued that one should not have to choose between approaches to teaching writing that stressed grammar, process, or "the therapeutic value of writing." In spite of her attempt, however, to define error as only one of a writing teacher's concerns, she helped construct a category of basic writer based on deficient, if logical, language use.

Thus, with the best intentions, she defined the basic writer in terms of error. Known and celebrated for her inquiry into the "logic of error," as opposed to rote grammar drill, her analysis of the students' writing lacked a contextual, sociocultural basis and, as John Rouse (1979) points out, ignored the overwhelming research evidence that grammar instruction is an ineffective means of teaching writing. Despite her genuine commitment to democratic ideals, her depiction of the basic writer has given us the following attributes: "severely underprepared freshman writers" who write "alien papers"; "true outsiders"; "strangers in academia." One telling metaphor is that of teachers as settlers of the frontier of basic writing, which is "unmapped, except for a scattering of impressionistic articles and a few blazed trails that individual teachers propose through their texts" (1977, p. 4).

Elsewhere she urges teachers to remediate themselves in the new discipline of basic writing—"not only suitable but challenging work for those who would be teachers and scholars in a democracy" (1988, p. 302). That work, according to Shaughnessy, centers on gaining mastery of standard written English:

> [A] person who does not control the dominant code of literacy in a society that generates more writing than any society in history is likely to be pitched against more obstacles than are apparent to those who have already mastered that code. (1977, p. 13)

Although Shaughnessy acknowledges that different codes compete with one another, she uncritically accepts the standard language as superior. As one of the most conspicuous border crossings in the academy, basic writing brings the conflict between dominant and subordinate discourses sharply into conflict. It is this contradiction that drives much subsequent basic writing research and theory.

In a 1992 issue of *College English*, Min-Zhan Lu and Paul Hunter debate Shaughnessy's legacy. Lu, arguing for a pedagogy that stresses conflict and struggle, criticizes Shaughnessy for advocating a strategy of accommodation in which students could "master academic discourse without forcing them to reposition themselves" (p. 906), what Lu elsewhere calls "the politics of linguistic innocence" (1991). Hunter bids Lu and other basic writing teachers to view "Shaughnessy's work not as 'innocent,' but as a politics of experience forged in a revolutionary struggle to open the doors of our academies" (p. 926). According to Hunter, Lu's "Marxist and poststructuralist" critique reflects a revisionist history of basic writing promulgated in a 1980 issue of *The Journal of Basic Writing* commemorating Shaughnessy. In a very interesting rhetorical analysis of the speeches published therein, he shows how Shaughnessy was cast as an upholder of conservative cultural values, rather than a pioneer in open admissions who fought for a more democratic educational system.

Despite his persuasive account of how E. D. Hirsch, a featured speaker, uses Shaughnessy to advance his own conservative agenda, Hunter's defense of her radical values underscores how contested her legacy has become. While Hunter is certainly right that Shaughnessy played an historic role in rethinking writing instruction for nontraditional students, initiating a process of curricular reform that continues to unfold, his own reading of the commemorative speeches demonstrates how readily her pedagogy was appropriated by the right. Given her revered status in composition studies and her influence on several generations of teachers, it clearly seems important to examine not only her "true" philosophy of teaching but also the various readings it has allowed. James Traub's (1994) account of Shaughnessy, for example, in his critique of open admissions in *City on a Hill*, echoes the conservative spin. He praises her "radical attack on conventional pedagogy" in the context of her belief in "the traditional mission of English departments." She was "the high-minded progressive and the radical populist" whose favorite authors, Milton and Bacon, redeemed her from the low-status "remedial underworld" to which she had descended (p. 115).

At issue for the basic writer is whether education is a means of empowerment or erasure, critical analysis or obedient conformity. Adrienne Rich (1979) gives a rather different picture than Shaughnessy of CUNY students circa 1970. Though Rich has nothing but praise for Shaughnessy, to whom she dedicates her essay on open admissions, she describes the students as witty and politicized. In contrast, Shaughnessy portrays basic writers as "[n]eglected by the dominant society," individuals for whom "college both beckons and threatens . . . to assimilate without acknowledging their experience as outsiders" (1977, p. 292). While Rich, too, is concerned about assimilation, she characterizes the students as agents of their own experience who revitalize the academy, rather than passive victims of its powerful allure. Says Rich:

> Many of our students wrote in the vernacular with force and wit; others were unable to say what they wanted on paper in or out of the vernacular. We were dealing not simply with dialect and syntax but with the imagery of lives, the anger and flare of urban youth—how could this be *used,* strengthened, without the lies of

artificial polish? How does one teach order, coherence, the structure of ideas while respecting the student's experience of his or her
thinking and perceiving. Some students who could barely sweat
out a paragraph delivered (and sometimes conned us with) daz-
zling raps in the classroom: How could we help this oral gift transfer itself onto paper? (p. 56)

Later, as she recalls the experience of "learning from and with our
students as rarely happens in the university," she documents the
impact on white teachers of *their* discovery of black literature, a
"submerged culture":

> . . . we were not merely having to confront in talk with our stu-
> dents and in their writings, as well as the books we read, the bitter
> reality of Western racism: we also found ourselves reading almost
> any piece of Western literature through our students' eyes, imag-
> ining how this voice, these assumptions, would sound to us if we
> were they. (p. 57)

And as she muses on the students' acuity and the intensity of their
response to that literature, she describes the political energy that
fueled their education, acknowledging:

> Writing this, I am conscious of how obvious it all seems and how
> unnecessary it now might appear to demonstrate by little anec-
> dotes that ghetto students can handle sophisticated literature and
> ideas. But in 1968, 1969, we were still trying to prove this—we and
> our students felt that the burden of proof was on us. When the
> Black and Puerto Rican Student Community seized the South
> Campus of C.C.N.Y. in April 1969, and a team of students sat down
> with the president of the college and a team of faculty members to
> negotiate, one heard much about the faculty group's surprised
> respect for the students' articulateness, reasoning power, and skill
> in handling statistics. . . . (pp. 57–58)

In "Putting Error in Its Place," Isabella Halstead (1975) quickly
disposes of what Rich calls "the bitter reality of Western racism,"
describing her entry into the classroom: "I began teaching writing six
years ago, first of all, doing my homework: *aside from reading the
popular classics on ghetto life*, I found articles about dialect and went
to lectures" (emphasis added, p. 72). Thus armed, she discovers:

> . . . our students recognize what they already have learned so well:
> this is what the teacher looks for, this is what writing is all about: The
> Avoidance of Error. Our students tell us so, in many ways. (p. 73)

Although Halsted makes no reference to Shaughnessy, as a CUNY
teacher she was presumably influenced by her work. Her deempha-
sis of error and concern about the students' alienation from writing

foreshadow some of the major trends in composition research. Yet her reading of student texts strips them entirely of communicative power. For example, she quotes a passage from "Sam's" freewriting exercise. Despite spelling, puctuation, and syntactical errors, Sam manages both to convey how difficult it is for him to write and to stress the importance of a college education and the ability to express oneself in writing.

Ignoring the fact that, by her own account, this was a freewriting exercise, Halstead tells us, "Sam, of course, has an *enormous obstacle: he lacks the basic skills required for communication in written standard English*, and knows this so well that it 'stops me from writing'" (emphasis added, p. 74). The exaggerated, absolute terms she uses to describe this student's writing make it seem more deficient and alien than it is. In fact, Sam communicates fairly well; he *lacks* experience and knowledge of conventions.

Language describing basic writers as deficient, abnormal, and alien can be found again and again in the writing of composition scholars, including many influenced by Shaughnessy and, like her, sympathetic to students. Andrea Lunsford (1978) laments the "awesomeness of the tasks" of researching remedial writing, a project that "could fill a lifetime of work for an army of pedagogical researchers and thinkers" (p. 47). Patricia Bizzell (1986), albeit ironically, calls basic writers "outlanders" whose "salient characteristic is their 'outlandishness'" (p. 294). Arguing that there is a style to basic writers' efforts "to make and transcribe meaning," David Bartholomae (1988a) terms their writing "apparently bizarre" and "incoherent" (p. 305). Alice S. Horning (1987), noting that Shaughnessy's "classic study" failed to provide a "comprehensive theory" of basic writing, proposes one based on second language acquisition theories. In her introduction, Horning describes basic writing students as "strangers in a strange land" whose "affective filter" must be reduced; she refers the reader to research articles that "suggest ways of tearing down the walls that students sometimes build between themselves and their instructors" (p. 5). Given the teacher assumptions described above, students might do well to defend against such pedagogical advances.

A Changing Perspective

As early as 1979, objections were raised to Shaughnessy's approach to teaching basic writers. In his essay "The Politics of Composition," John Rouse (1979) argues that Shaughnessy's program trains basic writing students "to follow authority, however willful or arbitrary," thus perpetuating their marginal status (p. 4).

Using Bernstein's theory of restricted and elaborated speech codes to characterize lower-class students in much the same way Lazere does vis-a-vis middle-class students, Rouse depicts basic writers as "young people formerly considered unsuited for higher learning or incapable of it, particularly blacks and hispanics" (p. 1). He goes on to describe them as students whose authoritarian, sociocentric family structures used a context-dependent speech code, typical of lower-class groups, as opposed to the elaborated code learned by middle-class individuals in order to communicate more explicitly and extensively. Thus, he argues, Shaughnessy's focus on error and surface reinforces the restricted speech code that had limited basic writers in the first place rather than enabling them to learn "an elaborated speech code and the habits of mind that go with it" (p. 4).

Yet Rouse, too, assumes a fundamental inadequacy in the language of basic writers and a need for them to adopt a superior linguistic code. Reflecting a trend in composition research generally of revaluing subcultural discourses, Bizzell (1986) argues that the tendency to see the problems of basic writers as rooted in either dialect, discourse conventions, or cognitive functioning has led to "an excessively narrow focus" of their experience (p. 296). The acquisition of academic language, she believes, results in the acquisition of a "new world view." It is this "biculturalism," not simply linguistic or cognitive differences, that makes it difficult for basic writers to succeed in college. In a similar vein, the shift to a process approach to teaching writing pushed researchers to examine acts of composing rather than written products. This work led to a more qualitative analysis of student writing. For example, Sondra Perl's (1979) study of unskilled college writers showed how their focus on editing undermined their ability to compose fluently, while their recursive style of writing proved them to be not beginning writers, but rather, writers whose "lack of proficiency may be attributable to the way in which premature and rigid attempts to correct and edit their work truncate the flow of composing without substantially improving the form of what they have written" (p. 328).

Further contributing to the changing perception of basic writers, Mike Rose (1985) criticizes the term "remediation" as a metaphor for medical diagnosis that "serves to exclude from the academic community those who are so labelled. They sit in scholastic quarantine until their disease can be diagnosed and remedied" (p. 352). Elsewhere, Rose (1988) challenges the view of basic writers as cognitively deficient, noting that to see such students as "locked . . . at the Piagetian level of concrete (vs. formal) operations" is to misinterpret Piaget, who assumed that normal functioning adults are by definition capable of analyzing and generalizing (p. 336). More recently, John Mayher (1990) examines the metaphors of skills and remediation, pointing out that, in light of our "very fragmentary understanding of how the mind works . . . what we do know shows even less promise for the 'skills' mavens in that we are discovering that many of the processes of language use are *necessarily* unconscious—and therefore not subject to the kind of conscious control that a drill and practice 'skills' model depends on . . ." (p. 4).

Underlying the cognitive/developmental approach to basic writing instruction is the widespread scholarly belief that literacy produced a "great divide" between oral and literate cultures in terms of cognitive abilities. Refuting this view, Scribner and Cole's (1988) study of multiliteracy in the Vai people of northwestern Liberia shows that "different types of text reflect different social practices" (p. 69). "Nothing in our data," Scribner and Cole conclude, "would support the statement quoted earlier that reading and writing entail fundamental 'cognitive restructurings' that control intellectual performance in all domains" (p. 70). Shirley Heath (1983) makes a similar point in *Ways With Words*:

> the different ways children learned to use language were dependent on the ways in which each community structured their families, defined the roles that community members should assume, and played out their concepts of childhood that guided child socialization. (p. 11)

It was the fact that the working-class children, both black and white, were socialized differently from the town children, who already spoke the mainstream language used in the schools, that placed them at a disadvantage in the classroom—not any cognitive deficiency.

Labov (1972), meanwhile, challenged the assumption that school language is preferable to other cultural languages. In his comparison of the verbal styles of a black, teenaged gang member and a college-educated black adult, Labov finds that the teenager's speech is marked by logic, mental quickness, and clarity, while the adult's is repetitive, full of qualifications, and verbose. Although Black English speakers, for example, may need skills typical of middle-class speech to excel in school, such as familiarity with Latinate words, what is commonly seen as linguistically superior in any cultural group may be verbose, turgid, even "dysfunctional" (p. 213).

Bartholomae's University

The word "basic" in the term "basic writer," says David Bartholomae (1988b), implies neither "simple" nor "childlike." Rather than learn language per se, basic writers have to learn written academic discourse. The sentences basic writers compose do not signify immaturity or "arrested cognitive development"; instead, they represent "a variety of writing," an "interlanguage," an "occasion to learn." Error analysis, Bartholomae suggests, provides basic writing teachers with both a technique for analyzing errors and a theory of error, based on second language acquisition. In "Inventing the University," Bartholomae (1988a) moves from the level of the sentence to the discursive conventions through which students do or do not appropriate academic language. Describing basic writers in respectful, admiring terms, he is "continually impressed by the patience and good will" of students; an essay is "[i]n some ways a remarkable performance" (p. 274).

Although Bartholomae's language in both essays reflects the evolution of an increasingly sophisticated pedagogy, his assumptions about the marginal status of basic writers remain unchanged. Accepting the status quo, he argues that successful writers must

> see themselves within a privileged discourse, one that already includes and excludes groups of readers. They must be either equal to or more powerful than those they would address. The writing, then, must somehow transform the political and social relationships between basic writing students and their teachers. (1988a, p. 277)

According to Bartholomae, the process of gaining insider status is more "a matter of imitation or parody than a matter of invention and discovery" (p. 278). The student writer, and by extension all writers, must learn to address a privileged insider with knowledge of the subject—"a way of knowing that is also a way of writing" (p. 277). To assume such a stance, students must locate themselves within a particular discourse community. Thus the movement of the basic writer, for Bartholomae, is from the outside—the margins—to the inside, a process he characterizes in "Writing on the Margins: The Concept of Literacy in Higher Education" as true of "most of us" whose "lives as students were marked initially by a struggle to enter into those habits of mind . . . that define the center of English Studies" (1987, p. 67).

Bartholomae's depiction of the margin is problematic for two reasons: first, he assumes an equality of opportunity between basic writers and "most of us," who, statistically speaking, in the academy are white and middle-class; and second, he sets up a binary opposition between the inside and the outside that ensues, as Foucault states in the epigram to "Inventing the University," from "the well-trodden battle-lines of social conflict" (1988a, p. 273). The absence of discussion of social conflict and structural inequalities in Bartholomae's analysis of basic writers is striking given his Foucauldian premise. Although he theorizes that the exclusivity of writing nearly always "defines a center that puts someone on the margins," he accounts for privilege solely in terms of knowledge rather than class, race, gender, or other social structures that over-lap the academic margin. Thus he concludes that the "exemplary culture" is "academic culture, with its powerful ways of represent-ing the world":

> It is not enough to imagine a world in which readers and writers are equals, particularly when the classroom is the place where this is not so, where there are people empowered by their knowledge and people who are excluded from that power. (1987, p. 79)

Rather than political oppression, it is the individual's failure to appropriate the knowledge and the discursive conventions of the academy that will result in his or her exclusion from it. Although Bartholomae acknowledges that once inside the privileged dis-course, it is not unusual to "push against that center—to debate, redefine the terrain" (p. 67), he does not question the oppressive structures that undergird the system as a whole, nor the fact that those who enter universities start out in unequal positions deter-mined by more than their familiarity with academic language. As Diana Fuss (1991) writes in her introduction to *Inside/Out: Lesbian Theories, Gay Theories*, about another experience of outsiderness:

> . . . the figure inside/outside, which encapsulates the structure of language, repression, and subjectivity, also designates the struc-ture of exclusion, oppression, and repudiation. This latter model may well be more insistent to those subjects routinely relegated to the right of the virgule—to the outside of systems of power, author-ity, and cultural legitimacy. (p. 2)

Moreover, she points out that the association of the "outside (of sex-ual, racial, and economic others) with absence and lack" has begun to be challenged:

> The greater the lack on the inside, the greater the need for an out-side to contain and to defuse it, for without that outside, the lack on the inside would become all too visible. (p. 3)

Such challenges promote the sort of oppositional world view that hooks learned as a child growing up on the wrong side of the railroad tracks. For Bartholomae, "all writers, in order to write, must imagine themselves the privilege of being 'insiders'—that is of being both inside an established and powerful discourse, and of being granted a special right to speak" (1988a, p. 277). To be sure, he frames this perspective by defining the university as a place where the student is called upon to "work self-consciously, critically, against not only the 'common' code but his own" (p. 283). The "inside" in the academy allows for "counterfactuality," the term George Steiner (1975) uses in explaining his notion that "through language, we construct . . . 'alternities of being'" (p. 473), and that Bartholomae and Anthony Petrosky (1986) adopt for the title of their influential book, *Facts, Artifacts, and Counterfacts*. Here the movement to the inside that Bartholomae and Petrosky believe possible for basic writing students is accompanied by a countermovement back toward the margin. Basic writers, they argue, "have learned (and perhaps in a way that their 'mainstream' counterparts cannot) that successful readers and writers actively seek out the margins and aggressively poise themselves in a hesitant and tenuous relationship to the language and methods of the university" (p. 41).

The potency of this theory of reading and writing helped create a nationally renowned pedagogy for basic writers, a thematic course modeled after a graduate seminar, rather than a laboratory for grammar drill, in which the students read whole books and become "experts" who theorize and debate subjects like adolescence or work.

Reconfiguring the Margin:
The Strategic Value of Basic Writing

And yet, despite the program's theoretical advances, the margin and center described by Bartholomae and Petrosky conceal the political basis for excluding social groups from cultural institutions like universities; their narrative of basic writing omits the race, class, and gender oppressions that pervade higher education. It assumes the academy is an ideologically neutral zone that fosters critical thinking and self-criticism, rather than a key site for the reproduction of the dominant culture, and that literacy is indeed a ticket to upward social mobility. In "On the Subjects of Class and Gender in 'The Literacy Letters,'" Linda Brodkey (1992) describes the ideologically driven responses of teachers to basic writers with whom they corresponded as part of a graduate class project. She found that both teachers and students told "class-based narratives" that for the teachers revolved around busy professional lives and for the students centered on external threats to themselves and their families or neighbors.

In one case, a student broke the pattern established by a teacher who had represented himself as "a complex subject . . . beset by personal failings his correspondent would find amusing," when she reported a tragic incident in her neighborhood. In a poignant run-on sentence, filled with spelling and verb errors, the basic education student describes a murder of a friend by a "good man" who she believes acted in self-defense.

The teacher's response to this news is a perfunctory three sentences, including the statement: "It's always hard to know what to say when the situation is as unusual as that one" (p. 104). Eventually, after the teacher's repeated failure to recognize the content of the student's letters, the student stops writing. The teacher's response, according to Brodkey,

> is characteristic of the kind of discursive uneasiness that arises whenever one of the students interrupts the educational practice that deems such working-class concerns as neighborhood violence irrelevant . . . we see that the teacher's desire to be preserved as the unified subject of an educational discursive practice that transcends class overrides the student's desire to narrate herself as a subject unified in relation to the violence that visited her working-class neighborhood. (p. 105)

Brodkey concludes that "To teach is to authorize the subjects of educational discourse" (p. 111). To that end, Nicholas Coles and Susan V. Wall (1987) observe, "The focus of metaphors such as 'initiation' and 'assimilation' is on what must change in our students, how they must become other than they are in order to accommodate our discourse" (p. 299). Instead, they propose to "focus also on those motives and abilities that grow from our students' histories and that may be sustained and extended, transformed perhaps, but not therefore abandoned in the process of accommodation" (p. 299).

Instead of the "critical detachment" encouraged in most academic discourse, Coles and Wall believe that "the more enabling path lies . . . through intensified engagement and even partisanship with the facts, experiences, and viewpoints represented 'in' books" (p. 303). This strategy of "identification" helps foster an ability "to imagine oneself in another's place," a necessary component of academic work. As opposed to the notions of "critical detachment" or "knowledge for its own sake," Coles and Wall stress "connection" and "commitment" (p. 307). Thus they reject the metaphors of the basic writer as an outsider, a "traveller to an unfamiliar country," in favor of the metaphor of living "between two worlds" (p. 313). For to become an "insider," as Bartholomae suggests basic writers need to do, one must assume the existence of outsiders and accept a system of exclusion, a proposition that subjects basic writers to a kind of cultural schizophrenia. Rather than undergo a "split" between one's culture of origin and the culture of the university, Coles and Wall argue, it is possible to enrich them through a process of mutual recognition.

Similarly, Victor Villanueva (1993), in his autobiography, *Bootstraps: From an American Academic of Color*, describes a basic writing program in which he "institutes a Freire-like dimension to the curriculum." As the new program director, he replaced sentence-combining exercises with reading Carolina Maria deJesus's *Child of the Dark*, the story of a poor, barely literate, woman of color from the *favelas* of Brazil. Although instructors seemed to like the book, Villanueva felt they depoliticized class discussions and reduced complex sociocultural problems to swapping stories about ghettos and suburbs, fostering dialogue but "no dialectic, no sustained probing into the conditions that relegate certain peoples to the ghettos and others to the 'burbs in disproportionate numbers" (p. 93). Villanueva, "an American success story" who made it from "GED to Ph.D.," grounds his theory and practice in the work of Freire and Gramsci, seeking to understand his own contradictions as an "academic of color," eager to assimilate yet constituted as "other," and placing that dialectical process at the center of the writing curriculum.

In her study of basic writing and student diversity, *A Kind of Passport*, Anne DiPardo (1993) points out the hurdles that students of color continue to face as accrediting institutions add "'progress toward multiculturalism' to their criteria" and college administrators fear that becoming "truly multicultural" will mean a loss of prestige and a tarnished institutional image. Unlike Villaneuva, however, who uses Bernstein's notion of a "restricted code" in his research on basic writing, and finds class rather than color to be the key determinant of students' difficulty with academic discourse, DiPardo sees the central problem as a "racial dilemma." Somewhat weakly, she concludes:

> [T]he problem lies not within equity students alone, but within all of us who struggle to promote interracial harmony in our classrooms and on our campuses, and who wrestle with our own ethnocentric biases and deficit-oriented assumptions about students whose backgrounds differ from our own. (p. 178)

While DiPardo's liberal perspective is limited, leaving out the issue of class almost entirely and making a "we are the world"-type plea for racial harmony, her story of a university's struggle to live up to its commitment to promote "educational equity" depicts the deep roots of racism in this country and the contradictory nature of much current institutional reform.

Thus, over the last twenty-five years in basic writing research and instruction, a complex picture has emerged of the relationship between language and identity, rhetoric and reality. As Susan Miller (1989) points out, "the basic writer became . . . an active emblem for contemporary writing and for all of its writers' entries into unfamiliar textual worlds" (p. 165). Using the experience of the basic writer as a metaphor for the condition of writers generally, Miller explains:

> Just as speech and primarily oral situations are always simultaneously confluent with, and alienated from, the fixed product of writing that attempts to record them, every writer is in some measure a basic writer. (p. 165)

Bartholomae (1987), too, sees basic writers in this postmodern light when he defines "the problem of writing to be the problem of appropriating the power and authority of a particular way of speaking . . ." (p. 70).

More recently, Bartholomae (1993) has argued that the basic writing curriculum perpetuates a top-down liberal humanism that erases difference and arbitrarily sorts students into basic and mainstream classes. Rather than "mark an area of contest, of struggle, including a struggle against its stability and inevitability" (p. 8), basic writing has become a fixture of the university. No longer a useful course, basic writing prevents mainstream and basic writers from coming into contact with one another. To illustrate what he means by "mainstream" and "basic," he compares passages by African American authors Shelby Steele and Patricia Williams. Steele tells us he struggles as a writer to "search out the human universals that explain the racial specifics" rather than be "overwhelmed by the compelling specifics—and the politics—of racial difference"; in contrast, Williams, writing *as* a black female legal scholar, unpacks the rhetorical gestures of the law that she says simplify the complex realities of life.

Bartholomae identifies Steele as a conventional "mainstream writer" and Williams as an unconventional "basic writer" to show what he means by a pedagogy that would encourage both kinds of writing in the classroom instead of erasing "the overwhelming specifics and politics of difference." To accommodate both discourses, he invokes Mary Louise Pratt's theory of the "contact zone," a social space like those produced by colonialism or slavery in which cultures, often unequal in power, come into contact with one another. Bartholomae suggests the contact zone could inform "a curricular program designed not to hide differences (by sorting bodies) but to highlight them" (p. 13), as opposed to existing programs that are "designed to hide or suppress 'contact' between cultural groups rather than to organize and highlight that contact" (p. 14). Further inspired by Carolyn Steedman's analysis of the writing of three working-class British girls, he suggests that "as professionals who manage writing in institutional settings we might see that writing as material for an ongoing study of American life and culture" (p. 17).

To teach in the contact zone and study American life and culture through student writing are appealing propositions that reflect a progressive impulse in curricular reform. However, the coincidence of the theoretical argument to abolish basic writing with political attacks against entitlement programs raises some questions. What is the strategic value of a critique of basic writing now, at a time when this sector of the university is most vulnerable to budget cuts and complete elimination? Is unconventional writing *basic* writing, and if not, which features of so-called basic writing are problematic and why? What criteria identify basic writing: organization of ideas, cohesiveness, surface features? Will writing in the "contact zone" or the mainstream class provide "basic writers" with adequate support to develop a range of rhetorical strategies and be able to choose which ones to use?

The emphasis of form over content in Bartholomae's gloss of the passages by Steele and Williams reflects the same kind of slippage so often found in discussions of writing pedagogy. Whatever rhetorical features of Williams' prose—and I would argue there are none, really—identify her as a basic writer, the more salient point is in the different positions she and Steele assume vis-a-vis race and racism. For Steele, identification with mainstream, universal values precludes a critique of racial stereotypes insofar as he aligns himself with the dominant culture and marginalizes his "black" identity. Williams (1991), on the other hand, in the final chapter of *The Alchemy of Race and Rights*, recalls the story of her great-great grandmother Sophie, who was bought and impregnated at age eleven by a white lawyer. When Williams' mother reassures her she is capable of succeeding in law school because law is "in her blood," Williams reflects that her mother asked her "to claim a part of myself that was the dispossession of another part of myself; she was asking me to deny that disenfranchised little-black-girl who felt powerless and vulnerable" (pp. 216–17).

Although basic writing is obviously not synonymous with racial and class subordination, it arises from the same structural and historical inequalities, and its position in the academy reproduces the same hierarchical arrangements of insider/outsider, marginal and mainstream status. However, basic writing has also evolved into a course that provides genuine support to students outside the main-stream, just as affirmative action, equal opportunity, and other enti-tlement programs have done, and consciously analyzes the margin-ality of both students and teachers. Neither academic nor social "margins" will disappear simply because we—or our students—wish they would. The contradiction remains between basic writ-ing's reproduction of the status quo and its potential to challenge existing conditions. If we simply eliminate basic writing courses, as Bartholomae suggests and politicians have begun to do, I fear the margin will simply shift, in many cases outside the academy alto-gether, as we return to a pre-open admissions, whiter, more middle-class university. If we reenvision basic writing, on the other hand, as a location in the university that we choose in solidarity with stu-dents whom it has historically served and teachers who have also been marginalized, then the margin can become, as hooks suggests, a site of resistance rather than deprivation.

There are two complications that need to be spelled out: first, basic writing students as a whole do suffer from the effects of struc-tural inequalities in social and educational spheres. Consequently, they need to confront their weak reading and writing skills in order to acquire the "language of wider communication" and participate in public discourse of all kinds. If such needs are addressed early in the educational process, so much the better. But if students reach college without strong literacy skills, then it is the responsibility of universities to reallocate resources and provide the best possible instruction and support services. Second, there *are* competing dis-courses in the academy that ask students to identify with the main-stream—white, middle-class culture and language—and deny the "disenfranchised" parts of themselves that feel "powerless and vul-nerable." Basic writing, as it has evolved, can be a productive mar-ginal space from which hierarchical insider/outsider versions of education can be critically opposed and students and teachers together can resist the logic of the center and the margins as inevitable representations of reality.

Part Two

Students and Teachers as Writers

Chapter Three

Surface Errors and the Female Body
Basic Writers Who Make Mistakes

> *The structure of political discourse possesses an isomorphism with the masculine sex; that is, working through an unstated correspondence—a "morphologic"—of sexuality and textuality, it privileges unity, form, coherence, oneness, the visible. Yet this morphologic has nothing to do with the female sex; it does not correspond to the feminine, because there is not a female sex. Irigaray uses the morphology of female sexuality—the logic of the female form, its multiplicity of erogenous places—to show that "it is possible to exceed and disturb this [masculine] logic." (1991, p. 88)*
>
> Lynn Worsham

The West Side Extension, one of DTU's three small branch campuses, is located in a working-class, predominantly Puerto Rican neighborhood where smoky Italian espresso shops still line the main street. I arrived on a winter evening looking for Inez Moreno, Anna Tremont's student who had agreed to participate in the study. Anna had described Inez as a very eager, diligent student, who worked hard but failed BRW-1, the first course in the basic reading and writing sequence. As I entered the community center that houses the college program, Inez greeted me at the door, where she had been keeping an eye out for me, her long black hair pulled back, her face drawn and tired. She smiled wanly and brought me inside. After negotiating for a place to sit, we settled down at a secretary's desk and began. As we talked, the busy reception area in which students congregated, many with small children, slowly emptied.

Among the first details I noticed were Inez's pressured, husky voice and the wetness of her eyes; she was very tense. I learned she is bilingual with a strong accent, in her late twenties, and a mother of five children, two from her husband's first marriage. She returned to school at West Side in the fall of 1991, a decision that reflects her determination to improve the quality of her and her family's life and to contribute more to their income. Both her writing and her oral commentary resonate with an awareness of social decay, especially the impact of budget cuts on social services. She feels grateful that her husband can support their family on his income as a city bus driver, in contrast to her mother's experience of raising six children singlehandedly on public assistance. But she wants to work, and a college education means a good job, preferably in accounting, rather than a factory job in which her salary would be spent entirely on child care. "I can't see myself doing that," she says, "working for $20, $30 a week. Okay, I'll get out of the house, but for what cost? It's gonna cost me too much."

Inez's account of herself as a writer is complex. According to both her and her teacher, Anna Tremont, she has difficulty writing, "just getting it down on paper," and makes numerous errors, only a few that she can correct. Driven by the belief that education will improve her life, she takes college seriously and confirms Anna's sense that she works hard. Despite her struggle with writing, Inez reports it has become a means of coping with her problems. Sometimes the writing she does for herself coincides with school assignments, but she has not written at all about several disturbing experiences she discusses in the interview. Nevertheless, she alludes to the value writing has for her, observing, "it helped me writing these papers" and has enabled her to retrieve lost memories and "face facts." Despite her diffidence as a writer, she feels she has made progress; while it will "take a few more years of practice to become a really good writer," she sees herself "in the near future writing, maybe writing about myself and my experiences, and even if I just write it for myself and keep a journal I would like to write about personal experiences and the way I feel like today and how I could, how to make a change."

In talking about her writing, Inez returned repeatedly to experiences of sexual abuse and physical injury. A serious accident detailed in one of her essays is precipitated by dizziness from skipped meals, which she did regularly during high school, striving to become thin enough to be a model. Just as writing illuminates "how to make a change" in her life, yet remains muddled on the surface by sentence-level errors or trapped as thoughts too complex to render in writing, her experience of her body teaches her not to starve herself, yet remains defined by the myth of female beauty and her sense of her own imperfection. This inscription of pain and error on the body—the surface—of writing and the physical female body resonates throughout Inez's stories. Even as she struggles to understand her situation, she remains subjected to the larger sociocultural forces that shaped her, and in particular, her concern with appearances. The near fatality of the "error" of fasting, which she writes about in her "fatal fall" essay, and that incident's lifelong consequences for her, set in motion a series of questions that indeed changed her and influenced her approach to rearing her own children.

However, just as she sees the grammatical and syntactical errors in her writing as separate from her thoughts—the problem is "just getting it down on paper"—she sees her errors of judgment, first as a teenager and later a parent, as momentary lapses or mistakes rather than manifestations of underlying cultural assumptions about women, discipline, and punishment. Thus Inez's description of herself as a writer and a woman suggests a correspondence between her conceptions of writing and the female body, both of which she describes as inner/outer dualities. In this chapter, I explore the dichotomy between surface and depth in Inez's thinking about her writing and her own body. I suggest that there is a palpable connection between attitudes toward surface errors in writing and attitudes toward the female body, and that we can better understand the punitive dimension of corrections of surface errors in writing when we see the consequences of the cultural propensity to "correct" the female body. Such errors, as Inez points out, may well be fatal if we view them, as she does, as empty forms, divorced from content, innocuous and meaningless in and of themselves; rather, we need to look at error, as Min-Zhan Lu (1993) suggests, as inherently semantic.

Received Knowledge

What Actually Happened

At first, in BRW-1, Inez says she "was reluctant to write about personal experiences. I felt kind of uncomfortable, you know, writing about people I knew or even family members or myself." But her teacher, Anna, "kept pressing for situations that had actually happened . . . and I couldn't see myself making up a story, even though a good writer will make up a story." Her discomfort with the personal aspect of the assignment seems to emanate not from the personal narrative itself but from her displacement of a central, secret episode in her childhood—sexual abuse—onto less highly charged, though still emotionally intense, material. That is, what she feels most compelled to write about—as becomes evident in a long, circuitous story about child abuse—she *cannot* write about; nevertheless, her pressing need to articulate what happened to her, first as an abused child, then a potentially abusing parent, motivates her to write about other incidents in her life and attracts her to the idea of writing itself, *for* herself.

Then what stops her? According to her teacher's direction to write about "situations that had actually happened," and her own inability to see herself "making up a story"—something she believes only "good writers" do—writing *is* "truth." The metaphor WRITING IS TRUTH seems to underlie Inez's sense of herself as a writer and renders her (re)construction of what *actually happened* problematic for both her and her teacher. In relation to her paper, "Drugs and Prostitution" (see Figure 3–1), she explains that she had "seen the changes in this neighborhood right in front of my eyes," including the erection of a hospital that "ruined the whole neighborhood, finishing the destruction that had already started." In order to capture this process of deterioration, she concludes: "So that's why I changed the paper a few times and put in the personal experiences." Apparently, Inez has understood her teacher's suggestion to tell about what *actually happened* as the key to writing: if she puts in personal experiences, then the essay will assume a shape, achieving the veracity of the eyewitness account, the conviction of personal testimony; indeed, this belief in the authenticity and authority of experience is implicit in the personal narrative assignment. In Inez's view, then, good writers may invent, but unpracticed [not good] writers must rely on true stories for authentification.

Two related responses to Anna's advice derail Inez in her "Drugs and Prostitution" paper: first, the invitation to write about what really happened opens a floodgate of memories about sexual abuse that she desperately wants to write about but never does; and second, the anecdotal material she associates with what happened conflicts with the task of developing an argument, precisely where the paper's logic breaks down. For Inez, writing about events that "actually happened" helped her to face . . . to think about certain people, you know, even your loved ones. They were in certain situations and you didn't wait to even think about it, just because it was so painful, and I found myself when I wrote that I eased the pain a little and I let go of that pain that I was holding inside.

Although she credits Anna with helping her "let go of certain feelings that I had so tied in . . . that were frustrating me and were holding me back from doing better," she also states that if she had been able to write about her most disturbing experiences, "I'm sure my writing would have grew better and I could have got into

continued on page 58

Figure 3–1
Inez Moreno's Paper: "Drugs and Prostitution"

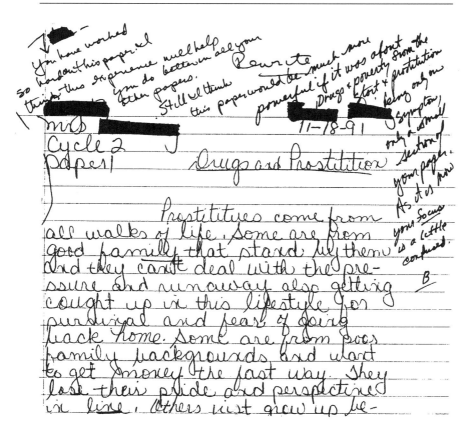

Figure 3–1, continued
Inez Moreno's Paper: "Drugs and Prostitution"

living–thats the way to make a living and follow in those footsteps. I think the problem with the prostitution in this neighborhood have a lot to do with drugs and economics.

Mostly the problem today with prostitution has a lot to do with Economics and drugs. The reason I say economics is because with the budget cuts today as they are everthing is being cut back, that includes places where prostitutes can go for help. For example, hospitals are cutting back on the services available. Treatment centers are forced to cut back there help.

Second of all most of these men and women are hooked on drugs of somekind. Some shoot up Drugs. Others smoke crack and do other drugs I know nothing about.

The men and women get involved with drugs. They lose their jobs and family. They are so hooked on the drug that whats left for them to do is sell their bodies for money and drugs. My friend Julio had a new food.

Figure 3–1, continued
Inez Moreno's Paper: "Drugs and Prostitution"

city job but due to cutbacks he got fired. He got so depressed that he got into doing crack. He felt that by getting high, he'd for- get his problem. He didn't sell his body but he started robbing his friends and family. It got so bad that his wife was going to leave and take the children with her and not let him see them. That's when Julio went for help. Two years later, Julio is still off the drug.

Economics is also playing a big rolle in the situation today. People are losing their jobs. They have no education or skills they are left jobless. With no job there is no money so they lose their homes. now they are homeless. Some of these individuals get so depressed that they start doing drugs to forget their problems. The problem becomes bigger and bigger and they turn to prostitution and drugs. My mother's friend Carmen lost her job due to cutbacks. She had no skills or degree so she got really depressed. Her family tried to help her get through

[right margin annotation:] utiadd to talk about Julio as on example in a paper on prostitution when he was never a prostitute

Figure 3–1, continued
Inez Moreno's Paper: "Drugs and Prostitution"

this but she got involved with the wrong people. She started shooting up drugs and soon after she started selling herself. She caught Aids and when she found out she had the Aids virus she got off the streets and got help to stop shooting up, but it was to late for her because she died about six months after she found out she had Aids.

    There should be a place were people go to get help before the problem gets any worst. Instead of cutting back on the budget and start closing down these places where people can get help, they (the government) should start cutting down their paychecks. Keep these places open for the ones who need and want help.

    A few of my ideas are:
    Open some place were the prostitutes could go for help. Walk the streets and talk to some of them who really want help

Figure 3–1, continued
Inez Moreno's Paper: "Drugs and Prostitution"

---

but don't know how to find it.
WoodHull Hospital was doing this
at Flushing Ave. Talking to the
girls and giving them condoms
for protection but the cutbacks
stopped that program. WoodHull
Hospital should get some budget
(money) help from the government
to start this program again.
        Have more drug treat-
ment centers available for the
drug abuses. Don't make them
wait or come back when they
have a space available because
they wont come back. Give them
counseling so that they will stay
off drug. I speak of the centers
available now, I called a few
places to get help for my brother
and all they told me was "call
back when we have a bed available'
Help is what is needed. Something
has to be done.

Figure 3–1, continued
Inez Moreno's Paper: "Drugs and Prostitution"

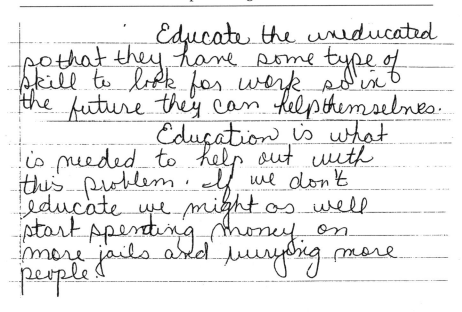

Educate the uneducated so that they have some type of skill to look for work so in the future they can help themselves. Education is what is needed to help out with this problem. If we don't educate we might as well start spending money on more jails and burying more people.

it." Significantly, Inez feels she has been given permission to write about her own experience. Yet the permission neither extended to the province of the classroom nor allowed Inez to write about sexual abuse, which seemed clearly to be the paramount issue in her life. Her discomfort in sharing her papers with her classmates, she says, led to a change in class procedures. "I don't mind *her* knowing," Inez explains, referring to Anna. In fact, Anna never referred to Inez's history of sexual abuse, and very possibly never knew about it. What Anna perceived as confused, unskillful writing may represent Inez's struggle with hidden psychic material, at once displaced by the safer essays she writes and apparent in them as a repressed wish to "face . . . certain people, even your loved ones . . . to let go of that pain I was holding inside." Her eagerness to talk about the subject of her sexual abuse underscores this hypothesis, as if she experienced the interview format as a kind of therapy.

After discussing her writing process, she summarized the content of "Drugs and Prostitution." The problem, she says, is not the story, which she knows all too well because her neighborhood is full of prostitutes, but "just getting it down on paper." Specifically, she explains, "I'll find a lot of errors, um, grammar errors," which she misses at first, "but once I read over and read over and read over, I'll catch a few." She worked very hard on the paper—"I must have done it like four different times, rewrote the paper, and I was sick and tired of prostitution after a while." She then turns to content, explaining that prostitution is related to social problems—"it has a lot to do with society and drugs . . . Economics also plays another role . . . loss of job, loss of home, no family support." Some prostitutes, male as well as female, "want help but don't know where to get it; sometimes they know where to get the help and just don't want it." Yet within this social context, she concludes, "It's an individual situation." These themes, enunciated in her oral remarks, recur throughout the paper. In the second paragraph, she explains what she means by economics:

> The reason I say economics is because with the budget cuts today as they are, everything is being cut back, that includes places where prostitutes can go for help.

Although Inez gives examples of two friends and one family member who were involved with drugs and/or prostitution, describing how their lives unraveled as a result of job losses and inadequate health services, she never situates herself—literally, authorizes herself—in the paper as she does here in her oral commentary:

> . . . when I wrote it I was thinking about the neighborhood where my sister lives . . . two blocks off of Flushing. They had a very very bad problem with prostitution and drug abuse. There was times when they would break down her door to her building to get into the hallway and shoot drugs and smoke crack and do whatever else they do in there. And I seen that so much that as I wrote this paper I just thought about my sister's building and I wrote about situations I seen there with my own eyes, not things that I'm making up . . . And you see all these women and men just deteriorate in front of your eyes. I mean today you might see them and tomorrow you might not, so you wonder, you know, are they dead? Did they get some help? And I really just wanted it to leave from that one particular neighborhood because that's where my family lives and I don't like the idea of walking through there and having my children see this . . . so when I wrote this it was more like it was hitting home for me.

Thus, orally, she sets the scene and locates herself within it, providing the context that impels her to write the paper and gives her the authority of an eyewitness. From her description of her revision process, the "personal experiences"—her stories of Julio, Carmen, and her brother—appear to have been incorporated into the paper in response to Anna's comments. While these stories infuse the essay with some anecdotal energy, undercut at least in one case (Julio's) by a disjuncture between the thesis and the exemplification of it, they do not provide the ballast Anna apparently hoped they would. While Inez endeavored to comply with her teacher's suggestions, Anna remained dissatisfied both with her own assignment and with Inez's essay.

All These Multiple Drafts

Before turning to a closer analysis of Inez's "Drugs and Prostitution" paper, it will be useful to introduce Anna Tremont and establish the context in which she recalls having made the assignment. I interviewed her in April at her apartment, not far from the DTU campus. We sat next to an open window, curtains billowing, the room, full of traffic noises, growing dim as night fell. During our conversation, her teenage son came home; her daughter, a high school junior, was out for the evening. A 43-year-old writer and teacher from a midwestern, white, working-class family, divorced, a single parent, Anna is a thin, energetic woman with straight, light brown hair and an expressive face, who refers to herself as "physically dyslexic." She moved to New York in the early 1980s to escape the Midwest and resume work on her Ph.D.

There is an aura of sadness about her, which she traces to both the death of her mother and an almost excessive compassion for students. As she says, "I start becoming upset with my own reading. You know, sometimes I think I have too much empathy." Later, she explains, "When I was a young girl my mother always told me, you know, 'I'm going to die before you grow up, you are going to raise the children. Be sure of one thing, graduate from high school.' That was my message." The text of the message is the parental value placed on schooling; but the tragic subtext, shaping her outlook from a young age, is the knowledge that, before she grew up, her mother would die. Disoriented by the loss of her mother, as well as the responsibility she assumed for three younger siblings, Anna's primary objective after graduating from high school was to leave her father and stepmother's home. Although she had been awarded a college scholarship, she turned it down, enrolled in a night course, and worked as a secretary, as her mother had done. "I never knew what I wanted to be when I grew up," she remarks, explaining that she only received her B.A. at age thirty. Soon after, she decided to get her doctorate in English, ultimately earning her degree in 1988.

As Anna discusses "Drugs and Prostitution," she informs me that Inez "does all her work and comes to class every single time";

the paper, Anna says, was "weird." Its problems, however, may have stemmed from the assignment, an experiment with Freirean generative themes inspired by a graduate course on literacy Anna was teaching that same semester. After the students in BRW-1 had read an article on prostitution and become engaged in a discussion of it, Anna recalled thinking:

> They're in [the West Side neighborhood] and there's prostitutes all over. In fact, a prostitute was killed in the school parking lot this week . . . so I thought it would be cool to write about it.

But the assignment "fizzled out," Anna said. "I worked too hard on it; I wasn't satisfied with the whole assignment." She read her comment at the top of Inez's paper: "You have worked so hard on this paper. I think this exp—." She then interrupted herself, affirming that "[Inez] did work; she kept rewriting and rewriting . . . [but] it was too hard of an assignment." After the first paragraph, she remarked on a long, packed sentence; after the second paragraph, she admitted, "Well, it's hard to comment on this paper. I have to say that I just remember all these multiple drafts and it's all screwed up still, and I think that's why I thought—gave up with them."

She then questioned the genre, speculating that the paper might have been more successful in letter form. Another problem, she reflected, may have been a lack of the trust needed to discuss community issues that affected many of the students personally. Inez's paper is "very uncomfortable." Interfering with the greater fluency she achieved in her other, more autobiographical papers is

> discomfort about essay form, discomfort with the subject, and "do I know all the people and can I talk about what really is happening in my neighborhood and what's going on because there's so much social stigma about it."

It is Inez's reference to her friend Julio—who "didn't sell his body but he started robbing"—to illustrate the chain of events leading to prostitution that triggers Anna's memory of the paper:

> See, what I really wanted her to try and figure out—she goes off the subject. I wanted her to write about whatever it was she was writing about. To either set it up and write about dru— I would keep talking to her and it would come back with, start with prostitution and go off into this friend that she really wants to write about, you know.

More specifically, Anna wants Inez to "talk about neighborhood problems or something, and frame it." But this is precisely what Inez fails to do in the autobiographical narrative as well; only there the omission is less glaring because the story structure conceals the absence of an analytical or argumentative framework. Moreover, it is clear from Inez's account of revising the "Drugs and Prostitution" paper that, in compliance with Anna's suggestions, she tries to incorporate personal experiences, such as her firsthand knowledge of Julio, into her discussion of social problems. But Anna has no idea Inez wants to—but cannot—write about sexual abuse, a theme that never surfaces in the interactions discerned from Inez's papers or those either she or Anna reports.

Reading "Drugs and Prostitution"

The first paragraph demonstrates several problems that permeate the paper: stance, genre, and logic. Inez begins:

> Prostitutes come from all walks of life. Some are from good family that stand by them and they can't deal with the pressure and runaway also getting caught up in this lifestyle for survival and fear of going back home. Some are from poor family backgrounds and want to get money the fast way. They lose their pride and perspective in live. Others just grow up believing thats the way to make a living and follow in those footsteps. I think the problem with the prostitution in the neighborhood have a lot to do with drugs and economics.

First, Inez assumes an objective stance, announcing in her opening sentence her theme of prostitution and then using a familiar construct—on the one hand . . . on the other hand—to substantiate her thesis. Clearly this is more than an abstract freshman theme for Inez: she knows firsthand about her subject. Even in its present form, the paper is more than what Jasper Neel (1988) calls "antiwriting"; indeed, a question it raises in light of her teacher's response and Inez's attempts at revision echoes Richard Ohmann's (1988) admonition to beware formulas for good writing that automatically value detail and specificity more than a writer's attempt to generalize, theorize, develop an overview. Inez's difficulty in "getting it down on paper" stems not only from her perspective, her authorial stance, but also from the genre she slips into which, like Neel's antiwriting, reads like a cross between a five-paragraph theme and a tediously written textbook.

The problems with perspective and genre are exacerbated by the illogical development of ideas, which forces the reader to slow down—a strain, given the sheer volume of papers most composition teachers grade—and glue disparate ideas together. In Inez's case, she moves quickly from discussing prostitutes "from all walks of life," rich and poor, to the problem in "*this* neighborhood" (emphasis added) caused by drugs and poverty. In an attempt to be even-handed and inclusive, fair and authoritative, Inez not only surrenders her actual authority as eyewitness, a member of the community, but also misleads the reader into thinking the essay is about all prostitutes, rich and poor, instead of the prostitutes in a particular neighborhood that is, in fact, impoverished. As Anna notes, Inez has trouble with focus, depicting the neighborhood's general state of decline from drug addiction and robbery to unemployment and homelessness—with prostitution only one of several social problems she has in mind. Indeed, the first and last sentences of the opening paragraph suggest opposing theses: the first, economics is not a determining factor in prostitution; the second, in this neighborhood, it is.

Despite Inez's difficulties with the paper, she gives voice to stark social realities faced by working-class people. She writes:

> There should be a place were people go to get help before the problem gets any worst. Instead of cutting back on the budget and start closing down these places where people can get help, they (the government) should start cutting down their paychecks. Keep these places open for the ones who need and want help.

And she concludes:

> Education is what is needed to help out with this problem. If we don't educate we might as well start spending money on more jails and burying more people.

Inez believes the U.S. government's failure to provide social services to its own people results from its readiness to send "food and medical supplies" abroad. As simplistic as this analysis may be, the underlying sentiment is her disgust with domestic policies that have turned her neighborhood into a war zone full of casualties. She says, as if to an imagined political leader:

> Worry about your own people. I mean help us so that we could keep producing a better life instead of wasting away. It's gonna happen—the human race gonna deteriorate and kill each other away, and it's gonna happen like the dinosaurs and there's gonna be no more humans.

Here, when she addresses a concrete audience other than the teacher, and speaks spontaneously rather than writes, Inez achieves a tone of authority and a clarity of style and purpose her writing lacks. Anna

Tremont's wish for Inez "to write about whatever it was she was writing about" can be understood in two ways: first, as advice to narrow and focus her topic; but second, and perhaps more important, to engage in the act of writing as generative and dialogic, writing not to capture an elusive, external truth but to construct knowledge through a dialectic between the writer, the word, and the world.

Constructed Knowledge

For Anna, writing serves as both trace and medium of her life, a way "to make a record about life and to affect the record at the same time. It's very important for me to write for my own existence and to continue to think through my life." Thus, learning to write is:

> learning how to make a record and change a record and how to make sense of your life by using writing so it becomes—once you're putting words down on paper you're questioning even how you speak, when you speak, what you do, what's being said to you.

Inez appears to have understood and benefited from this conception of writing in regard to her personal life; she says she would like to keep a journal to write not only about her feelings but also about "how to make a change." However, she has difficulty transferring the knowledge she has gained from journal writing to that required by her "Drugs and Prostitution" paper. Clearly, neither anecdotal material nor personal narratives alone can unpack her complex perceptions; rather, what she must do here is *construct* an argument about her neighborhood, a task that calls on her to "make a record and change a record" of social events or phenomena just as she would do in regard to her own life. A key difference between Anna and Inez as writers—in addition, of course, to Anna's experience— is that Anna constructs the record that Inez tries to locate elsewhere. Both necessarily rely on already existing discourses—the discourse of the media, for example, in Inez's case; however, for Inez, the truth remains external to her, couched in a language that she quotes but never engages with dialogically or critically. Given the complexity of the assignment, which Anna admits, the question is what sort of pedagogy can help Inez make the material her own.

Along the lines suggested by Mary Belenky et al. (1986) in *Women's Ways of Knowing*, Anna's perspective is one of *constructed knowledge*—a way of knowing "in which women view all knowledge as contextual, experience themselves as creators of knowledge, and value both subjective and objective strategies for knowing" (p. 15). In contrast, Inez still operates in terms of *received knowledge*—a position in which women feel they can receive and reproduce but not create knowledge. As Belenky et al. point out, these categories are fluid. In Inez's case, firsthand knowledge of social conditions in her neighborhood gives her a "double consciousness" about American society. But she can only engage in a dialogic writing process when she writes about herself. When she writes about the world she is unable to "talk back" and the dialogue is cut short. She becomes passive, surrenders authority, and cannot sustain the logic of her thinking. Ideally, what she learns about writing for herself will infuse her writing about the world, enabling her to move from a position of submission to the Truth to one of critical reflection on her perceptions of reality.

Anna as a Writer

Anna's history illuminates this process of intellectual growth. Her ardent, intimate sense of connection to writing and teaching seems to arise, in part, out of her troubled childhood—particularly her mother's death and her father's emotional distance—and her working-class roots, which together foster depression, insecurity, and disbelief in her professional success. Once she decided, fairly late, in her early thirties, that she wanted to write and teach, she was "very serious about everything I did to the nth degree." Her studies were "life and death" matters; she liked what she was doing; it deeply involved her. Asked to articulate what it means to her to have thus shaped her life, however, she sets her love for her work, children, and companion in the context of her emotional life:

> I'm very depressed a lot in my life but it doesn't have anything to do with the quality of my life . . . I love studying and I love writing and I love teaching; I love Paul, I like Katy, I like Joey, and I'm still depressed ninety—no, I'm still depressed thirty percent of the time . . . I'm glad that I went ahead to do what I wanted even though I thought the whole time I will never be able to make a living doing this—I mean really, I'm only doing it because I like it and I want to do it. And I'm glad I did that. And I can't believe I actually ended up with a job . . .

Except for the memory of a few teachers who encouraged and supported her, Anna recalls herself in high school as a "definite outsider." She says, "I always felt out of it because I was never that social. I was more social with kids who would hang out in dimestores and skip school and smoke cigarettes and run off . . ." Explaining further, she attributes her outsider status to the fact that "after my mother died I felt so unable to deal with anything that that sort of escalated." Nevertheless, once she decided to apply herself to her studies in tenth grade, up to which time she "wasn't into it," she became and remained an "A" student.

Her earliest memories of school are entirely negative until the third grade when she "might have had a nice teacher." She hated the early grades because "I didn't like the teachers. I wanted to be with my mother. I remember that, crying, and I used to wet my pants on the way to school and back . . . I had very mean first and second grade teachers; I remember them, thinking, God, who are these people, you know? They would just like be there, gnnaaa, yelling at me and telling me to shut up." Her next vivid memory of school coincides with her mother's death. In spite of a kind sixth-grade teacher who "tried to help" her, Anna recalls having had to assume parental responsibilities for younger siblings whose teachers would "call me in like I was an adult." This role had its limits, however, according to Anna, who recalls that "I used to tell stories to my brother and sisters all the time and I would make up horrible nightmarish stories." Sometimes teachers would inform her, "Your sister is telling the strangest stories in class."

During her high school years, Anna received praise from teachers for her writing but seemed to seize control of her life by switching from an academic to a business track. A tenth-grade English teacher who taught students to write haikus read Anna's poem aloud to the class. "That had a very big influence on me. I think I started writing again," Anna recalls. "I think they were sad little things, too, you know, like falling leaves or something." This gentle self-criticism of her early writing as precious, maudlin, diminutive, is also evident when Anna talks specifically about her development as a writer in her early twenties: "I had a little journal full of things . . . but they're really horrible if I look at them now . . . they were just kind of like expressive things, you know."

Two moments in her life lead her to identify as a writer. The first, in her early twenties, occurred while she was living with a man who ordered her, "Get me a beer." Anna recalls, "I'd go get him a beer. I mean, I was his fucking slave. I can't believe I did those things in the past. These were my models of my past." Eventually, she had an argument with him precipitated by a television program that featured two feminists and impelled her to write. Looking back, she says, "I don't know—something about that. I started writing poems more . . . I would sit and write them and figure out my life." The second moment, the defining one for Anna in terms of writing, happened the day after her second child's birth, at her mentor's house, where an author was discussing a book she had recently written about having her baby. "Oh my God," Anna recalls having said to herself, "I can write about my own experience." Explaining how this insight helps her to teach writing, she describes an "incredible feeling that my domestic experience . . . that realization that I could write, that every single little thing that happened to me in my life made a big difference . . . it was *my* material. I didn't have to write about somebody else's life. Anyhow, so that was a big turning point."

Inez as a Writer

The turning point for Anna is the moment she realizes she can write about her own life *because* what happens to her "made a big difference," meant something, counted. By her own account, Inez, too, seems to claim an authority of experience that perhaps will eventually infuse her writing with greater consciousness and control. For the time being, however, her writing about herself seems more grounded and engaged than her writing about the world; even though she bears witness to scenes of contemporary life that need to be reported and analyzed, she has yet to claim sufficient authority to do so effectively. Certainly, one issue for Inez is her dialect, evident in her speech as well as her writing, which impedes her fluency in what Smitherman calls "the language of wider communication"—the standard language; but the fact that she is more fluent and has greater syntactic control writing so-called personal narratives than expository essays indicates that dialect is a secondary issue, one that is likely to diminish as she becomes a more practiced writer. How then does the authority of self-knowledge relate to authoritative knowledge of the world?

For Anna, the process of internalizing theoretical concepts and making them her own is analogous to the process for Inez of critically interacting with the complex world around her. Says Anna of her early encounters with theory:

> I didn't think I really wanted a Ph.D. because I was really starting to be very skeptical about theory; in fact, I think I was being jarred and I was thinking well, you know, if I can't live with this theory. . . . See, for me, deconstruction and all these things, I didn't figure that I could somehow get it into my art and my way of living because it seemed contradictory to me, and it was so drastic. That's really why I quit graduate school. I know this sounds weird now because it was so radical but I couldn't—and the people who were teaching that weren't willing to make that leap between life and theory. I understand, well I could apply it to this text but I couldn't—they weren't making some real bridge to talk—to try to

get people to see how theory related to life, which I had to spend lots of time writing and thinking about to do.

One wonders if the bridge Anna describes needing between life and theory would serve a similar function for Inez in linking self-knowledge and knowledge of the world. Of course, by the time Anna quit graduate school, she was already a self-identified poet/artist whose resistance to theory was to some degree a conscious one, while Inez is just starting to see herself as a writer at all and does not have comparable skill or knowledge. Nevertheless, the experience Anna recalls of having "had to spend lots of time writing and thinking" to relate life to theory highlights the trouble an unpracticed writer like Inez seems to have in moving from a view of knowledge as given to understanding it as constructed and subject to criticism. Such experience points, for one, to a problem with the institutional expectations implicit in semester-driven curricula that students move in a predictable, linear, and relatively speedy fashion from one level to the next. Especially for nontraditional students like Inez—or Anna, for that matter—this assumption is a crucial one to challenge and replace with a deeper understanding of the uneven, unpredictable ways people learn.

In keeping with the metaphor of a bridge between different types of knowledge, one can see both Inez and Anna in their respective situations as located on various borders. For Inez, one border is between received and constructed knowledge, or, put somewhat differently, between tenuous knowledge of the world and increasingly authoritative self-knowledge; another is between home and school, the impoverished community she describes in her essay and the branch campus, which connects her through DTU to mainstream values. The borders Anna describes between life and theory, art and intellect, must be navigated, temporarily, outside the academy, perhaps because inside the institution Anna continues to feel class divisions that, if anything, are more rigid for the predominantly white, male, middle-class faculty, invested in maintaining its privilege, than for the overwhelmingly working-class, African American and Latino student population.

For both women, the borders are permeable, their positions in flux; they lose the stability of fixed social boundaries and identities, but gain the potential for more radical change, personally and politically—in Anna's words, "to create a record and change it." Thus, as Belenky et al. would acknowledge, it is wrong to place Inez or Anna in fixed epistemological categories. For one, we can see many similarities between them, including their female, working-class backgrounds and their struggle with the academy; for another, Inez's cultural location allows her a vision that middle-class America, urban and suburban, sees on local evening TV news or, worse, through the lens of hatred, fear, and resentment created by the politics of race and class. Nonetheless, Inez's testament to social decay, however raw and unmediated by critical reflection, is easy to disregard as a poorly written school essay by a basic writer, while Anna, as a credentialed professional and published poet, escapes some—though by no means all—of the strictures of working-class identity.

As Linda Brodkey (1992) points out in "The Literacy Letters," well-intentioned, middle-class teachers tend to misread and ignore concerns articulated by working-class student writers. The voices of such students are routinely silenced and dismissed as illiterate or unsophisticated in order to defend middle-class myths of stability and normality against the encroaching realities of poverty, socioeconomic injustice, and social breakdown. Even a teacher as sympathetic as Anna becomes fixated—especially in her written commentary—on Inez's errors and syntactical confusion rather than the story she tells. Inez *is* an authority on drugs and prostitution in her neighborhood, whose apocalyptic vision of social decay in which the human race disappears like the dinosaurs echoes the dire predictions of some leading environmentalists; but she is *also* a writing student whose ability to articulate what she knows is mediated by stock concepts and images derived from the media and other cultural reserves, and delimited by her struggle with the symbolic realm of written English.

Surface Errors: Writing the Body

Along with class and ethnic codes, Inez's writing is shaped by the rhetoric of gender. A crucial, unresolved experience for her as a child was sexual abuse, a subject she returns to again and again, circuitously and obsessively. She never names her abuser, nor specifies the nature of the abuse, but her repeated references to her choice *not* to write about being abused, along with her focus on abuse throughout the interview, indicate the internal pressure she feels to talk or write about her experience, as well as, speculatively, the degree to which the repressed material blocks her other attempts to write. For example, she says:

> I really didn't want to get into the sexual child abuse issue just yet, so when Tremont said to write about something that happened to, you know, yourself in the past, it was either those two issues [sexual abuse or an accident in which she injured her teeth].

Early in the interview, after first disclosing that she was sexually abused, Inez explains the psychology of sexual abuse in therapeutic terms:

> I just don't want to deal with people questioning me cause it had nothing to do with—it was something I couldn't control. I was only a child. It wasn't like it was my fault and most of the time with children that's what happens: they grow up always thinking it was their fault. And then it's very hard to let go of the guilt.

She goes on to attribute her understanding of this dynamic to psychological counseling and to acknowledge her inability to discuss the problem with her mother, an idea that presumably was suggested to her in counseling:

> With me, see, I have a cousin who's a counselor; she helped me through this and then I seek counseling on my own; I see a counselor twice or three times a week, a month, and I spoke to her about it so I'm able to let go of it now. I still never confronted my mother about it, you know, she doesn't know about it. Maybe she knows but I've never—it never came out of me—and that's something that's very difficult to deal with.

One sees here the process of internalization Bakhtin describes as external authoritative discourse becoming internally persuasive. The words of the counselors enable Inez to see her situation in a larger social context in which she gains both independence from her mother and knowledge about therapy as a way "to let go of it."

But her understanding of sexual abuse does not extend to a critique of the gender stereotype of the thin female model, described in another essay in which she describes her "fatal fall." This fall, a physical accident in which she is severely wounded, bashing in her upper teeth, reverberates with a more metaphysical fall from grace, innocence, and purity into a state of sinfulness. Inez writes in the opening lines of her essay:

> I remember that cold, snowy January afternoon as if it were yesterday. (It actually was 15 years ago) when I had that fatal fall that ruined my four upper teeth and any chance that I had of becoming a model or entering the "Miss Teen Pagent" which was my dream and goel in life.

In addition to casting herself in a stereotypically female role—the sexual objectification and spectacle of a beauty pageant—she goes on to explain that the fatal fall was caused by skipping breakfast and lunch to "avoid gaining any weight, which I often worried about." She repeats the excruciating details of the fall in her oral commentary on the written passage. First, she writes:

> I heard the school bell ring. "It's time to go inside", my friends called out to me, "Put on your coat". Let's walk back to class. All I remember after that is looking at the sun and then being awaken by my friends screams and crys.

A moment later, she *says*

> . . . so I'm just like saying, "What are these stars in front of my eyes?" And I hear the school bell rang and when I go to walk, all I remember is stepping a foot forward. That's how I figured I must have passed out on my face because I remember sticking my foot forward to walk and I don't remember anything else after that.

The repetition is powerful, even poetic, especially in light of Inez's claim that "writing has helped me deal with problems and not repeating them again. Not doing the same mistake twice." She must retell the incident again and again in order to escape it; yet there is a quality in her rambling narrative about the fall, child abuse, and, as we shall see, her fears of abusing her own children, that suggests an obsessive compulsion to repeat the story of the "fall" until she learns something from it besides the loss of her beauty and her chances to model or win the pageant. But the story never changes; the ending remains the same, its significance fixed, already decided by a cultural hegemony she fails to recognize, much less resist or challenge. For she cannot rewrite a story, except superficially, premised on unchallenged assumptions about female beauty and worth. The one mistake she can recognize, that of starving herself, she does not see in the larger context of sexism and the social phenomena of anorexia nervosa, bulimia, and other eating disorders suffered primarily by women.

The Other as Mirror

Like the fairytale queen, threatened by Snow White, who asks the mirror to tell her who is the fairest of them all, Inez relies on mirrors to affirm her status, whether elevated or fallen. The dominant metaphor that emerges in this paper and throughout the middle portion of the interview is that of mirroring, how Inez sees herself reflected in others' eyes: "the shock and hysteria" in her friends' faces; "the guard's panicked look"; the nurses' "pessimistic look"; the guard's assumption she fainted because she was pregnant or on drugs; the literal covering up of the mirrors in the nurses' station to prevent her from seeing her own fearful image; and her compulsion to look. In the interview, she describes how she tricks the nurse:

> "Look I need some water, I need to spit." So she forgot that the mirror was there and I went to the sink and when I looked up I just

> went hysterical, I mean, there was no controlling me. I was scream-
> ing, I was crying . . .

Then she is mistreated by hospital staff who view her as a "spoiled
brat," she believes, because her mother is on Medicaid. The doctor,
a "tall, slim, white man in his mid-thirties with blue eyes," looks
down at her and makes her uncomfortable, calling in what "seem
like the entire hospital staff," who make her feel like a "freak from
another planet" and conduct a "three-ring circus" to decide on her
treatment. She fears her classmates will see her as "a monster, a horrible thing" because that is "the way I saw myself." Finally, in
describing the scene of writing and rewriting this paper, she con-
jures an image of herself reflected in her children's eyes:

> I cried as I wrote this paper, and I read it to my children and they
> were like, "Mommy, is that true?" And I says, "Yeah, that was
> true." And they was like, they felt bad and they could understand
> how I feel sometimes and why I'm so strict with them . . .

She insists that they eat every meal "because I learned the hard
way." She had "nobody to tell me what I was doing was wrong."
Her own mother didn't notice that she "faked" eating. Now, she
adds, giggling, she knows about nutrition; if she wants to lose
weight, the only meal she will skip is lunch. In psychological terms,
she has learned to face

> the fact that you know if you want something, you want it so bad,
> like I wanted to be a model so bad . . . that I couldn't go about it
> the way I was doing it cause all I did was hurt myself. And starv-
> ing wasn't getting it.

Economically, she realizes that the ill-fitting implants she got in the
hospital were "all my family could afford." Now, fifteen years later,
she will have to pay $6,000 to repair the damage from the poor med-
ical care she received as a teenager, a fact she sees in stark class
terms: "If my family's situation had been better off and I would have
received expert dental treatment, I would not be facing this
dilemma today." But despite her insight into the dynamics of
instant gratification, her awareness that starving herself is self-
destructive, and her class-conscious critique of the medical profession, her view of gender stereotypes remains uncritical and simplistic. The image she sees of herself reinforces her sense of lost
beauty and her complicity with her fall from grace; her inability to
question gender roles in turn produces confusion about her role as
a parent.

Inscriptions: Burning, Spanking, Writing

In the midst of discussing her "fatal fall" essay, Inez makes a long digression about a fire. The connecting thread is her observation in regard to her own traumatic experience that the educational system is unequipped to deal with the serious problems that affect children's lives. To mitigate these problems, she argues, schools should provide counseling—at least referrals—to children and parents. In her segue into the story of the fire—which becomes a story about child abuse charges, counseling, and Inez's own defining experience of sexual abuse—she states: "That's the way, with my counselor—I started going to my counselor because my daughter was playing with matches." Her daughter inadvertently set her bed on fire while Inez was cooking, then remained silent, leaving Inez's four-year-old son to run to the kitchen and announce, "Mommy, there's fire over there." Inez screamed, "Get out of the house, get out of the house right now." She moved the baby to the hallway and returned to extinguish the fire, making "a whole mess of the room and the living room and everything."

This episode, which scared Inez, led her to invite a fire marshall into her home for a prevention class for the children. In the course of the two-and-a-half hour class, Inez's daughter told the fire marshall that her mother "whipped her"—terminology Inez objects to, explaining, "I didn't consider it a whipping; I spanked her because I was scared that she was gonna do it again." Ironically, her concern for her children's welfare resulted in an investigation of her for child abuse. The fire marshall had no choice, according to Inez, but to call the Bureau of Child Welfare (BCW). The BCW worker who visited Inez's home declined to prosecute her, since the children seemed "well" and "healthy" and she understood Inez "was really scared." Her account of her interaction with the BCW worker occasions a retelling of the story in greater detail, culminating in the object of the entire digression, that is, Inez's request for counseling "just to even improve our daily life, just to be able to deal with certain things because kids have it rough, you know, and it helps them and it helps me."

Counseling helps Inez deal with her accident as a teenager and with having been sexually abused. In a poignant description of denial and acceptance of personal trauma, Inez compares the benefits of therapy to those of writing:

> I spoke to her [the counselor] after about six months about the sexual abuse. It took me a long time to be able to put it that way, you

know just to be able to say it, cause then I couldn't even say it. I just would dream it and for a long time I couldn't tell whether they were dreams or they were real. . . . It was just that I was so small I had blocked it out; when I started to know what life was about, it started to come back up. I just didn't know what to do. You know, I can't deal with it; I can't see myself telling my mother, you know, because I was too afraid of what she was gonna think. She was gonna say it was my fault or she was gonna accuse me of something, you know . . . she was the last person I wanted to tell, which is really wrong because she should be the one you confront . . . I won't confront her, you know, I'll talk about it and everything but I won't tell her. And it helped me writing these papers.

Anna's Reading of Inez's Papers

Unlike Inez, who neither confronts her parents nor gives an analysis of their problems, Anna rebels against her oppressive father and offers a detailed history of her parents' lives. Her father earned his General Equivalency Diploma (GED) after quitting high school and went on to become a first-rate draftsman for a Detroit auto company. Her mother's French Catholic family—turned Presbyterian—was shaped by her grandmother, a gentle, quiet, caring woman. In contrast, Anna says, "My father comes out of this dark German Swiss background. I mean I always thought there was more of an involvement with money and a lot of pain in that family." Thus she gives some sense of history in her description of her family: her paternal grandfather an alcoholic, her grandmother—already on her second husband by the time Anna's father was born—divorcing and remarrying three or four times, a "wild cookie." There was "weird incest" in the family involving an aunt and a cousin and "all these secrets." Her father's response, Anna thinks, was to insulate himself. She wonders "what it was that would make that—that he would be so scared of others. He won't go into the city, he won't come visit me. He's very frightened of the world."

Her mother, the only one of nine children to graduate from high school, expected Anna to persevere alone, take care of her siblings, and pursue her education. Although her father also encouraged Anna in school, offering her help in his forte, math, and teaching her the alphabet—a scene she recalls in a recent poem—his efforts were thwarted because, says Anna, "I never had a very good relationship with him." The conservative Protestant work ethic both her parents embraced takes diametrically opposite forms in their attitudes toward race: "My mother was a definite anti-racist and so always raised me to think that you do not be biased against anybody. My father was a total racist." Presumably, these differences between her parents' world views caused Anna to feel the loss of her mother even more keenly.

As she reads Inez's papers out loud, elements of which perplex her, Anna's attention shifts from the text to Inez, whom she remembers as "a young woman with a million children." It is as if her memories of the writer can answer questions about which the problematic text remains silent. For example, in Inez's essay about her accident, Anna stops after the first paragraph, at Inez's description of the "fatal fall that ruined my four upper teeth and any chance I had of becoming a model or entering the 'Miss Teen Pageant.'" She explains that the assignment, modeled on the narrative structure of *How the Garcia Girls Lost Their Accents*, was "to write a story about their life in the present tense and then in the past." (It is interesting to note here that Inez's peculiar—almost modernist—shifts from first- to third-person pronouns appear to be caused by confusion between verbs and pronouns, so that she performs the correct task on the wrong part of speech.) Anna has conflicting responses to Inez's opening paragraph—sympathy for her suffering and irritation with her embrace of stereotypical gender roles:

> . . . I feel compassionate at first with her and then I'm distanced from her which I wouldn't even say to her actually because she starts writing about "Miss Teen Pageant," and as I read that, I remember so many kids writing about "Miss Teen Pageant" at [a nearby] College . . . I'm always like "oh" you know but then I go back and realize that even though I hate that whole thing that you have to be beautiful to succeed—I just don't understand the disappointment.

At the same time, her interpretation of the paper depends on her knowledge of Inez as a student in her class, a knowledge that shapes and is in turn shaped by Anna's reading:

> I look over and I see Inez who doesn't look like any of the girls I've ever known who've written about doing this, so I know, and she's really struggling; I know something's going on, and then I start understanding her in class better, why she's quieter.

As Anna reads through the essay, she refers to errors as discrete problems Inez is not ready to tackle. However, for Inez, errors are paramount in her efforts to revise her writing. About her "Drugs and Prostitution" paper, she says:

> I had done it four times and I couldn't find all the errors she had found the first time and I was like, my God, but it seems so well written, and I kept reading it, and then after she pointed some of

them out, then you know I started seeing them myself and I started writing, and I rewrote it four times before she gave me a good grade.

Significantly, Inez misunderstands Anna's philosophy of teaching writing, not only that Anna would have postponed dealing with error but also that she believes error alone does not determine the value of a piece of writing. Although she will ultimately need to produce relatively error-free prose if she wants an audience, the biggest obstacle to her at this point in her development is not grammatical error but lack of control and fluency.

Anna also notes techniques she might have taught Inez to improve the paper: "to make it more descriptive and to include dialogue." However, she counterposes, her aims in the assignment were to give students an opportunity to write about their own experiences, to work on verb tenses, and to talk to each other. Ultimately, she praises Inez as a good BRW-1 student, maintaining tension in her paper that "keeps you reading." "A very good paper," she concludes. "Too bad you even have to grade 'em." This contradiction surfaces later in the interview when Anna describes Inez as a student and writer: "a very good student" who will "probably succeed despite all her problems. . . ." Inez will "be like a 'C' writer unless she gets herself really freer so she can be more intellectual." Thus what prevents Inez from developing her potential are her family responsibilities in conjunction with "some block that stops her from being really inquisitive . . . she stays on the surface a little bit, she doesn't like instantly click off into question"—the inner, often conflicting voices of a Bakhtinian dialogue, Anna reflects, that can transform external authoritative speech into internally persuasive speech. In light of Inez's account of her personal history, "some block" immediately brings to mind her discussion of having been sexually abused.

The lack of depth in Inez's writing is underscored by Anna's more penetrating analysis. In her essay on her accident, Inez describes an exchange with the school nurse in which she mentions she has no home telephone. For Inez, not having a phone is incidental, a given, insignificant except as a narrative truth, part of what she remembers happened. But for Anna, "here's right when you start getting into what the real situation is . . . that she's falling down and hurting herself, wants to be in a beauty contest, and she doesn't have a telephone at home."

It is through a broader perspective that Anna interprets Inez's words, imbuing them with meaning derived from the sociohistorical context that she supplies to the narrative:

> I start seeing what the situation is, that her life's surrounded by—
> she may not have even thought about it though that she reveals by
> saying "I don't have a phone at home" that she's coming from a
> very poor family.

This sort of analysis is exactly what Anna wishes Inez could provide:

> I wish she had some kind of social crit—, more of a social criticism
> and could see it a little broader.

But unlike Inez, Anna's impulse to link the personal to the social is
habitual, reminding her of an approach she developed several years
ago in her composition classes based on a rubric she refers to as
"self-world-text." At the end of Inez's paper, Anna reads her own
comment out loud: "Someday we'll have socialized medicine and
teeth will count, I hope." The final grade for the paper, Anna recalls,
was a "B+" because Inez "fixed everything," not an "A" "because
she's still struggling with grammar" and the paper lacks "sophistication." The social critique Anna would have liked Inez to under-
take remained unspoken in the dialogue between them, only
referred to obliquely in Anna's written comment.

Thus there appear to be two types of miscommunication. First,
Inez displaces her feelings about the central trauma in her life—sexual abuse—onto other material that remains entirely on the periphery of the student–teacher relationship. Inez reports discovering
"when I wrote I eased the pain a little and I let go of that pain that
I was holding inside." It was "Tremont," Inez says, who "helped me
let go of certain feelings that I had so tied in, that were frustrating
me and were holding me back from doing better." But she never
writes about her experience of sexual abuse, which emerges
strongly as we talk as the nexus of the "certain feelings" that hold
her back; instead, she imagines that "if I would have wrote on experiences like that [sexual abuse], my writing would have grew better
and I could have got into it."

The second miscommunication can be seen in the discrepancy
between Anna's written response to Inez and her conversation with
me about Inez's writing. First, as already mentioned, Anna's oblique
end comment in "The Fatal Fall" about socialized medicine is based
on an analysis she never communicates to Inez, nor does she convey her belief that more "social criticism" or a stronger conceptual
framework would have strengthened the paper. Similarly, although
Anna quite clearly identifies the problem with the paper on prostitution as lack of focus and organization, Inez understands that Anna
wanted her to "put in personal experiences." Anna believes Inez

really wants to write about . . . the problems in the neighborhood and how they're related to economics and not to depend on just prostitution to organize it. But once she got started with the draft, she wasn't skilled enough to go back.

The subversive writing of *ecriture feminine* might build a bridge for Inez between her experience and rhetoric, calling into question pedagogical assumptions about "unity, form, coherence, oneness, the visible" (Worsham, 1991, p. 88). As a teacher, Anna feels remiss for having failed to constrain Inez to a single focus, a manageable topic. But perhaps Inez and other students would benefit from allowing "the multiplicity of erogenous places" (p. 88) to exceed and disturb the masculine logic of traditional rules of writing. Of course, as Lynn Worsham suggests, were we to embrace the philosophy of *ecriture feminine*, "we would cast such suspicion on the whole enterprise of composition studies as an accomplice of phallocentrism that composition would be transformed beyond recognition" (p. 94). Nonetheless, rather than second-guess what Inez "really wants to write about," an admission of the unmanageableness and multiplicity of Inez's themes might encourage her to develop a strategy of writing that could accommodate complexity and tolerate ambiguity. Instead of asking her to conform to the constraints of her topic, her thesis, we might recognize that she has already begun to explore its contradictions, excesses, and disturbances.

Anna's theory of teaching writing, influenced by Mikhail Bakhtin and Paulo Freire, is "based on reading, writing, talking about things that are important to you, and so that you write and write and think and talk." Yet she suggests her theory may be changing: "I might work more with like weird exercises and things and playfulness with words." As a corollary, she thinks "there should be a break between talking about social problems in writing . . . and then come back to it." Her theory of teaching basic writing is the same except that she is more patient, "don't cut off, don't be arrogant, really talk to them, same thing only it's just that you can't move as fast." For her, basic writing simply means "inexperienced writers and readers." She likes teaching basic writing students "because they change so much if they stay with it." But she recognizes social realities that impinge on their development:

> . . . on the opposite side, the thing that's worst is that they're usually very poor, their lives are really hard, they can't come to class, they don't stay with it, they give up easy because they have bad habits of schooling and they have messages from their past that say, "I'm a bad student, I can't do it, I don't know how to speak proper English blah blah blah" . . . you know, they have lots of tapes going in their heads that make it hard.

But while Anna enables Inez to claim writing for and about herself as therapeutic, she seems to reinforce Inez's difficulty in writing for and about others by inadvertently separating language and thought and assuming that Inez will never become more than a mediocre student and writer. For Inez to develop as a critical thinker capable of questioning and rewriting the central events in her life, she will need to assume an authoritative voice stronger than those she hears who insist it is her fault—for having been abused, female, and lacking. Rather than being surface errors, Inez's "mistakes" in writing and life are deeply embedded in language, culture, history, and politics. It is from this point of view, I believe, that Inez and other students like her will be able to understand the logic of their errors and explore the deeper structures of language and life.

Chapter Four

Writing in an Alien World
Basic Writers and the University

> *That invisibility to which I refer occurs because of a*
> *peculiar disposition of the eyes of those with whom I*
> *come in contact. A matter of the construction of their*
> inner *eyes, those eyes with which they look through their*
> *physical eyes upon reality. (1947, p. 3)*
>
> Ralph Ellison

I take the words "in an alien world" in this chapter's title from a paper on the invisibility of blacks in science fiction by Joe Baxter, an African American student at DTU's South End branch campus. Joe wrote the paper in a BRW-1 class taught by Sandra Bennett, a young African American teacher, aspiring writer, and science fiction enthusiast. I was so impressed by the depth and eloquence of Joe's writing—in addition to his papers from BRW-1, he has completed the first hundred pages of a novel about cyberfighters —that I wanted to test my own and Sandra's excitement about it with another teacher's response. Since I also wanted to include more men in the pool of volunteer teachers, most of whom had been women, I asked Thomas Riley, an Irish American, senior faculty member in the English Department, to read Joe's paper. An alumnus who graduated twenty-five years ago, Tom was the oldest participant in the study and had the longest association with DTU; he also, like Sandra, shares Joe's interest in science fiction.

Joe's placement into a basic writing section raises two key questions: 1) what criteria for evaluation—implicit and explicit—do we use to assess writing? and 2) what contexts for learning do we—and can we—create for diverse students? More than any other student who participated in the study, Joe defies the typical linguistic profile of a basic writing student, yet shows how traits like open resistance to schooling and labored handwriting identify students as basic writers nonetheless. The issue of racism, which emerges clearly here with the topic of Joe's paper, becomes paradigmatic of the effects of social exclusion on any group. Indeed, Joe's paper on the invisibility of blacks in science fiction can be read as analogous to the situation of basic writers—many of whom belong to other socially marginal groups as well—in the university; yet his anomalous position as a novelist in a basic writing class suggests a view of academic life as heterogeneous and fluid despite a hierarchical structure that remains stubbornly resistant to change. No sooner is the hierarchy contested by students like Joe—or policies like open admissions—than the institutional codes are reasserted and the boundary lines redrawn.

Joe came to the main campus for the interview. A large man in his mid-twenties, tall and very heavy, he was wearing an African medallion and spoke in a fluent, confident tone of voice. Perceptive, articulate, voluble, he was extremely charming; one question could elicit a wide-ranging, half-hour response. For privacy, we sat in a colleague's office with the door shut, traffic faintly audible outside the fourth-floor window. South End, the branch campus that Joe attends, is located half an hour away from the main campus in an inner-city neighborhood that made headline news soon after our interview when a teenager gunned down two of his classmates in the corridor of their high school. I have heard similar stories from many students, including Joe, who speak of themselves as lone survivors of childhood friends now dead, on the streets, or in prison.

Joe was born in the Bedford Stuyvesant section of Brooklyn, raised by his mother, aunts, and grandmother in what he describes as a "matriarchal" family. He has a very protective attitude toward his younger sister, whose high school and college education has been a priority for him. Says Joe, "Me and my mother would share the housework. I would wash the dishes, sweep, vacuum, whatever, just so that when my sister came home from school she could go out and join extracurricular things." But his sister, despite having graduated from a college bound program was, like Joe, financially unable to attend college. "So in a way," Joe explains, "I kick myself for that because I was thinking that, you know, if I make sure that she can do everything she wants to do, then she'll go to college. Then again, I did the same thing my friends did. I didn't think about tomorrow, and I didn't do anything to make sure she had enough money to take classes." Fortunately, the college program gave Joe and his sister as well as their aunt the opportunity to return to school. "So far," Joe says, "college has been everything I wanted it to be."

Several themes emerge in Joe's depiction of his family and community: 1) his close, caring relationships in a family he defines as matriarchal; 2) the strong value the family places on education and racial tolerance; and 3) the struggle he and his friends endure in a social environment that obscures and often obliterates any vision of the future. The countervailing forces in Joe's life to despair and decay, in addition to his close-knit family, appear to center on literacy: reading *and* writing, especially science fiction, as well as visual media—in particular, television drama and comedy. It is the imagination of the future either as more just and equitable, or as a grimly brutal technocracy, that seems to attract Joe to science fiction. Science fiction provides him with a vehicle to project the outcome of the drama of the struggles for social justice he observes. Indeed, the genre of science fiction, with its visions of a future world, can be seen through Joe's eyes not only as a metaphor for hope—that we have a chance, at least, of preserving the planet and cultivating a more ethical human sphere—but also a metaphor for writing itself as existing in time, suffused with a sense of futurity.

Social Contexts for Writing

Joe's World: "Tomorrow's Not Promised to You"

Joe describes how his friends laughed at him as a teenager because of his love of reading: "My peers, they were on the basketball court playing basketball and I'm sitting on the bench reading a book, watching everybody's coats." "Man, you're dreaming," his friends told him. "You know you don't have no time for that . . . You gotta make sure that you have a hustle and that you put food on the table." Joe's analysis of this attitude reflects a deep despair: "Most teenagers act the way they do because they don't think tomorrow . . . The saying now is 'Tomorrow's not promised to you,' so they don't live for tomorrow, they live for today, for the here and now, and that's why I think they have so many problems because they don't make plans for Friday. They make plans for Tuesday and then they make plans for Wednesday. They go on like you can get blasted and you'll be d.o.a. tomorrow."

He tells the story of a friend, Peanut, who would ask Joe, "Why have you always got your head stuck in a book, man?" Joe says he told Peanut:

> . . . a book is more than just pages and letters and words, man; it's, if you read a book and it's a book that you really enjoy, you don't just see the pages, you could see what's really going on in your heart.

Since Peanut liked horror movies, Joe recommended Stephen King's *It*. So enthralled was Peanut by the book, says Joe, that upon seeing the two-part television adaptation, "I couldn't keep him in his seat. 'They didn't do that in the book!' [Peanut said]." Although Joe "tried to pull him in," Peanut was shot and killed by a local drug dealer. Confirming statistical reports of the high rate of homicide among young black men, Joe admits, "I been to more than my fair share of funerals, and these people were young." But he places this phenomenon squarely within a social critique, asserting that the drug trade is strong in his neighborhood because local residents "see people like Michael Milken and Ivan Boesky making big money, okay, and basically getting away with it."

In his paper entitled "Blacks in Sci. Fic.: Why Are We Invisible" (see Figure 4–1) Joe provides a deeper analysis of his peers' alienated lives. He begins by inviting us into a "typical scenario" in science fiction novels:

> Picture an alien world. A sleek craft touches down on the forbidding surface. A hatch opens and a small group of people exit the vehicle, they check the atmosphere with strange instruments. The air is fit for them to breathe so they remove their helmets. All the people are human and all are caucasian.

Commenting orally on the paper, Joe extends his critique of science fiction's limited vision of humanity to women—"I think women should be just as heroic as men"—and to the disabled, including the blind, paraplegics, and people with Down's syndrome. As he puts it, "If you're writing about the future, you have to put all of humanity in there, everybody, you know, you can't just have the heroes all being white, blonde-haired, blue-eyed males." In his paper, he theorizes:

> Science fiction is a medium where you create a vision of what will be, what could be, or what may have been. To exclude any group of people is to say they do not exist in the reality you create. If you

write about the dreams of the human race, you should include the whole human race.

It is Joe's ethical stance that links this powerful vision to a commitment to social justice. In addition to his watching progressive television shows like "Star Trek" and a proclivity for reading that broadened his world view, Joe's perspective seems to have been shaped by growing up in what he calls a "matriarchal" family in which women were strong role models. For example, he describes his maternal grandmother: "She's a stroke victim and she can't talk anymore but she still runs the show." Another important family value is a capac-

continued on page 86

Figure 4–1
Joe Baxter's Paper: "Blacks in Sci. Fic.: Why Are We Invisible?"

Blacks in sci.fic.: Why are We invisible

Picture an alien world. A sleek craft touches down on the forbidding surface. A hatch opens and a small group of people exit the vehicle, they check the atmosphere with strange instruments. the air is fit for them to breathe so they remove their helmets. All the people are human and all are caucasian.

This is a typical scenario for many science-fiction novels. In the future it seems that many novelists view only caucasians making the leap into space or across time and alternate realities.

In the book *Logan's Run*, you have an example of a utopian society where people live a life of leisure and all are physically perfect, or can become physically perfect by means of surgery. In this book whites are the only ones who live in this perfect world, and even the aged are excluded because the lives of the "perfect" people are terminated at thirty.

Sandra Bennett's comment, on a separate page, for "Blacks in Sci. Fic.: Why Are We Invisible" reads as follows: "Joe: Nice paper. An issue you might have adddressed is the possibility that there are many black writers exploring science or speculative fiction, but it just isn't classified that way. Toni Morrison, for example, deals with alternate realities in *Beloved*."

Figure 4–1, continued
Joe Baxter's Paper: "Blacks in Sci. Fic.: Why Are We Invisible?"

Science-fiction is a medium where you create a vision of what will be, what could be or what may have been. To exclude any group of people is to say they do not exist in the reality you create. If you write about the dreams of the human race, you should include the whole human race.

This tunnel vision I used to attribute to the fact that the majority of science-fiction authors are Caucasian, and therefore mold their characters after themselves. If you are for the general public, you should represent them in your writings. Some Caucasian writers will add a "token" black character to their stories but the characters are usally little more than parts of the scenery.

Sometimes other ethnic groups are portrayed with attention payed to their customs and the lifestyles they lead, while black characters are usually one-dimensional analogs of white characters and without substance.

My young cousin, to whom I have passed my love of science-fiction, asked me a question that I couldn't answer to his or my own satisfaction. That question was "why do none of the humans in these books look like me?" I felt that he should have characters he can identify with, being that he is a young child of ten. He cannot read the more advanced books by black authors like Samuel Delaney, and the books he is equipped to read, blacks are not represent

When I first acquired my love of science-fiction I was five years old. I was viewing an episode of Star Trek "Amok time". I was captivated by the ethnic diversity of the characters who made up the crew of the ship. They were black, white, asian and non-human races. The series was created by Mr. Gene Rodden-berry who had vision of all races of people working together to bring man as one race into the future. This idea has made Star Trek the most popular of all science-fiction stories. His characters have endured for twenty-five years in novels, film and television.

Figure 4–1, continued
Joe Baxter's Paper: "Blacks in Sci. Fic.: Why Are We Invisible?"

By no means am I saying that there are no black writers of science-fiction; Samuel Delaney and Octavia Butler are two examples of blacks in the medium. Until other writers share the same vision of Roddenberry and Butler, that all races of humans can be explorers of time and space and are capable of dealing with the unknown, blacks and other ethnic groups will be invisible in science-fiction.

As we come to the end of this century and move into the 21st century, people who write about the future have a unique chance to affect change in the science-fiction industry. I say to them this; let the future generations read your work and learn that for mankind to have any future it must be united and see past color and religious beliefs.

ity for hard work and responsibility, what he calls the "American work ethic," for which one earns praise, in contrast to the tendency to "judge people by the color of their skin." This anti-racist view is reinforced by the physical diversity within his family, in which some members have straight hair and light skin and others have "more what you would say the norm of a black person is." Like his grandmother, his mother dislikes "prejudging," which means:

> It doesn't matter what you are; I don't care if your family come—if your heritage is African American, Irish, Korean, whatever, you should be proud of that, you should never try to hide that fact, you should never dismiss any part of your heritage. And she's really almost religiously strong on that. Always be proud on what you are and where you come from.

That this stance is generational and historical—both in his biological family and the larger sociocultural groups with which he identifies—can be seen in Joe's attitude toward his young cousin Jimmy, who asks, "Why do none of the humans in these books look like me?" Although Jimmy only appears in the sixth of nine paragraphs in Joe's paper, Joe foregrounds the significance of their relationship in his oral introduction to the paper: "I chose this [paper] because mainly why I wanted to be a science fiction writer is I've enjoyed it my whole life but I have a younger cousin. . . ." His cousin's questions about the omission of black characters in science fiction provoke Joe to explore further: "I started to look and I said, I know there's got to be more [black characters and authors] out there but it's like they're invisible."

Thus, there is not only a critical impulse in Joe's writing but a didactic one as well. Just as he is concerned about the future of humanity, he expresses compassion and caring for those younger than he: his then-six-year-old cousin, his sister, and another small cousin whose precocious ability to take apart a radio earns the father's rebuke but praise from Joe: "What amazed me is he took it all apart and didn't break anything." In his essay, Joe refers to his cousin Jimmy as someone "to whom I have passed my love of science-fiction," a line that delighted Tom Riley, prompting him to exclaim, "I love this paper!" Later, discussing the paper as a whole, Tom pretended (unasked) to address his remarks to Joe: "I think I like best the paragraph about your young cousin, but your opening was so good that I could hardly wait to read the rest."

Tom, an English professor of Irish-German descent in his late fifties, is a heavy smoker with thick-lensed glasses and a habitually disheveled look. He grew up in Brooklyn, New York, where his father was a journalist, a "rewrite man" for the *New York Times* and news agencies, and then an associate editor, "fourth from the top," at *Newsweek*. Unemployed during the Depression years from 1929–1938, and lacking a high school education, his father gained a foothold in journalism "as soon as the war started looming." Repeatedly, Tom describes his father as an exceptionally smart, humane man and himself as "very, very lucky" to have been his son.

Along with Tom's strong praise for Joe—"Obviously a good reader . . . an intelligent kid . . . Given the subject matter of the paper, a very, very reasonable, what do I want to say—moderate person," a strong selling point for him is Joe's reasonable attitude toward racism. Says Tom: "It would be so easy to stress racism, racism, racism." He then declares, "I would give at least my left arm, and maybe my right, to have this student in my BRW-1 class." Many BRW-1 students, Tom continues, had difficulty reading Ursula Le Guin's *The Word for World is Forest*, a novel over which he believes "this guy [Joe] would be going bananas." Le Guin, he explains, is "one of the best at bridging the race gap." He praises her treatment of race in *The Left Hand of Darkness* because "You don't learn until about the middle of the book that the main character is black because it's not important, you know, it's of no consequence."

Sandra's World: Dealing with Ghosts

Perhaps race would be of no consequence, according to Sandra

Bennett, Joe's teacher, "if more representation were given to people of color in this society. I don't think that anyone should necessarily have to write about a particular person if they choose not to." However, she concludes, "on the flip side, if representation [of authors of color] is going to be deliberately suppressed, it does become problematic." Sandra started teaching in 1990 as a workshop instructor in DTU's basic reading and writing program. Although she has a B.A. in journalism, she never worked as a journalist; during and after college, her interests shifted from newspaper journalism, which wasn't "creative enough," to magazine writing, which was "too corporate," to a commitment "to get any old job that would allow me to be a creative writer." It was at that point that she got her first teaching job at DTU, "a godsend" that enabled her to pursue her own writing and now to apply to doctoral programs in American studies.

A tall, striking woman in her mid-twenties who once considered becoming a professional dancer, Sandra is the oldest of three children, with one brother and one sister. Her parents, as well as her grandmother, are college-educated—an accomplishment for her grandmother that Sandra only recently understood as unusual. Self-employed entrepreneurs, her parents strongly value financial security, a goal that for Sandra "didn't really wash because it didn't give me the things I needed, a sense of personal fulfillment." She attributes her disagreement with her parents' priorities both to the confidence she gained living in North Carolina up to age ten and to her retreat into literature in the ensuing unhappy years after her family moved north to New Hampshire. It appears to be the contrast between the two periods—the security of her early years and the isolation she later felt—that created her need for more than what her family life had given her.

The North Carolina community she thrived in was integrated, middle-class, blue-collar; she recalls herself as extroverted, even "unruly," but not "in a negative way—it was like you know I just always had something to say." In New Hampshire, where she was frequently the only black student in her class, she became introverted, silent, and "only did enough work to get by." Because she didn't understand the rules of Northern white society, Sandra says she "looked to books for a place to exist." Reading was a "lifeline . . . a world that I understood so well because I spent so much time there." Asked to describe her post-high school educational experience, she admits she "carried a lot of the same demons" with her to college, a subject that

> opens a whole can of worms—my experience with, interaction
> with . . . other African American young people had been very neg-
> ative because of where I was brought up, and the rules for the com-
> munity where I was brought up were not the same rules that
> applied to an urban environment peopled by African Americans.
> It just—the two did not jibe.

Sandra's explanation of those rules illuminates her current emphasis on the development of a sense of self in relation to writing, a
theme that recurs throughout the interview in statements such as,
"ultimately, all writing comes from the self," and, "the whole idea
is to get away from being defined by others and work on self-
definition." The impact of the rule system she entered into in New
Hampshire was devastating; the first rule

> was realizing who you are, I mean, as soon as we moved into a
> white community, it wasn't a matter of who you were; it was a
> matter of who you had to pretend to be. Otherwise you were gonna
> be nowhere. You know, so that's what it was about. And coming
> into the urban environment in my freshman year of college with no
> sense of self, even at like a basic level, was just like people thought
> they were dealing with a ghost and they treated you as such, you
> know, like a non-person.

For the past year and a half, at South End, Sandra has been
teaching in an urban environment very much like the one in which
she once felt like a "ghost." The ironies are manifold. Her experience of attending a white high school rendered her a non-person
with "no sense of self" when she entered an urban college. This
mutability of color is characteristic of the construction of race in the
U.S. As Ralph Ellison (1947) says,

> Thus one of the greatest jokes in the world is the spectacle of the
> whites busy escaping blackness and becoming blacker every day,
> and the blacks striving toward whiteness, becoming quite dull
> and gray. None of us seems to know who he is or where he's
> going. (p. 564)

In her more recent discussion of "whiteness" in American literature, Toni Morrison (1992) explains white America's projection of
its own psyche onto an "Africanist persona":

> Black slavery enriched the country's creative possibilities. For in
> that construction of blackness *and* enslavement could be found
> not only the not-free but also, with the dramatic polarity created by
> skin color, the projection of the not-me. The result was a play-
> ground of the imagination. (p. 38)

She unpacks the classic liberal response to racism that Tom Riley invoked:

> Statements . . . insisting on the meaninglessness of race to the American identity, are themselves full of meaning. The world does not become raceless or will not become unracialized by assertion. The act of enforcing racelessness in literary discourse is itself a racial act. (p. 46)

Tom's World: "A Kennedy-Eugene McCarthy Liberal"

As much as Tom Riley admires Joe's paper—which explicitly protests the invisibility of blacks in science fiction—he concludes that race is unimportant, inconsequential. For Tom, this attitude toward race is a mark of tolerance, fairness, and broad-mindedness. He recalls, for example, that in addition to his father's intelligence—"he was the smartest man I ever knew"—his father repudiated his own family's bigoted attitudes. With the loving self-deprecation that often characterizes ethnic humor, Tom describes himself as having a "thickheaded, Irish-German nature." His father's family, he says, "in general, is just a deplorably, typical shanty Irish— shanty Irish, you know they were all bigots, they were all racists, they were all stupid." His grandfather was a steelworker in Youngstown, Ohio, where "the black section was elegantly called the Monkey's Nest." As a young man, Tom saw himself as more progressive than his father; now he remembers that "by the time I was about twenty I thought my father was outrageously reactionary . . . but he was obviously very progressive." In addition to being a cofounder of the CIO "when it was thought to be a communist union," Tom's father was "miraculously free from the anti-Semitism and racism that was so pervasive in the family." This freedom meant having black friends from the newspaper business at a time "when what white people had black friends?" His father also fought with Tom's brother, who experienced a "brief anti-Semitic phase that I [Tom] found appalling."

His own youthful disagreements with his father centered on whether the Monroe Doctrine applied to post-revolutionary Cuba: "my father's going on about the Monroe document and I'm saying, 'What the hell, we wrote the Monroe document. Who says we have the right to secure the Caribbean from communism?'" Making a distinction between shades of liberalism, Tom characterizes his father as "an old New Deal liberal" and himself as a "Kennedy-Eugene McCarthy liberal." The whole family was expected not only to vote but to work for Adlai Stevenson; they were "kneejerk Democratic liberals." Tom now identifies himself as a "moderate liberal . . . a terrible term," and names Senators Paul Simon and Bill Bradley as his "closest analogues." Although he had a beard, demonstrated, "and even got teargassed a couple of times" in the 1960s, he says he was no more a radical then than now. He was "deeply involved" in the antiwar movement and the "Eugene McCarthy insurgency." He even "wound up president of a reform Democratic Club," he adds, self-disparagingly. "Jesus. But anyway, you get the stereotyped idea, I'm sure."

The Effects of Schooling

Joe's Background: Learning to Resist

So why was Joe Baxter placed in a basic writing course? A closer look at his writing and his educational history suggests two reasons that may account for his becoming a BRW-1 student: first, his labored, lefthanded penmanship is accompanied by scant margins, idiosyncratic hyphenation, and indistinct spacing between words and sentences; and second, he was identified early on in his school career as a student with behavioral problems, culminating in a scuffle with a high school math teacher in which Joe recalls he started "destroying the classroom; I started throwing chairs and there was just a lot of frustration . . . and I still, like right now, I'm starting to learn but I had a hard time." According to Joe, he was bored and easily distracted in school because he found the work too easy; to his teachers, such behavior meant a poor attention span and an arrogant attitude. As Joe puts it:

> When I was—I think from first grade on I had—I got sent home from school a lot. Basically what they said were behavior prob-lems, what they said was I didn't pay attention . . . I guess they took it that I was being arrogant or whatever, but when I got into junior high school, I didn't have a good time in school. Basically, I felt like with the exception of math, I was being not held back but I wasn't being challenged. I could do what I had to do, as far as the work was concerned but things didn't really hold my attention; if it doesn't hold my attention, I tend to shut it out.

Since his turbulent high school years, Joe has apparently learned to channel his resistance to the repressive aspects of school-ing into more productive political and creative forms like writing and a rather developed social critique. He says he felt encouraged by both his teachers and his peers at South End:

> That was one of the best experiences I ever had. I learned a lot; I learned how to write more descriptively. . . . And my instructor, Miss Bennett, I really liked this lady. She was in there, she knew what she was talking about; she let everybody express their opinion. And she was a real strong lady. She never told anybody, "Well, you're wrong, you're totally off base." She was always, you know, "That's your opinion; it's a good opinion."

As much or more than his teachers, it is his peers at South End who boost his confidence about himself as a writer:

> That was really the first time I had shared anything I had written with a large group of people, much less people who weren't my family, and the feedback I got was positive, they liked it . . . My peers, they became curious about the stuff that I wrote and they wanted to read it and I enjoyed that. I really enjoyed that people liked what I wrote, and that made me feel a lot better and that made me want to write more.

One wonders, then, how Joe would have fared in a more traditional classroom driven by teacher authority and attention to surface errors rather than South End's strong sense of community.

Despite Tom's enthusiasm for Joe's writing, his commentary on "Blacks in Sci. Fic." is laced with surface error corrections. Although he repeatedly describes the paper as "excellent," seventeen out of twenty-six responses to the text, as he reads it aloud, refer to errors, including underscoring, apostrophes, usage, and misspellings. Indeed, while reading the paper, Tom describes himself as "pretty picky, particularly if somebody is obviously good." Specifically, he says:

> If it were early in the term, I probably would have the student revise it because, although the grammar is very good, syntax isn't terrific and the punctuation is a little bit uncertain. I was in fact happy to see a couple of sophisticated semicolons in there toward the end. That's not important in and of itself but it tells you that he has some idea of how punctuation marks work. The run-on sentence early in the paper was inconsequential because it was two short clauses; the correct semicolons. Later on [he reads]: "By no means am I saying that there are no black writers of science-fiction," semicolon, "Samuel Delaney. . . ." That's terrific. That's just what a semicolon's for, right? Wonderful student, wonderful paper.

Tom's Background: A View of Basic Writers

As a senior faculty member, Tom provides an historical overview of DTU that sheds light on his attitude toward the students he currently teaches. A decade before Tom got a faculty appointment at

DTU, the university was accredited—"I think in '54"—despite its poor reputation. At that time, many of the students were returning G.I.'s; the school was mediocre but several of his colleagues in the English faculty were "wonderful." When Tom arrived at DTU in the mid-1960s, after teaching "white, affluent, middle-class kids with good basic skills but generally kind of uninspired" at the midwestern university where he got his master's degree, he says the school was "referred to as 'DT-Jew' . . . the kids who didn't quite make it into [another college] when the admissions standards were very high." These students, too, were "mostly middle-class kids with decent basic skills," who failed to prepare Tom for a student population that was increasingly "more black and Hispanic, and now ESL students, with weaker basic skills." Tom says he was "slow to adjust and very stubborn in my kind of disciplinary approach." Drill, review, and strict rules resulted in a high pass rate on the exit exam matched by an equally high dropout rate—as high as fifty percent—each semester.

What Tom has learned, he says, particularly from a younger colleague trained in composition and rhetoric, "is that bullying and coercion are not going to work with students whose primary impulse when they're under pressured situations is to give up." Furthermore, he recalls that until quite recently—the mid-1980s—a dominant view in the department held that content was irrelevant in developmental courses and that instruction should focus exclusively on sentence structure and basic grammar, "a mind-boggling negative concept as far as I was concerned," says Tom. He remains torn, however, between what he sees as opposing positions: those who believe "that what you say makes no— has no importance at all as long as you say it with minimal correctness" and those "who pay, in my opinion, insufficient attention to the fundamentals."

Thus he understands that the goal of BRW-1 "is to have got the students engaged with what they're writing, comfortable more or less with writing as an act and interested in their own writing." More "old fashioned" than some instructors, however, he also believes it important to tell students, "If you're still writing at this level at the end of BRW-2, you will be repeating the course because there's no way you would pass the department exit exam[6] with all these grammar errors." Tom feels that he now has

> a better understanding of how to communicate with developmental-level students without crushing their spirits, though I think I still do to some degree, more in BRW-2 than BRW-1, for the reason . . . that a student comes out of BRW-1 thinking that he is not just

6. The exit exam was recently abolished and replaced by portfolio assessment.

a competent writer but an excellent writer and he just isn't. And I have to tell him that, and I need to figure out a way of telling them that better.

As Tom has striven to adjust to the needs of his students—to become less "bullying" and more "understanding"—he has grappled with the contradiction between content and form, hoping to engage students and make them comfortable with writing while he dispels them of the illusion that they might be more than, at best, competent writers. This contradiction is a familiar one in writing pedagogy, insofar as content is at once idealized and ignored (the student—an empty receptacle, as Freire describes in the "banking concept" of education—has nothing to say) while the gross body of writing is regulated and denigrated. Such thinking leads to the construction of a new generic student: for Tom, the basic writer is "someone whose primary impulse under pressured situations is to give up" and who must be reminded that she is not an excellent writer.

Two types of response to students follow from Tom's pedagogy: first, he reverts to a "disciplinary approach," complete with red pen corrections, in more advanced classes, despite complaints from his sophomore students that "I hurt their feelings with all that red ink and stuff"; and second, in practice, even with basic writing students—at least in Joe's case[7]—he focuses overwhelmingly on surface feature errors. The binary oppositions that seem to define Tom's perspective as a teacher depict students, language, and learning in rigid categorical terms—marked by "either/or" rather than "both/and" habits of thought. The multidimensionality of the student's—and the teacher's—identity is obscured by a set of educational goals predicated on models of accommodation and homogeneity. Like Shaughnessy and others who view education as accommodation, Tom illustrates what Min-Zhan Lu calls the "politics of linguistic innocence," a view of language as essential and given rather than constructed, contested, and inherently social. The dilemma for such liberal educators is that they want to enable nontraditional students to enter the academy but cannot relinquish their belief in a culturally superior language and literature. From another vantage point in composition theory, Tom can be seen as adhering to current-traditional writing pedagogy mitigated by cognitivist and expressivist beliefs that push him to construct both a "kinder, gentler" classroom and an impotent student who "just gives up."

---

7. Tom Riley does specify that he pays more attention to surface correctness with more advanced writers like Joe.

Asked if he identifies himself as a writer, Tom replies, "Oh boy, that's kind of a painful question because I don't believe in writer's blocks." After nearly publishing a novel he wrote in his thirties, he says, "I haven't written anything creative to speak of in 15 years . . . I guess I have to identify myself as an ex-writer." He attributes this to "a lack of determination to go on with it" that has resulted in "six hopeless works in progress." This contrasts sharply with his feeling when he completed the final draft of his unpublished novel: "Ah, I knew I was gonna write more novels; I knew just what they were gonna be and just how they were gonna go. And somehow I lost that. Where has it gone? That visionary gleam . . . ?"

Sandra and Joe occupy a different cultural space than Tom, certainly as African Americans whose relationship to the dominant culture is mediated by race, but perhaps also as members of a generation influenced by a media-based, pop-cultural consciousness that situates them in a postmodern world whose boundaries have blurred. As Donna Haraway (1992) puts it, describing a 1989 painting by Lynn Randolph called "Cyborg," in which a Third-World woman sits at an earth-encrusted keyboard with a circuit board on her chest, a tiger skin on her head, and graphic displays of the galaxy behind her, "These borderlands suggest a rich topography of combinatorial possibility. That possibility is called the Earth, here, now, this elsewhere, where real, outer, inner, and virtual space implode" (p. 328).

A Basic Writer's View: "Cyberfighter," a Novel in Progress

Joe is currently working on two books, one set three hundred years in the future, about a multicultural crew on an Earth spaceship forced to land on a planet still gripped by segregation, the other about the effects on civilization of the depletion of the ozone layer. *Cyberfighter*, the story about ozone depletion, illustrates the power of Joe's imagination. His first question is how people will deal with the cancer-causing effects of ultraviolet rays. A protective shield at the city's center radiates outward, becoming weaker the further it extends. Predictably, the rich and powerful live in the inner city and the poor live in the outskirts. Advances in cybernetics allow for a renewal of sports entertainment in which robots fight like gladiators. Bands of outlaws in the unprotected periphery, populated by poor people, sell drugs and buy cybernetic body parts for self-defense. Meanwhile, a young man gets caught in crossfire while attempting to save his sister and is himself rescued by a cyberfighter named Winter Hawk. Together, they confront a villain heavily addicted to a drug Joe calls "warp." Winter Hawk has to go underground with the cyber-gangs to find out who sold warp to his foe.

So far, Joe has written about a hundred pages of this story. Asked at the end of the interview to describe himself as a writer, he paused, thinking, and replied, "Eccentric." He went on to explain that he meant "just a little off center. I don't write about what most people write about . . . I don't like to use what's at hand. I like to create everything from the ground up . . . What I'm doing now, *Cyberfighter*, it's more like it's there already and I'm just putting it down." Joe traces his desire to write science fiction and his vision of a more equitable future to his early exposure to "Star Trek," recalling that he was only five years old when he saw the well-known episode "Amok Time." As he explains,

> I enjoyed it because I saw when they showed the bridge crew, okay, the communications officer was black, the helmsman was Asian, then the other helmsman was Russian. You know it was like at that time of my life there was a lot of conflict going on between races and the Vietnam war, and everything was going on, and I saw the war every night on television but then here it is in this show, here everybody's living together. Nobody call anybody racist slurs or anything, these people all work together to do what has to be done, and I felt, well, the future was going to be a good place if this is what it was supposed to be, and from then, as I got older I just got more and more involved in science fiction.

A Basic Writer's Vision of Himself: The Nebula Award

In addition to Joe's multiple strengths as a writer and reader—his analytical ability, his compassion, his engagement in the world around him, and his linguistic skill—his desire to become a writer positions him differently from the majority of students in basic writing classes. He sees himself as a writer in the most concrete terms, as exemplified by his conclusion to an essay for which he was assigned to rewrite the ending to a real event in his life. He tells the story of his relationship to a young woman who

> wore her hair in short dredlocks with sides cut low. Her eyes were almond shaped and dark brown. . . . Her lips were full and seemed to smile without effort. Her skin was the rich brown of cocoa or mahogany. She was wearing the bluest blue cowboy boots I have ever seen and jeans that had been bleached and decorated with red and blue daisies. She was wearing an over-sized Spiderman t-shirt and a blue denim jacket.

The rich detail is matched by repartee in which Joe describes their first encounter in a comic book shop, where Tiye's interest in a vintage collector's item impresses him:

Her always-smile exploded into a grin that could have lit Carlsbad Caverns up. "Paydirt!" she yelled. She laughed like a lotto millionaire . . . "Oh, I'm sorry, my name is Tiye Cooper." She thrust her small hand toward me. "Joe, Joe Baxter," I said taking her hand. "Good to meet you, Joe, Joe Baxter." I laughed. "That's an old joke," I said. "Hey, it was an old set-up line," she said still laughing.

After a brief summer romance, however, Tiye asks Joe whether she should abide by her father's wish to return home to the West Coast to attend college. Confused but honest, Joe responds, "Tiye, not many of our people get a choice whether or not they can go to college. I think you should go." In real life, this ends their affair; she refuses even to speak with him again. In the essay, he imagines a future with Tiye and their son ("kinetic energy incarnate") in which they are both writers:

> That was five years ago. I think about those days when I'm blocked and can't write. I stare at my computer screen trying to think of something to tap into the keys and finish this book. I sigh and rub my eyes. She's sitting on the couch. . . . She's dangling her shoe with her foot. That was her signal for I'm bored. "Can't think of anything huh?" she said. "Well everybody can't be as prolific as you," I teased. I look up at the shelves at the two Peabody awards (hers) and the Nebula Award (mine). . . .

Of course, there are countless would-be writers, but Joe's imagined life as a writer is not wholly romantic. His portrait of his and Tiye's world, despite its rewards, suggests an understanding of writing as hard work and slow gain, mitigated by humor and love. Unlike his peers who live only for the "here and now," Joe projects himself into the future, envisioning himself as a writer with study, desk, computer, and awards; a lover whose partner matches, even exceeds, his intellectual and creative talents with her own; and a father delighted by his son. At the end of the story, Tiye persuades Joe to stop working so they can pick up a Christmas tree.

> "Okay Speedball let's go," I say rising from the desk. I grab him by the arms and raise him over my head. I look into his face and see my sister and grandfather in him. His eyes are brown like his mothers. She enters the study with our coats and says "I hope there are still some trees left." I cross to the window and look out. "This is New York, you can find a tree at 4 o'clock in the morning." She comes to stand beside me and our son squeezes inbetween us. "You know," Tiye says "It doesn't snow much here." "Sorry you stayed?" I ask. "No" she says looking at the reflection in the window of the three of us. "Not at all."

In his fictive version of his relationship with Tiye, Joe enunciates his desire for her and for writing. Although he cannot change what actually happened, he articulates a vision not simply of what he wants from life but what he values and, in some sense, what he already has: a sense of connectedness to others, especially his family; generational continuity; and an understanding of the human condition—more particularly, a writer's—as cleaved between being and consciousness.

A Language of Possibility

Learning in the Community:
Playing the Dozens, Living for Today

Joe's visions of the future—his own and the world's—inspire him to read and to write, to imagine the world transformed into "a good place," free of "racist slurs," where people of diverse cultural backgrounds cooperate to do "what has to be done." In addition to the influence of "Star Trek," science fiction in general, and comics on Joe's development as a reader, he recalls "literacy events" such as learning to read can labels as his mother put away groceries. He also recalls playing the "Dozens," which he describes as "little insults on each other . . . you get real creative, you know . . . 'you flatfooted this and that.'" Asked to define the Dozens, Joe says, "You use words descriptive[ly] and to blow somebody's clothes or physical attributes way out of proportion." He gives examples: "You got big feet like a duck. Your head is wide as a mountain. Your ears stick out like airplane wings." He and his cousins also enjoyed comedy; avid fans of TV shows like "Saturday Night Live," they delighted in family in-jokes, were quick at repartee, and rewrote song lyrics.

Joe's reading habits and idealism, however, caused tensions between him and his friends in Bedford Stuyvesant, who

> didn't understand, you know, they felt that you supposed to deal with the here and the now today. . . . Most teenagers act the way they do because they don't think tomorrow. They say—the saying now is—"Tomorrow's not promised to you," so they don't live for tomorrow, they live for today, for the here and now, and that's why I think they have so many problems.

At the same time, his class and racial identity put him at a disadvantage in a school system defined and controlled by the dominant culture. While the content of what he says about inner-city youth shows deep insight into his own development and the social problems of his community, Joe speaks a form of Black English, evident in the deletion of the "s" in phrases like "nobody call anybody racist slurs" and the omission of "be" from constructions like "you supposed to deal with the here and the now." To middle-class teachers, Black English dialect often marks students as different—or worse, deficient.

Basic Writers in the University: Entering an Alien World

In his essay on the invisibility of blacks in science fiction, Joe describes the genre as "a medium where you create a vision of *what will be, what could be* or *what may have been.*" There is in this grammatical progression an eerie reflection of the tension often experienced in the writing class between actual and potential outcomes. In *The Knower and the Known*, Marjorie Grene (1974) explains the philosophical shift from Aristotle's view that the actual precedes the potential to Michael Polanyi's contention that it is the other way around: the potential precedes the actual. As Grene puts it, elucidating Polanyi's description of human beings as a "society of explorers," "rooted in potential thought,"

> The power of what is not yet draws us on, whether to achievement or to failure, to knowledge or to error. From that ultimate dubiety there is no escape, [just] because it is in the last analysis process, not eternity, contingency, not necessity, in which we have our roots. But if there is no end to our peril, neither is there any end, so long as life lasts, to our hope. (p. 250)

This view of learning as moving toward a future of contingent realities, of actualized potential, is a crucial concept for writing teachers, enabling the shift in emphasis from product to process, what James Britton called "shaping at the point of utterance." Accordingly, all writers move toward the unknown, actualizing "what may be" through a dialectic between individual consciousness and the system of language. What Grene calls the "protensive pull of the future" loses meaning for those whose survival— whether emotional, intellectual, or physical—is in jeopardy, just as writing loses meaning when severed from the subjective conditions out of which it arises. Subjective and objective forces interact. Just as women may protest sexism yet recognize their own construction as female, black youth like Joe's friends "speak" from—accept, resist, or negotiate—institutional positions in a dialectic between their consciousness of themselves in a hostile world and a system that continually confirms their despair.

Joe's critique of science fiction suggests a rich metaphor for the writing class as utopian and transformational. In imagining a future world, which writers invariably do every time they address a reader, the student (or any other) writer, like the science-fiction writer in Joe's critique, is confronted with both rhetorical and ethical choices: his or her position as author, purpose, audience, style, voice, contingent meanings, omissions, and effects. Just as Joe believes authors are responsible for including blacks and other minorities in science fiction, educators—as authors of syllabi, curricula, classroom practice, and policies—are responsible for diversifying higher education through admissions and hiring, as well as through scholarly journals, textbooks, and required reading lists. "To exclude any group of people is to say they do not exist in the reality you create," writes Joe. For many basic writers, the university is an "alien world" like the one Joe depicts in his essay, populated by white professors and dominated by the strange language of academic discourse. Historically, like Joe's "alien world," higher education has excluded the vast majority from "making the leap into space or across time and alternate realities" as students. One difference is a growing number of teachers of color.

Sandra's Pedagogy: A "Two-Way Flow"

Impressed that South End campus students manage to attend classes at all in a high-crime neighborhood suffering from social service cutbacks, Sandra finds it "phenomenal they engage in this kind of dialogue and they're willing to put this much effort into trying to understand what's happening; what's this whole—you know—analyzing a text, interacting with a text about?"

She describes her class as dynamic and class discussion as powerful. The students' writing improved—"everyone grew in some way," exuding "energy to make education work for them on a very personal level," not just in terms of the job market but "growing as a person and sharing ideas with other people around them." The students developed "a willingness to look at things through different lenses." Dialogue, interaction, reciprocity—a "two-way flow"—are key concepts for Sandra as a teacher.

Her response to Joe Baxter, whom she said she would place in the top third of the class, exemplifies this reciprocity: he "represents the dynamic I strive for in a classroom . . . giving something to the students and them also giving something back to me." According to Sandra, Joe initially lacked enthusiasm and submitted mediocre papers but then responded to her marginal comments and "blossomed—it was amazing." What Joe has given her is the pleasure of reading essays that are "powerful," "special," and provoke ideas and personal associations for her. For example, in a paper on gender roles in the pre-civil rights-era South depicted in Maya Angelou's *I Know Why the Caged Bird Sings*, Joe describes Clidell, Maya's stepfather, as

> a self-made man. He had very little education but he wasn't ashamed of it. Clidell, like many black men, had to give up an education to help support his family. Even though he had almost no formal schooling he became a success in business. Clidell was intelligent despite his limited education.

Sandra reflects that:

> Joe is talking about one of the strong male characters in the novel, and I think he really draws out the strengths of this character and kind of puts him out there, so that . . . maybe someone who had less interaction with the text would have said there are no strong male— black male—role models in the text. And that's problematic because it's something that you know a lot of students will just read . . . and will just take for granted that that's the way it's going to be.

Sandra then goes on to connect Joe's ability to draw out the character's strength to her own "experiences with male role models," from which she learned to accept their weaknesses and "take from" their strengths, a connection between her own and Joe's experience that "hit home" for her; it was "special."

Sandra's Vision: Alternate Realities

Sandra's identification with Joe is even stronger in response to his paper on science fiction—she was "really excited"—because she shares his love of the genre. She praises his trenchant analysis of the effects of the exclusion of nonwhite and other minorities from science fiction—"it's really powerful that he points all this out." Yet she also becomes a sort of coauthor, extending his discussion of the psychological effects on the reader of being unrepresented (or misrepresented) in literature to any act of reading:

> Everyone is Caucasian so immediately if you're of a different ethnic background, you like take pause, you know like wait a minute, where am I? And that same difficulty in being able to orient yourself in . . . a physical world takes place when you're reading a text . . . you're being drawn into this physical world and you just really can't find a place for yourself.

Although her emphasis is on the effects of social exclusion, she also seems to be commenting on the alien world of language itself. If we assume language mediates reality and multiple social languages compete in a vast array of social contexts, then some sociolinguistic experiences will affirm and console while others challenge and disturb us.

For Sandra, the sort of alternate realities associated with science fiction are present as well in the work of writers like Toni Morrison. But, unfortunately,

> her work is looked at as, you know, folk fiction or coming from this mythological place that African Americans inhabit on occasion and maybe—maybe it has something to do with their African ancestry . . . a little hoodoo something.

In contrast to this patronizing view, according to Sandra, the alternate realities that Morrison embraces involve "the legacy of monotheism and polytheism taken from African culture." In addition to influencing Judaism and Christianity—an influence that is "never credited"—African religious beliefs emerge from "a strong tradition of a people who believed deeply in alternate realities and their function in society as a means of allowing people to live together in harmony." Sandra believes the loss of this tradition has resulted in a "schism within the self" destroying "very strong mythological beliefs" that allow "a people to be themselves, to realize the importance of who they were and what their culture was all about."

Had the tradition been better sustained, she suggests, the reality experienced by African Americans might have been different: "maybe these things wouldn't have happened or happened to the degree that they did if people hadn't been so quick to give up their beliefs and allow someone else to define them." Thus the notion of alternate realities permits those who have experienced social degradation and suffering a vision, as Joe puts it in terms of science fiction, "of what will be, what could be, or what may have been." On the other hand, Sandra points out, the imaginary world that white science fiction writers give us—even in those works meant as social critiques—often reproduce the dominant culture's "experiences of oppressing other societies, going to another world and conquering it, suppressing the peoples."

This same argument for an alternative vision of history, located outside the dominant culture, extends to composition instruction. As Sandra says when asked to describe her relationship to DTU, "I think I can look at it in a similar way to how I look at my philosophy of what goes on in the classroom." She describes the developmental reading and writing program as "multicultural" and sees herself as a new teacher initially accepting the "constraints of this new curriculum" and then "finding a place for myself within it that was more autonomous." Asked what she perceives to be the program's mandate and how her perspective differs from it, she explains that, as with any "institutionalized philosophy, it's going to be kind of unbalanced, and especially at an institution like DTU where there's a concentration of white males in high positions . . . it goes without saying that all of the desire can be strong but the result may not reflect that."

Asked what she perceives that desire to be, Sandra replies:

> The desire for multicultural education, you know, realizing that something needs to happen, that there is a lack of something in the classroom but not really understanding all sides of the issue—how it just can't be tackled in one place, like you can't keep hitting at the same place and hope for success.

Pressed for specific examples, Sandra echoes her own remarks about white science fiction writers and the alternate realities emanating from African traditions. Starting with the issue of "self-definition," she argues:

> . . . in all the texts that we're using it's basically looking at how Eurocentric ideas defined different peoples around the world . . . In looking at African Americans and how they were shaped by European ideals, I think that that in itself is really one-sided when you look at how self-definition is something to strive for. In an extremely integrated or homogeneous society, it's still an issue. So that's something that could be confronted in the text and that is not; it's all of, well, this is how African Americans were deprived by the Europeans . . .

Authors like Frederick Douglass and James Baldwin—both on BRW-1 reading lists—record "how white society acted on" African Americans, reflecting an "overwhelming feeling of Europeans having to be in the mix for us to be able to look at this issue" of self-definition. "One of the hazards" for educators, Sandra warns,

> in addressing [self-definition] solely from that place is that the students get the feeling that people of their own ethnic group have never tried to define themselves aside from oppressive constraints.

How then does Joe's critique of the exclusion of blacks from science fiction relate to the experience of basic writers in the academy? Like black readers of science fiction novels, basic writers enter an alien world in which they must "find a place" for themselves. For working-class, immigrant, black, and Latino basic writing students, the paucity of other students and teachers with similar cultural backgrounds has made that entry a difficult one. Even more damaging, they have encountered class and racial biases in teachers, curricula, and literature throughout their school careers. These social problems, in other words, are not confined to any one arena—science fiction literature, the mass media, or basic writing—rather, they permeate sociocultural and economic life. In the field of basic writing, the recognition of the effects of social exclusion and inequality might lead teachers and researchers to question assumptions about class, race, language, and privilege; tolerate the tension between nonstandard and standard forms; explore the contradiction between postmodern views of identity as fluid and decentered, and political exigencies that require us to take a stand against socioeconomic injustice; defend the rights of oppressed groups, especially self-determination; and theorize a "language of possibility" that gives voice to those rendered silent and invisible.

When I embarked on this research project, I was concerned about the tendency in higher education to objectify the basic writing student as "other." Such students, I feared, would be kept on the margins of a society structured by gender, class, and racial divisions, a society that denigrates linguistic and cultural differences in order to substantiate the dominant cultural myths of freedom, individualism, and democracy. In order to renew belief in the possibility of success, of upward social mobility, as well as justify the systemic need for cheap labor, it would always be necessary to construct an "other" against whom those more privileged could measure themselves.

Joe Baxter, Sandra Bennett, and Tom Riley both confirm and deny this analysis. Each one, for example, possesses a love of reading, especially science fiction, and a desire to write, which might in itself be called "a language of possibility." They share, too, a history of resistance to fairly negative school experiences and a reliance on other cultural forums—home, street, books—in their personal development as readers and writers. One might ask, with Joe a hundred pages into his novel, *Cyberfighter*, and Tom calling himself an "ex-writer," what does "basic writing" mean? One answer is simply that for many basic writers, reading and writing cause more pain than pleasure, and classical literature seems as distant as Mars; they do not have the same resources as Joe, whose position is anomalous, nor can they cross the academic border of basic writing with such ease.

Nevertheless, as this chapter shows, these boundaries shift, break down, and reform elsewhere; like the borders between self and other, those between teacher and student, male and female, black and white are neither fixed nor linear, but fluid, recursive, and complex. While this complex view by no means erases sociohistorical realities of racism, sexism, and class oppression, nor by the same token the struggle to create a just society, it does suggest ways of reconceptualizing them. Tom Riley's desire to deracialize science fiction, the academy, and the other worlds he inhabits reasserts the dominant discourse and suppresses real and bitter social conflict. But although white teachers remain the majority in most institutions, the presence of teachers of color invalidates the still prevalent use of "we" and "them" in reference to ourselves and our students with different linguistic and cultural backgrounds. As Sandra proposes, those of us who teach, administer, and research basic writing can develop a "two-way flow" and help students realize their potential to retell history from perspectives outside the dominant culture.

Chapter Five

Multiple Teacher Responses
Authorizing Words and
the Discipline of Writing

> *Language is not a neutral medium that passes freely*
> *and easily into the private property of the speaker's*
> *intentions; it is populated—overpopulated—with the*
> *intentions of others. Expropriating it, forcing it to submit*
> *to one's own intentions and accents, is a difficult and*
> *complicated process. (1981, p. 294)*
>
> Mikhail Bakhtin

I had called Ethel Martin repeatedly to arrange a second interview, almost giving up after several brief conversations in which she would answer the phone, I would ask for her, and she would say in a small voice, "Who is this?" I would reply, and she would whisper, "Ethel's not here." I was obviously making her uncomfortable, but I wanted to be sure she was all right and I still hoped she would read and comment on her paper, "Complexion," to which her teacher, Karen Stein, had responded intriguingly. Finally, I got up the nerve to say, "Ethel, I know it's you. How are you?" "Oh," she said. "I'm fine, I had the baby." I congratulated her—though her pregnancy had been so inconspicuous I had no idea she was pregnant—and explained that I wanted to visit her and that it would only take a few minutes for her to read the paper. She agreed, gave me directions to her apartment in a working-class section of town, and hung up quickly.

On the appointed day, I packed a gift for the baby and my tape recorder in a bag and started off in the hot afternoon, taking buses through parts of the city I had never seen before. I had tried to call to confirm our date, but her line was continually busy. Worried that something would go wrong, I crossed the highway and found the address. Sweaty, nervous, I climbed five flights of stairs to her apartment, knocked on the door, and was greeted by a short young man who I assumed was the baby's father.

"I'm looking for Ethel Martin," I explained.

"She's not here," he apologized. "She had to go to a funeral."

Trying to conceal my disappointment, I reached into my bag and gave him the gift. "It's for the baby. Will you give it to Ethel? And will you tell her I'll call her?"

I never saw or heard from Ethel again. All I have are her papers, her interview transcript, responses to her writing from several teachers, my memories of our brief encounters, the image of her apartment building baking in the hot sun, and my questions about her evasiveness, her acute shyness, and her retreat from me and the university. For her interview, we sat in a small, undecorated cubicle; her discomfort was evident in her bodily stiffness and an expression of fear on her thin face, accentuated by large eyes and a sharp nose. Wearing a scarf on her head and a blue jacket, she curled up in her chair. Her voice was very soft, musical; she kept asking if I understood her, almost panicking sometimes, ashamed of her writing errors and her confusion.

Ethel is in her early thirties, raised in the Guyanese countryside, the second of sixteen children (two of whom died), in addition to five children from her father's first marriage. She came to the United States in 1986, sponsored by her husband who, at the time of the interview in the spring of 1992, had just gained temporary custody of their two sons. Visibly distraught over her loss, Ethel declared, "I'm not gonna give up my children. I'm gonna fight to the end to get my children back." About a month after this conversation, Ethel appeared unexpectedly at my office door to register for tutoring at the Writing Center. Hesitantly, she entered and said in an apologetic tone, "I don't know if you remember who I am. . . ."

"Why, of course I do," I said.

"I don't know," she explained. "A lot of times people don't remember who I am."

The portrait that emerges of Ethel in this chapter is a troubling one. Acutely shy and understandably distressed over her personal circumstances, she also seemed linguistically pressured, disoriented by the demands of a basic reading and writing class. Her profile is complicated by the bewildered, uncomprehending reaction she provoked in her teacher, Karen Stein. Karen's markedly different attitude toward Ethel and another student from her class who participated in the study, Rivka Minsky, creates a lens through which to examine the process of identification and the politics of location. These discursive and ideological processes have implications for the teaching of writing and the construction of subject positions that enable or disenable communication. To investigate these processes further, I asked several other teachers to comment along with Karen on Ethel's paper, "Complexion" (see Figure 5–1). Through these multiple perspectives, the picture of Ethel as a writer

continued on page 111

Figure 5–1
Ethel Martin's Paper: "Complexion"

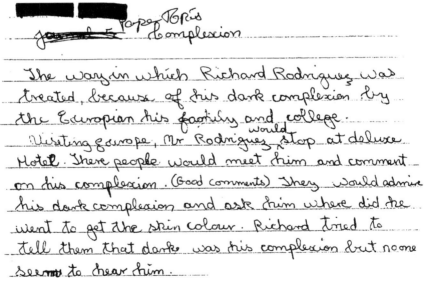

A subsequent draft of "Complexion," the original copy of which was unfortunately lost, was retained in the transcript of the intertextual dialogue. It is the same as the earlier draft reproduced here, except for minor word changes and an additional last paragraph that reads: "When I came to America to live the only problem I had was understanding what the American was saying because it seemed as though everyone was speaking very fast. I can remember listening and could not understand anything but I just said yes to make the person think I understand."

Figure 5–1, continued
Ethel Martin's Paper: "Complexion"

Richard mother never like to _{see her} son look dirty or because of walking in the sun, he might look a little darker. She always reminded Richard about complexion. It was a very part of life in those time. The more white you where the better were you chances. The more black you were the more inferior you was in people eyes. Mrs Rodrigues even showed her son what type of work people with complexion were doing. Some was farmers who came mexico with license to work, some was construction worker _{who worked} all day in the sun. These were the dark skin people who worked very hard and hardly can survive on on the little they made because some had wives and children to help in mexico. These were the dark skin frightening, powerless and poor people.

Richard relative never wanted to have dark skin children because they knew how much the white skin was counted. Like his aunt who had a dark skin little daughter would call her (my little ugle one) That little girl was smiling when her mother called her false name but in later days she will confront on mother to stop calling her ugle one because of dark complexion.

Figure 5–1, continued
Ethel Martin's Paper: "Complexion"

In College Richard saw what his mom was talking about especially when his friend told him about the construction job, which he accepted because he really wanted to know how hard is eight hours of physical labour. He was now to like a bracero. That is his mother words for dark skin hard working people.

Like Mr Richard Rodriguez I am dark in complexion and people often stop me and ask which country am I from. I would tell them Guyana and they would begin to make comment on on skin texture. (Good comments) which I feel very proud of, to know that although I am not white in complexion, there are many thing people can see and tell you about yourself by just looking at your skin colour.

My mother was not a person like Richard mother. I think its because she was also dark in complexion. She had fourteen children some dark and some fair, but never made any difference between us. Sometimes she might say (you look like your grandmother or something that will make you think you have a part of your early generation).

becomes clearer, providing insights into the development of linguistic competence and the realization of student potential.

The multiple teacher responses to Ethel's writing, along with the teachers' reflections on their own linguistic development, raise the question of how we become—or do not become—authorized as writers, as speaking subjects. Entry into the symbolic world of language, as theorists like Bakhtin have shown, is strongly associated with actual fathers and authoritative father figures. Discipline, punishment, ridicule, and shaming, as well as identification and desire, forge linguistic subjectivity; whether we identify ourselves as writers seems contingent in part upon whether and how we have internalized the notion of discipline. When discipline in regard to linguistic performance remains externally imposed, we resist its power and repudiate writing as punishment—indeed, it is often punitively taught; once internalized, this force can become the discipline of writing, an enabling, sometimes even joyous drive to write. But how does this "expropriation" of another's words, another's intentions, transpire? Who and what authorizes us to speak, write, and assert ourselves, our beliefs, our desires?

Student Portraits: Ethel and Rivka

Ethel's Family Ties

At the time of our interview, Ethel was a second-semester nursing student who worked part-time as a geriatric nursing assistant. She and her oldest son had moved to the U.S. in 1986, sponsored by her husband, who announced upon her arrival that she could continue to live with him if she accepted his two girlfriends. As Ethel put it, "I prefer to move out and get somebody else." Already pregnant with another son, she separated from her husband and has since had a third baby with another man; meanwhile, her husband has gained temporary custody of the boys. In Guyana, he had supported Ethel financially, urging her not to work, and indeed she dropped out of a secretarial training course when she met him. Now, along with two younger sisters whom she sponsored to move to the States, Ethel is studying to be a nurse; she wants to make as much progress as possible in her program so she can help her sisters with their studies. Nursing, she believes, will give her more freedom than secretarial work, which she now rejects because she doesn't "like people ordering [her] around."

Her father, a bauxite mine operator, died when she was eighteen years old; her mother supervised preparing meals for farm crews.

According to Ethel, her father was more lenient and easygoing, her mother more demanding. Her father, for example, never pressured the children to complete school, but after he died, her mother insisted that Ethel's younger siblings attend college. Ethel recalls having sided with her father when her parents fought; she liked to hunt with him in the country, "all these wild turtle and wild things, you know, birds and so." But "when Daddy's with Mommy, well sometimes you don't get to go because she might want to go." The fundamental value she ascribes to her parents is the importance of family—"a family should live together"—exactly what she has lost in her own life with her divorce and her ex-husband's temporary custody of her children.

Ethel's Classroom Lessons: "I'm Gonna Whack You"

A theme that recurs throughout her interview is punishment, having been physically disciplined—ordered, pushed, hit—and in turn disciplining others, first her siblings, now her sons. In her account of her life, education and punishment are intertwined. Over and over, she describes having been "whacked" by teachers and her mother, and in turn whacking others. A note of terror can be detected in her story of how her first-grade teacher, Miss Roberts,

> used to call out like dictation and when you get like five errors wrong or four errors wrong you got to stand up because when she pass around with that cane she's gonna hit you, and I used to, I used to r—, sometimes I used to duck under the desk . . . and sometime I used to end up running home and my mother would bring me back and tell Miss Roberts, "You do what you got to do."

But she never consciously resists, much less repudiates this punitive approach to learning. In teaching her older son, she tells him, "I'm gonna whack you . . . Turn your butt, give me your butt, just give me your butt." Interestingly, she spares—in her mind, spoils— her younger son, who is "thin like me" in contrast to the older boy, who is more like his father with "big skin and thick skin."

Ethel describes herself as a writer "not so good but neither poor so it's in between" and seems to concur with her teacher Karen Stein's assessment of her writing as confused and off topic. Her goal in BRW-1 was "to do better in English . . . to try my best," which would mean to "stop making these mistakes." Her accomplishment in BRW-1 was "I learned to write a lot." Asked what she thinks accounts for this, she explains:

> Because I was pushed to do it, you know, 'cause I was pushed to do it. If I didn't do it, I wouldn't have got my grade and I wanted to pass, I wanted to pass BRW-1, so I was pushed to do it and I had

to do it. That's like in Guyana my mother tell me, "You got to read, if you don't read, if you can't read that—I read it four times with you, if you can't read it now, I'm gonna whack you, and you better read it. You got to do it." She sit down and she read the book with us and she tell us how to write it and everything and she just give us and say, "Write it, and if you write it good, you're gonna get a good grade, if you don't write it good, you're not gonna get a good grade." So that was it.

Frequently, while reading her papers out loud during the interview, she seemed confused, anxious, as if the words on the page simply failed to make sense to her. However, in addition to learning to "write long," she says that BRW-1 helped her to read: "I read more now; I never used to read so much; I think it helped me a lot."

Rivka Minsky: Jewish Identity and Anti-Semitism

Ethel's classmate, Rivka Minsky, is a 32-year-old Russian Jewish immigrant, married, with one daughter. A second-semester freshman at DTU, she has been working for a year and a half in a medical clinic as a receptionist, nurse, and translator, a job she found through an agency for immigrants. She immigrated to the United States in 1989, but had wanted to leave Russia when she was eighteen years old because, as she puts it, "I was offended by my school, by my college, because it was six girls in our group who claimed for a diploma." Despite having received "A's" on her exams, Rivka was denied the high honors the other girls received. "I was offended by that," she explains. ". . . [I]t was done because I was Jew." She was also denied entry to medical school.

The theme of anti-Semitism pervades Rivka's account of her life as her primary reason for leaving the Soviet Union and the basis of her identity—more through the negation of her Jewishness than its realization. Her identity as a Jew remains a central concern for her. She describes a void in her life created by her forced identification with Russian—"goy"—culture and the negation of Jewish traditions. Now, although she hungers for a sense of community that she believes Judaism might offer, she feels cut off from Jewish culture. Even though she enjoys greater religious freedom in the U.S., she continues to feel this schism deeply:

> You know, I don't know history enough; not that I don't know—I don't feel that; that's not mine. I feel myself—not I feel myself, right, that I am Russian, Jewish: Russian because I have Russian culture but I know I am Jewish. You know, these two things they cannot live together, and I'm not Russian but I am not Jewish. And I want my daughter to be Jewish.

Thus she describes a gap between interior and exterior perceptions of social realities: "We lost our roots . . . Yes, my face is Jewish but I don't know anything about Jewish." Functioning as a sort of empty sign, her knowledge of being Jewish, looking Jewish, resides outside her experience, marking her without giving her life meaning, except in terms of absence, a lack of content; indeed, she has been shaped by a culture—Soviet culture—that rejected her and that she in turn repudiates. She would like her daughter to enjoy a stronger sense of Jewish identity but she seems to be thinking more generally when she says she hopes her daughter will feel "more free than I . . . I'm so inside of myself." Asked to explain, she replies:

> Because all the things, I don't know, I cannot explain that—you have to feel it, you know, the conflicts, yeah. I don't think about it a lot now. I feel more free now. I know that I can go to the college—it depends on me, you know, to do that. That I think nobody will force me and nobody will put me down here, you know. I'll try my best.

Rivka's parents divorced when she was in her early teens but, despite some retrospective understanding of their marital problems, she remembers her childhood as unconflictive. Her only complaint about her family, originally from Odessa, is that they traveled too much, uprooting her from friends. Her mother was an engineer, her father a dental technician; it was her grandfather, a doctor, however, whom she emulated. Her desire to follow in his footsteps with a career in medicine compounded her disappointment when she was rejected from medical school.

Four Teacher Portraits: Writing and Sense of Self

Karen Stein: "With No Erasures"

Karen Stein is a 48-year-old Jewish American woman who has worked as an adjunct in the BRW program since its inception. Although she identified closely with her father, who aspired to become a writer and died when she was five years old, she only began to see herself as a writer recently. As a young child, she retreated into a world of books, drawing solace from the "people" she met there. This experience inspired her to want to become a reading teacher, first as a volunteer in high school and then, more seriously, as a graduate student preparing to teach remedial reading. Her mother, a secretary, literate despite a ninth-grade education, encouraged Karen's early attempts to write: diaries, poems, notes to friends. Karen would read her "works" to her mother.

She remembers feeling anguished by her father's death and, somewhat later, a sense of awe toward his library, which was in her bedroom. Under the wing of first- and fifth-grade teachers who gave her special attention, she thrived; she says learning to read empowered her. But in between these positive experiences, she describes school as having been isolating, at best neutral; and she sees herself as having been a good but not an engaged or rigorous student. This sense of isolation continued in college where, except for a crush on an English professor, she recalls having "floated," unmoored, through four years in an honors psychology program.

Her discovery of sensory awareness work in her late twenties appears to have given her a philosophical and spiritual foundation; along with meditation, which she began ten years ago, sensory awareness is a primary influence on her life and her teaching. Like her attitude toward writers as special, outside the realm of the ordinary in which she places herself, she saw sensory awareness teachers as beyond her reach. Now, however, in part due to her experience teaching writing over the past three years, she feels she has achieved some degree of integration between writing and sensory awareness; she has also undergone a transformation from silence to volubility, and from seeing herself as incapable of the achievements she admires in others to seeing herself as both an artist and a writer. This change in self-perception marks a philosophical shift (though by no means a complete one) from a romantic view to a social theory of cultural production: she now believes that everybody is, broadly speaking, an artist and writer.

Underlying her spiritual experience is an earlier identification with freethinking. Despite her mother's stress on traditional Jewish values—education, family, customs—Karen reports that her mother "gave up" on her early because she was a freethinker. Reasserting a romantic perspective, she recalls how reading *Tess of the D'Ubervilles* led her to value love over marriage. In regard to herself, she emphasizes her satisfaction in sensory awareness work, drawing, and now teaching and writing. An important avenue of expression for her has been drawing; she draws freely, *with no erasures*, trying to capture lived experience, what she describes later as "that living quality."

Given her attraction to spiritual and romantic teachings, it is not surprising that she gravitates to composition theorists like Peter Elbow. Unlike Elbow, however, her approach to teaching writing centers on discrete words, and she uses the dictionary as a tool for building vocabulary. But she enthusiastically embraces Elbow's work with freewriting: for example, she reports that, while freewriting in her BRW-1 class, she became conscious of her lefthandedness and its significance to her—her mother refused to teach her skills she saw as distinctly righthanded. This insight led Karen during the freewriting session to explore the constraints of writing by foregoing letters altogether. Elbow's theories coincide with sensory awareness training in promoting the experiential component of writing. Karen says she wants to empower students by changing their attitudes toward reading and writing. She says she does not focus on grammar; however, her comments on both Rivka's and Ethel's papers contain repeated references to error.

John Ross: Dueling the Father

John Ross is a 43-year-old poet and teacher, a second-generation New York Jew whose grandparents were Eastern European. He is working on his doctorate in psychology and has been influenced by theorists like Sylvia Scribner; his dissertation focuses on revision in writing. He has been teaching for ten years, mostly adult basic education and developmental writing courses, but also a creative writing class at a prison. For two years prior to teaching at DTU, he was the academic coordinator for a Veterans' Education program. He started teaching BRW workshops in the fall of 1991 and went on to teach BRW-1 the following semester.

John's stories about his name are prophetic of his own identity as a writer: his paternal grandfather, for whom he was named, won a language prize in Romania, a one-way ticket to the U.S. "So language brought me here," John grins. One of his earliest memories of writing is the occasion he first wrote his name in kindergarten:

> I can remember the sun coming down onto the desk, you know that little square, the sun coming down onto the page and there was my name, so it was sort of like this revelation—some kind of theological thing, like light, sun, you know, light, page, me, a kind of very primal connection, like some kind of Lacanian thing. You know, there's the name there, here I am, so I think I learned I was a person if I had my writing.

This knowledge, he says, came relatively late, a delay he speculates was due to his being the second child and having a "receptive vocabulary" that allowed him "the luxury of living off other people's language." Once he started speaking—entered the symbolic register—he progressed quickly, if only to compete with his father's "inordinate vocabulary." Thus, in grade school, he knew he was "alienated" because he had learned sophisticated words and concepts "to be able to duel" his father. Learning "discursive strategies is—was" a matter of survival. Like many of the teachers (and the more linguistically confident students) interviewed in the study, literacy skills were learned at home or elsewhere outside school, exemplified in John's case by the fact that he knew at age ten what a "parasitical leech" was when his father called him one. Language then for John is a means "to support and defend yourself, and figure out who you are."

Elaborating on his relationship to authority and how language has empowered him, he traces his antagonists from his father to the Vietnam War to American culture generally. Having language skills has helped him "figure out how to fit into . . . [society] and not be completely marginalized by being silenced. So being a writer to me is being able to have an identity and being able to have someplace, space, where I—there's an 'I' to respond from."

Miriam Goodman: "When I'm Writing I Feel Alive"

A 38-year-old Jewish American woman, born and raised in New York City, Miriam Goodman has been teaching in one form or another since 1974, starting as a reading teacher in the public schools, then tutoring ESL and writing, and since 1980, teaching all levels of composition and some literature courses on the college level. In addition to teaching and working on her doctorate in American literature, Miriam is a playwright, wife, and mother. Her identity as a writer has caused family conflicts in several ways: being a writer and teacher has not satisfied her parents' high expectations; her father, having "no idea what goes into writing," has competed with her; and everyone in her family, including her sisters and brother, has discouraged her about her writing.

It is this experience of discouragement, despite which she continues to write and identify as a writer, "that's probably part of why I'm very encouraging to my students," says Miriam. Her nurturing attitude toward students also appears to be rooted in her training as a tutor. Her approach to teaching writing, modeled on tutoring, is individualized, holistic, and respectful. A key responsibility, she believes, is to ensure that the class is interesting enough to elicit student response. Rather than teach grammar per se or "fix" students' papers, she says, "I will circle things and I'll ask them to fix it." In addition to peer response, she "believe[s] in reading aloud," which often results in students restructuring a piece of writing as they talk. She takes their writing seriously,

> a lot more seriously often than they take it. And I try to give them a sense that it's important, important to be able to write well and to express yourself well and to develop things. But I also think that what's important is to be able to write about things you care about.

Miriam recalls that her mother taught her to read at age three by using the phonics method. She was a "voracious reader" and started to write her own books at age five. Her high I.Q. test results have been "the pride and bane" of her existence. She describes herself as an underachiever, the family "rebel," the "black sheep." Her father grew up in a poor family on the Lower East Side; her mother, more middle-class, was from the Bronx. The families are Russian Jewish, and both parents—professionals—identify themselves as socialists, although Miriam believes they have "become a little more conservative." They have homophobic and racist attitudes, she says, noticeable in their social isolation from people of color, but they are not aware of the contradiction between their professed values and their experience. Miriam identifies with her parents' political beliefs, she says, but not with their personal values except for their generosity. "It's important in this world not to be cheap, emotionally or financially." Her parents "hope for the best in the world . . . They have a lot of sympathy for people who have less than they have."

Describing her relationship with her students as one of mutual respect, Miriam admits one reason she has enjoyed teaching is that she gets approval for it in a way that she has not as a writer. As a student herself, she started school early and then skipped a grade, causing her to feel socially isolated. Coursework has always come easily for her so she "never took classes seriously." Her MFA program was marred by "terrible teachers because they were all writers; they were all very competitive." She first identified herself as a writer at age sixteen, when she left home. Asked what it meant to her to be a writer, she says, "If I didn't write, I'd be a very miserable person. It means being happy. It's an obsession; I love it and it dictates my life." Writing plays is "one of the reasons I'm alive . . . when I'm writing I feel alive."

Learning to write means "revision—it means being able to look at something and step away from it" and to "be impressed with something you've done even though you feel insecure as a person." Writing requires patience. For Miriam, it was "the only thing in my life—one of the few things that has not come easily . . . writing has taught me how to be patient."

Clinton Crawford: The Humiliation of Basic Writing[8]

Clinton Crawford is a black man in his thirties from Guyana who has been teaching college writing in the United States for five years, mostly to older adults; he completed his doctorate in sociolinguis-

---

8. As earlier stated, Clinton Crawford asked to be referred to by his real name rather than a pseudonym.

tics in the spring of 1992. His childhood was marked by immersion into books, especially the Bible, and his grandmother's evangelism. Along with his two older brothers, he was raised by his grandmother in a rural area and remembers being wakened at 5:30 every morning "to read passages from the Bible. I learned to read by reading the Bible." In addition to being "very religious," his family strongly valued education; Clinton recalls

> two statements that resonate with me growing up as a child: honesty is the best policy; and learning is better than silver and gold . . . those two [are] the sum total of the world that was created for me as a child.

Because it was a small town, "whatever you did was reported . . . If you misbehaved, the reports got to your home before you got there, so by the time I got home, she was waiting by the door for me, saying, 'Yeah, I heard what you did,' and so on . . . She was a disciplinarian because she had a responsibility of raising four boys and two girls."

He also reports experiencing an innate impulse to paint, an impulse so fierce that he literally painted on the walls of his grandmother's house until she bought him a set of oil paints at age nine. Early on, he connected images to words, creating cartoons with "soliloquies," indicating an interest in the relationship between images and language that has continued: in his doctoral dissertation, he proposes a multicultural high school curriculum that recasts images of ancient Egyptian art in light of African history.[9] However, his identification with writing did not spare him from the "humiliation" of being placed himself in a basic writing class at a large, midwestern university when he returned to school in the United States. His problems with writing emerged in his late teens and persisted through his twenties—problems with confused ideas rather than grammar, he believes, attributable to the circumstance of having had to assume care of his family at age fifteen. At the university where he got his B.A. in literature, he describes how

> being in a basic writing class, I started to put things together for myself. You know I tried to understand, how do I go about this whole process of writing . . . It took me almost eight years before I developed some kind of confidence as a writer again.

This experience mirrors that of students he now teaches and identifies with closely; however, unlike Ethel, whose writing remains externally driven by classroom assignments and teacher expectations, Clinton claims that his confidence grew as a result of

---

9. See Crawford (1993).

a one-to-one correspondence with what was going on in my life over these eight years. One becomes more introspective and more reflective when you leave your country and come someplace else. So, you know, in times of despair, really, when I got a little uncomfortable or felt some nostalgia, I wrote. . . . I guess that's what helped me in my writing during that period of time.

By writing on his own in journals, he was able to deal with the sadness caused by leaving Guyana and adjust more easily to life in America.

Teacher Responses to Ethel's Paper

Karen's Response: "Not English"

Basic writing teachers often experience a sense of frustration with students like Ethel, whose problems feel overwhelming and seem to extend beyond the province of the writing class. As she reads Ethel's paper, "Complexion," Karen remarks:

So I guess I was still struggling to find out what this all was. Was this a title or not? . . . First of all, what I'm relating to now is her handwriting, which is so, it has so many swirls; it reminds me of Ethel somehow. It's very confined and so I'm just noticing that and it's bringing back Ethel . . . So right off there's something that's an incomplete sentence and she hasn't really communicated to me as a reader . . .

Here the burden is on Ethel, the writer, to communicate to the reader. But when Karen reads Rivka's paper, "A Human Being Is Supposed to be a Human" (see Figure 5–2), she generously attributes the awkward title to "her language translation." In contrast to her impatience with Ethel's writing, Karen praises Rivka's attempt, explaining:

Here is Rivka struggling with the language . . . she just came here a couple of years ago and she's really struggling with this language and doing wonderfully.

Although Karen knows Ethel is from Guyana, she wonders if English is her first language and concludes that her failure to communicate "what she meant" goes beyond "language difficulties." Ethel seems to concur when she says, "I don't think a good writer might try to confuse themself by their writing but sometime I try to write the best I can and still sometime I put some confusion in the middle or somewhere and I don't really see it until somebody tells me."

But when she is told her writing is confused, "it really gets to me . . . When you think you write it all good and everything, then

continued on page 123

Figure 5–2

Riva Minsky's Paper: "A Human Being Is Supposed to Be Human"

Paper grade ✓

A Human Being is Supposed To Be Human. ✓

There are a lot of people who believe that they have to obey

all laws. On the one hand, probably, they are right, because if

everybody would begin to go his own way it would be no State, but

but just could bring everything to chaos.

Everything has to be in order. Everybody wants to live well,

in peace. Who has to make this order, whois making rules?

I think – people themselves. Everyone even not being in Congress,

can bring one's mite to the life. We do it by voting. If we get
have power might

on the top of the government the right person it can help a lot
what is

to get desired. But even after that we have to have sober look
at

on the things. We have to be able to estimate our claims, not

think just about what would be right only for me or my family,

but not to forget about other people. I am not offering prin-

ciples of Communism, I had enough of it. But simply we have to

be aware that we are surrounded by another people, who could have
other   There   ground

another opinions. It has to be found some middle, some situation

in which everybody could live and to be happy.

I do not know how to do it. This is why I felt that I have to

study, in order to do (well) my part in life.

I think that students of professor De Anza also were just the

people (young people) who wanted to know, to try everything. And

they trusted their professor and believed that they could get

true with his help. But that was not the right person to be taught

by. At first, he was the coward person, "shallow soul", who could

Figure 5–2, continued
Riva Minsky's Paper: "A Human Being Is Supposed to Be Human"

not stand against the law. I am not sure that he even thought

about the situation seriously, so far it did not touch him perso-

naly. But suddenly it could . And he was scared of it to the death.

He was ready to expose his students(whom he should feel at that

time as own children) to the regime. He knew what it meant for

them- it was equal to murder. But he already had no time, he was

afraid that somebody would go ahead of him, and he was in a hurry

to make a call first.

His role was to teach, to help his students to get the answers

to any questions. If he thought that they were on the wrong way,

he should try to persuade them ~~in his rightfulness~~ *otherwise.*

There were a lot of cases in my country when people turned out

in situation like Lawrence Thornton describes in <u>Imaging Argentina</u>.

It was time of WW!! which became the tragedy for whol*e* ~~my~~ *my* country.

And the time between 1937-1939 years, which were exactly the same

for my country as for Argentina, as though it was repe*a*ted in

~~some~~ *different* decades with ch*a*nged names,

From the books and people who were eyewitnesses of that events,

I heard many cases when people had chances to show their faces,

Sometimes people could discover in quite strangers the people,

with whom they tied for all the future.

Those ~~It~~ were times when people almost lost their belief even in close

relatives. It was *a* time when nobody could imagine what other had

in one's mind. There were enough cases when fathers or wives

exposed their children or spouse*s* to the enemy or regime*s*

But in other cases people commit*t*ed deeds: who under the mortal

fear hide~~d~~ in their homes refugees or *J*ews from *F*ascists;

who subjected danger not only themselves but also own children

and relatives just to save the life to stranger.

Th*e*y did noble steps not thinking to get something back, they just

did, just saved others lives.

I never found in my heart excuses for traitors.

you see that whatever you wrote wasn't so good." How does this make her feel? "I don't really like that," she says. "I try my best sometimes to do it over, to do the best, and sometimes come out like the same way or worse, so, for me, I don't like that."

Karen states a desire "to get [Ethel] to have more confidence in herself," to "feel that she could express herself and be heard . . . literally and figuratively." But Ethel's writing and demeanor in class confound her; Ethel is introverted, confused, and uncomprehending. Says Karen:

> She would just put something in that didn't belong and not quite realize it. I mean there were just like separate things a lot in what she wrote. So I guess that I gave her a check minus . . . I don't know, maybe I was being hard on her. I mean she does . . . stick to the topic most of the time, but there were a lot of, there was confusion at one point . . . maybe she just ran out of words, you know, because she had a lot of trouble writing at length so she just wanted to stick something in—I don't know. But to me as a reader, there were enough things that technically and in terms of sticking to the topic . . . for me to give her a check minus at that time. I mean, now I might give her a check.

The check minus is for the paper "Complexion," in which Ethel states:

> I am dark in complexion and people often stop me and praise my complexion. . . .

Reading this passage aloud, Karen says:

> Now, I have to smile because I was one of those people and I have never done that with any student but I just thought her complexion looks so beautiful; there's something about the darkness and . . . I don't know, I didn't know whether I would offend her, but I just felt when I first met her, you know like after the first class or something, I just said, "Your complexion is so beautiful, Ethel." So I guess I'm not the only one who did that.

One wonders if she *was* the only one, given that students often address their teachers in assigned papers and that the compliment itself, which Karen apparently does not believe provoked Ethel's statement, is by her own account unusual: "*I have never done that with any student.*" Not only does she tell Ethel she has a beautiful complexion, but she adds, "there's something about the darkness," a remark that evokes loaded literary and sociological constructions of race. Ethel's paper continues:

> people . . . ask which country am I from. I would tell them guyana and they would begin to make comment on on skin texture. (Good

comments) which I feel very proud of, to know that although I am not white in complexion, there are many thing people can see and tell you about yourself by just looking at your skin colour.

Assuming her own reaction to Ethel's complexion is typical, Karen cannot appreciate Ethel's resistance to Rodriguez's shame about his skin color. Karen remarks:

> I have in the margin, "I'm confused about this statement," that *"There are many things people can tell about me by just looking at my skin color."* So at this point she doesn't really explain that other than to say that she's from Guyana, but she doesn't say what people know by looking at her, so I have no idea what that was, so I questioned that.

Given Rodriguez's discussion of the social stigma of dark skin color and Karen's remark about Ethel's (dark) complexion, her inability to conceive the subtext of the above italicized statement is surprising. Rather than probe the statement's meaning, perhaps by questioning the implied link between skin color and character, Karen can only express confusion, frustration. That is, she misses the connection that Ethel is striving, however falteringly, to make between her personal experience—she receives *"good comments"* (from Karen) about her complexion *"although [she is] not white"*—and the significance of skin color in American culture. Indeed, the irony here is that our cultural lexicon does tell us—stereotypically—about a person *just by looking* at skin.

It is as if Karen literally cannot understand Ethel, partly because she seems to have constructed a linguistic standard that Ethel does not meet, but more significantly because she avoids the content of the paper—race—by focusing on surface errors. In response to Ethel's statement that "Richard mother never like to see her son look dirty or because of walking in the sun he might look a little darker," Karen metaphorically throws up her hands:

> Okay, so this is a kind of an English as a second language problem or something. It's not English . . . I know what she means. She means that Richard's mother did not want him out in the sun for a long time and she'd always make him use a towel so that he wouldn't—and we talked about this a lot in class and it left an impression—so that I know what she means as a reader only because I know it within the context and I've read it but I would not probably understand this if I did not know all that. So these are two common student errors, the possessive, which is very—it runs through most of the students' papers—and the verb tenses.

In sum, Karen describes Ethel's writing as incoherent, disconnected, not English, a misinterpretation of the reading, unintelligible. She sees Rivka's writing, on the other hand, as mature, thoughtful; Rivka struggles to translate from Russian into English; she has nice rhythm, sentence variation; she takes risks; she writes from the heart. Ethel is "not too bright" perhaps, but Rivka is a "basic American" rather than a "basic writer."

John's Response: "A High-Skilled ESL Student"

None of the other teachers who read Ethel's paper was as critical of it as Karen. An interesting aspect of John Ross' response to the text is commentary that takes the form of questions as he reads, using language such as: "I'm trying to figure out if this is . . ." and, in response to a parenthetical phrase, "Who wrote that?" Other rhetorical features of exploratory analysis include "seem like" and "I wonder if." Although he frequently refers to the problematic surface features of Ethel's writing, these remarks are offset by his belief that "there's a lot here to work with." Thus, unlike Karen, John brackets Ethel's grammatical and syntactical problems and stresses the content of her thinking, categorizing her as a "high-skilled ESL student who's probably got a lot to say about intercultural racial relations but doesn't have the organizational structure to do it yet in English." Specifically, in response to Ethel's comments about skin color, John says that "outside of the order, the grammar, the tense problems":

> This is the first time there's really personal reference, I think— maybe there was one before this—but this is the most situated writing so far. . . . The personal commentary is the power—the power comes out of the personal reflection. I'd like the author to have situated herself first and then put her experiences in relationship to Richard Rodriguez's.

In characterizing Ethel in relation to other BRW-1 students, John refers to "the real person behind the text" as a typical basic writing student. Of course, John is only guessing about this "real person," extrapolating from words on a page, while Karen's response to Ethel's writing problems is based on actual encounters with her. Nevertheless, John's inclination to see Ethel as typical and to recognize "the real person" as *behind* rather than *in* the text suggests a basis for establishing a rapport with her that eluded Karen. He certainly responds generously to the student writer he imagines (as well as the teacher), describing her in the following terms:

> I think the person is analytic; I think they're having difficulty with the genre in terms of framing—knowing how to frame their analysis in terms that are meaningful to them and also meaningful to the

teacher. I think there's some kind of . . . I'm just inferring there's the common experience of someone who's been out of school for a long time and is just returning or is not familiar with standard English conventions in terms of putting that analysis of the written text into their own culturally salient terms.

Miriam's Response: "Poor Grammar, Good Content"

Miriam Goodman's approach to teaching basic writing and freshman composition differs, she says, only in her choice of texts and her lower expectations. At both levels, she integrates reading and writing, relies on conferencing, and reviews student drafts individually. In remedial classes at a local community college, during conferences,

> I'd say do this, do that, fix the grammar, strengthen this, these are my responses, and so on.

In her reading of Ethel's paper, however, a dichotomy emerges between form and content, grammar and meaning, that seems different—at least in the concrete emphasis she gives to correctness in practice—from her account of herself as a teacher. Although she stresses meaningfulness and engagement, she is primarily concerned, as she reads Ethel's paper aloud, with surface errors. At the outset of the interview, she states her understanding of my instructions: "Right, so as if I was grading it, in a sense, but not grading it in terms of grammatical content, in terms of what really is being said in the paper." In fact, my instructions were to:

> respond to [the papers] as you're reading, to read aloud but stop yourself and comment on something that you question, that you like about the paper, that you don't like about the paper, that troubles you about the paper. It could be on form, it could be on content . . . Whatever comes to mind.

After I reiterated that she could comment on any aspect of the paper, including grammar, Miriam reads through the second sentence of Ethel's paper and admits, "It's hard not to comment on the grammar for me." Reassured she may do so, she says, "Okay, all right, so that would probably be—my approach also would be to talk about the grammar . . . " In response to the paper's content, Miriam struggles to understand Ethel's writing, praises it as interesting, and points to details she likes, such as the use of the term "*bracero*" to describe Rodriguez's experience as a construction worker, and thinking she respects, such as Ethel's analysis of Rodriguez's commentary on racism. Asked to describe Ethel as a writer, Miriam says: "grammatically poor but I think in terms of content really pretty good." She notes that, in her view, Ethel is presently a better reader of texts than of her own life, a task at which "usually students do better."

Later she says she thinks teachers shape the content of students' writing more than the grammar, which is "very hard" to do. She believes writing is a response to what is said and read, and college writing instruction that helps students "learn how to express themselves and think as individuals" can help build "a body politic in this country" of "questioning adults" rather than "sheep." Asked what "basic writing" means to her, she refers to clarity of expression but shifts gears midsentence and declares, "It's a societal phrase, I guess. The word 'basic' is derogatory. It has no validity because each student is so individualized. One person's basic writing is definitely not another person's basic writing."

Clinton's Response: Guyanese as Exotic Other

Clinton Crawford's reading of Ethel Martin's paper is especially compelling because of a correlation between his and Ethel's experiences—so much so that he assumed she was a male writer—of growing up in Guyana and immigrating to the U.S. He speculates that the favorable response to her dark complexion in the U.S., which she reports in her paper, could be because Guyana is seen as exotic; and he wonders whether African Americans would be so complimented. Thus he attempts to construe Ethel's meaning in "Complexion," exercising what Wolfgang Iser calls a "wandering viewpoint," a transaction between reader and text that "tends to . . . proliferate the meanings a text proposes" (Salvatori, 1987, p. 179). Conversely, an inability to read Ethel's paper could be a reliance on "consistency building," an activity that confirms familiar meanings—in this case, a perception of Ethel herself as unreadable, an exotic "other" produced by a racialized construction of Guyana.

The difference between Clinton's and Karen's responses to Ethel's paper is striking. Clinton responds almost entirely to content, Karen to the paper's surface confusion and errors; Clinton identifies with Ethel, Karen is baffled by her; Clinton credits her for making the connection between skin color and social status, Karen ignores it; Clinton sees organizational skills rather than grammar as Ethel's primary problem, Karen mistakenly attributes her problem to speaking English as a second language (although certainly issues of dialect are involved). Where Karen relies on her version of a process writing approach with emphasis on the word—freewriting, sensory awareness, dictionary exercises—Clinton is concerned with positionality, how the writer positions herself in relation to her subject and reflects on her experience and her writing: is she external to it, observing, or internally experiencing it?

In order to share her ideas—which Clinton says he assumes all writers possess—she must learn to organize them coherently, moving from the global to the specific, from the world to the word. The writer moves along a continuum from experience to language in this effort, as well as a linguistic continuum from nonstandard to standard forms. In this sense, Karen's focus on words, the dictionary, vocabulary, divorced from the writer's experience in the world, may reinforce a tendency to atomize meaning, to become fixated on specific words rather than to see them in relation to one another.

Rhetorics of Basic Writing: Teacher Assumptions

Traveling Between Worlds: A Sociohistorical Perspective

Both John Ross and Clinton Crawford reflect a philosophical perspective that assumes a dialectical relationship between individuals and social systems and promotes a reflexive, critical consciousness. Clinton Crawford sees writing as a matter of positioning oneself. For example, he praises Ethel and explains that he would give her a "B" on her paper

> because she relates the issue of complexion to a social—she is doing some very, very complex things. She is making a commentary on the society in which she lives and how they view people with dark complexion, and she's also saying, although some people view it negatively, she still views—Ethel has a pretty clear positive image of herself. So this person's thinking; this is a thinking writer, and so she needs to be credited for that.

He suggests that students who are able to position themselves on a "continuum of language" from nonstandard to standard dialects find writing less threatening. Understanding that "Black English or Puerto Rican English is as viable or as good as standard American English sparks a whole lot of twinkle in their eyes," he says.

Of all the teacher participants, John seems to be the most developed in terms of a high level of sociohistorical awareness *and* knowledge of critical writing pedagogy. A key concept for him is *situatedness*. John's view of language derives from a social theory of discourse that has permeated composition studies over the last decade. Social constructionist, Bakhtinian, and critical education theorists, among others, have argued that language is inherently social, ideological, and multivoiced. As Min-Zhan Lu (1992) has pointed out, educators who have made efforts to acculturate or accommodate nontraditional students to the dominant culture have been unsuccessful, in part, because they have failed to understand the conflicted nature of language itself. Sympathy for the plight of such students has been undermined by an essentialist view of language in which thought, meaning, and content are seen as preceding or separate from linguistic forms. Alternatively, Lu's rhetoric of basic writing instruction utilizes the metaphor of a borderland. By engaging in linguistic conflict and struggle, students are empowered to make their own discursive choices and define themselves through language. John's metaphor of enabling students "to travel between worlds linguistically" echoes Lu's description of a borderland. Says John:

> I'm concerned with sociohistorically situating a writer. I'm concerned with how a student learns to use their knowledge to trust their linguistic repertoire and to utilize it and be able to manipulate the various demands made by a student in encountering both different genres and different conventions and different ideologically invested encounters, including grades, writing letters for jobs . . . in dealing with the pressure of moving between various dialects and various subcultural language uses to standardization, to be able to travel between those worlds linguistically.

Who's in Control? Expressionist Assumptions

Although Miriam Goodman's response to Ethel's paper is both more positive and politically astute than Karen Stein's, both teachers view writing as self-governed; their talk about writing pedagogy resonates with metaphors of control, mastery, and self-expression, rather than social location, intertextuality, and dialogism. Karen articulates an expressionist view of teaching writing that leaves out a social critique altogether, except perhaps to give lip service to "the empowerment issue." This omission prevents her from reflecting on her assumptions about Ethel—especially racial and class biases—and diminishes her considerable effectiveness as a teacher. Asked to describe her theory of teaching writing, she replies:

> I guess I consider myself a writer, I mean, you know, in the larger sense I consider everybody a writer, I do, but I know that I'm a writer, I know that I get joy out of writing, I know that I need in a way to read and write, and this is—I'd probably be crazy if I didn't, you know, that I have to use my mind in these ways. And I guess I'm trying not to have other people duplicate me, but I'm

trying to get across some of that spirit and I'm trying to get across—I can only go from myself in a way—I mean, I'm not saying *I* can only go from—you might be able to go from a different direction, but the way I am, I'm trying to break down what it is that has helped me along the way, what tools have helped me along the way.

These tools include the dictionary, vocabulary, and freewriting, each of which allows for word play, a "playfulness" with language. The theorists, and associated key concepts, who have influenced Karen include: John Mayher's notion of "productive chaos"; David Bartholomae and Anthony Petrosky on "the empowerment issue," i.e., students "*are* readers and writers"; and Peter Elbow on the "balance between being a student advocate and upholding standards," as well as freewriting and revision.

While Miriam's political orientation primes her to view students, including Ethel, in a social context, her background in literature has not exposed her to the theories of discourse that have shaped contemporary composition pedagogy. Her knowledge of composition derives from practice more than theory; the only theorists she refers to are Bartholomae and Petrosky, whose *Facts, Artifacts, and Counterfacts* she read because of its influence on the DTU Writing Program. She says they reinforced a perspective on teaching she had developed in twelve years of experience. For example, a former writing center mentor taught her "how to help people write better in ways that I think were not intrusive." As opposed to "slashing across their paper"—what she calls a traditional approach—this mentor's philosophy gave "people the idea that they were in charge, that they were in control. Because of course they were; after all, they were writing this thing." Especially appealing here, for Miriam, is the assumption of equality in the classroom in which the teacher's role is not to impose her will on students but *to give them the idea they are in control.*

The notion that we can simply transfer authority from teacher to students is problematic because it decontextualizes discourse and presumes that classroom dynamics and acts of writing are independent of larger social systems, not the least of which is language itself. Teachers, like anybody else, are caught in the contradiction between attempts to control discursive systems—language, educational practices, classroom relations—and the control they exert over us. For example, the ultimate authority of grading in a college writing class, no matter how experimental assessment may be, almost always remains with the teacher. A social constructionist pedagogy might enable Miriam to approach the question of "who's in control" by viewing language as a zone of conflict in which students—especially basic writers—struggle to make semantic and syntactical choices and internalize what Bakhtin calls "internally persuasive speech." Once language is viewed as dialogic, the "I" who speaks is always interanimated with other voices. In this sense, authority, like ideology, inheres in all discursive relations, and rather than either surrender or claim authority, we constantly engage in its negotiation.

Authorizing Ethel To Write

I started this chapter by asking who and what authorizes us to speak and to write, to "come to voice." Let me conclude by framing an answer in the context of Ethel's experience. She enters the academic world with little exposure to the types of thinking, speaking, reading, and writing that will be expected of her. Her rural background, huge family, and punitive school experiences put her at a disadvantage in a college environment in which she will not only be required to read and write, but also to follow the academic rules. Such rules or codes at DTU, while perhaps less strictly enforced than elsewhere, remain in effect, however tacitly, weeding out those who speak too softly (or loudly), tentatively, perhaps with a nonstandard dialect too pronounced, too alien to a teacher's ear, or who write too briefly, in prose too fragmented, broken, "not English," unintelligible, frustrating, beyond the teacher's patience to decipher. Ethel dropped her "h's" and could barely be heard when she spoke in class; she does not expect to be remembered, recognized.

The drama in her life centers around her children, the sons who have been taken away from her, leaving her anguished, and the new baby who presumably comforts her. She wants to become a nurse, to help her sisters with their studies, to have a family. Education enables her to achieve these personal goals; but in order to learn, one must be punished, "whacked." Such external punishment is a given for Ethel, an instrument of learning she believes in for herself and her children. She feels no pang of conscience when she "whacks" her oldest son; it is a duty, a parental responsibility she shirks when she spares her younger son who looks like her. Discipline is external, physical, frightening, but unavoidable; the punishment that Ethel received as a child she now expects from her teachers and administers to her own children.

Enter Karen. Born and raised in New York City, she loses her father, an aspiring writer, at age five and grows up in a room surrounded by his library. She never realizes her first ambition of becoming a reading teacher and gets an administrative job after college. A self-professed "freethinker" who believes in love rather than marriage, she finds meaning in a spiritual quest that leads her to sensory awareness and meditation. In her mid-forties, she discovers teaching writing, which she does in the BRW program, excited by the connections she begins to realize between her spiritual work, creative endeavors, and teaching. The concept of freewriting, in particular, inspires her, liberates her own writing, and clarifies her goals as a teacher: "It changes that stopping pattern, it changes that intellectual negativity that you don't have anything to say, or that you've said it all, or that you're not a writer that can write for very long."

Karen can identify with students like Rivka Minsky, whom she sees as bright, mature, engaging. Rivka could be a friend, a colleague. But toward Ethel she feels a sense of frustration, bewilderment; she cannot fathom Ethel's shyness, her silences, her difficulty speaking in class. Although Rivka's English is still broken, heavily accented, it is familiar to Karen; she knows Russian students like Rivka, how they speak, think. Ethel is alien, "other," a puzzle. Rivka's English is a "translation"; Ethel's is simply "not English." How does race figure into Karen's relationships with Rivka and Ethel? Karen asks the students to respond to Richard Rodriguez's discussion of skin color; she compliments Ethel's nice complexion; she then has "no idea" what Ethel means by her statement that "although I am not white in complexion, there are still many thing people can see and tell about me by just looking at my skin colour."

The three other teachers. For John Ross, learning "discursive strategies" enabled him to survive his father's verbal punishment; language skills give him an identity and "someplace, space, where I—there's an 'I' to respond from." Miriam Goodman's sympathy with student writers stems from her own struggle to continue to write in the face of her family's discouragement. Writing means "being happy. It's an obsession . . . one of the reasons I'm alive . . . when I'm writing I feel alive." Clinton Crawford recalls that his problems with writing, which eventually placed him in a basic writing class, started with "confused ideas" in his mid-teens. Like Ethel, he is Guyanese, but his literate grandmother teaches him and his siblings to read the Bible, and he identifies himself as an artist at a young age.

Each of the teachers, including Karen, is a self-defined writer and/or artist who sees language, writing, and creativity as essential components of identity, even of existence. They see themselves as constituted through language and they use language self-consciously, reflexively, to assert themselves in the world, sometimes combatively, sometimes exploratively, often—as when Clinton painted the walls of his grandmother's house—through a sheer impulse to create. Neither Rivka Minsky nor Ethel Martin seems to possess a drive to write or a strong connection to language. Rivka has some literary background, as she makes clear in the epigraph to one of her essays in which she translates a Russian poem about war: "We cannot forget/The unforgivable early/We cannot forget/For tomorrow's sake." Of herself as a writer, she says:

> It seems to me I never wrote anything. Just in the school when we had to like journals work here. I don't remember like to write. I wrote letters for all my friends when we moved from one town to another, you know, but no I never wrote something. I tried to write poetry because my friends did and I wrote one about cat, about little cat something, you know I was ten years old, and it was creative. I don't do it now. I don't write now, just for school.

For Ethel, as we have seen, the experience of writing and reading is always connected to punishment. Asked if she read much as a child, she recalls that her mother would read to her:

> When like she read something to me and she give me it like two days after, and I make mistake in whatever I read and she whacks me, she would just give me some licks and I remember, I remember afterwards when she hit me or something like that so I remember everything.

Given the students' prior experiences with reading and writing and their current attitudes toward them as exclusively school-based activities, it is not surprising that as college students they placed into a basic writing course. However, Rivka is clearly more apt to succeed than Ethel: she has had a good education in the former Soviet Union, despite the anti-Semitism she faced there; she grew up in a literate household; and she is acquainted with literature and history. For Ethel to succeed in college she will have to make a leap from a rural, backward childhood, in which literacy and learning were closely linked with physical discipline, to an urban college environment in which, at the very least, she will be expected to motivate herself and assume responsibility for her own learning.

What and who can authorize Ethel to write, speak, participate in an academic community? To begin with, Karen has by no means completely failed her. In enabling her to "write long" through the freewriting and journal exercises she assigned to the class, she has given Ethel a sense of herself as a writer that she never before had. However, her negative assessment of Ethel as a reader and writer contrasts sharply with her appreciation of Rivka. Indeed, she acknowledges that:

> I can see that in fact I was penalizing Ethel for probably the same things that I wasn't penalizing Rivka as much for in terms of language. But somehow I didn't see her as an ESL student, and I think maybe a lot of these errors and things came from that. . . .

Thus she admits she treated the two students differently, reflecting that her expectations may have been higher for Ethel because she did not view her as an ESL student. But while Karen was "always impressed with Rivka that her thinking was right on," she describes Ethel as follows:

> As a reader . . . there was a lot of misinterpretation, and I remember her not understanding a lot of what she read which may have been the language barrier. I mean, I don't know, but she had a lot of trouble comprehending and she would be really off in space in her comprehension sometimes. . . . As a writer, again, like with that last paragraph [of "Complexion"] that came from nowhere. I mean there was just not even a connecting sentence to talk about where it came from. There would be this kind of struggle in all her papers.

Each of the other teachers who responded to Ethel's paper characterized her in positive terms: as a "high skilled ESL student" with "a lot to say about intercultural racial relations"; a better reader of texts than of her own life; and "sophisticated" but lacking control over her writing.

Although Karen's divergent responses to Rivka and Ethel cannot be neatly summed up as a case of identification with one and alienation from the other, the social and historical contexts of the study provide some clues to her negative response to Ethel. Such responses may reflect embedded racist assumptions that infect American society generally as well as, more specifically, in recent years, increased tensions between Jews and blacks. Moreover, while race is clearly not the only factor that shapes Karen's response to Ethel's personality and writing, her discussion of Ethel is laced with racial connotations. One conclusion that can be drawn from this chapter is the need for writing programs and other educational projects to confront racist assumptions and attitudes directly through workshops, study groups, and discussions that probe connections between discursive and social structures and practices. Also important, however, is to stress that the problem is not Karen's affinity for Rivka; for the point here is obviously not to deprive Rivka of a sympathetic teacher nor to pit students against each other, but to ensure that such support is available to Ethel as well, and to develop pedagogical perspectives that enable cross-cultural identifications.

All of the teachers who participated in this case study describe a process by which they internalize a sense of themselves as language users, readers, writers, an identity that in turn empowers them as individuals. Although Rivka discusses her development as a reader and writer in more pedestrian terms, without the teachers' intense identification with language, she is well-educated and literate, more of a "basic American," as Karen says, than a "basic writer." The first crucial step in developing linguistic competence for a student like Ethel, on the other hand, is for her to engage in a self-reflexive process in which she can begin to see language not as given, outside her own subjective world, imposed by parents and teachers through discipline and punishment, but as constitutive of her world and therefore within her power to know, use, and question. However, as Bakhtin reminds us, to force language "to submit to one's own intentions and accents is a difficult and complicated process."

Part Three

A Writing Pedagogy for the Nineties

Chapter Six

A Two-Way Flow
Social Construction Theory and Critical Pedagogy

As a living, socio-ideological concrete thing, as het-
eroglot opinion, language, for the individual conscious-
ness, lies on the borderline between oneself and the
other. The word in language is half someone else's. It
becomes "one's own" only when the speaker populates it
with his own intention, his own accent, when he appro-
priates the word, adapting it to his own semantic and
expressive intention. (1981, pp. 293–94)

Mikhail Bakhtin

Perhaps our greatest challenge as writing teachers, particularly in working with students with different linguistic and cultural backgrounds from our own, is learning how to read student texts and the discourses in which they are embedded. Recent composition theory has appropriated ideas from diverse sources that give value to student writing and reveal how we and our students are historically and socially situated. An understanding of the politics of location can give us critical insight into the production, distribution, and reception of texts (material objects) and discourses (social processes). In this chapter, I examine social construction-ism and critical pedagogy; in the next, postmodern and feminist pedagogies. Together, these theoretical perspectives illuminate the discursive and material structures and practices that constitute us and our worlds, including the field of college composition. In a period of rapid global change marked by massive immigration from the periphery to the centers of world power and increased competition for resources,[10] such perspectives help forge a writing pedagogy for the nineties and the fast-approaching millennium. They embody a convergence of political, linguistic, and pedagogical schools of thought that emerged from the watershed of the 1960s and strongly influenced the generation now redefining college composition.[11]

This intellectual convergence combines: Marxist theories of social and economic systems; psychoanalytic theories of the human subject; postmodern theories of language and other semiotic systems, the politics of race and gender that emerged from the new left in the 1960s; and a Freirean-inspired "pedagogy of the oppressed." An adequate theory of basic writing would create the "two-way flow" Sandra Bennett described in Chapter 4 and foster genuine dialogue in classrooms, the academy, and local communities. To build such a theory, the sophisticated view of reading and writing delineated in the Pittsburgh BRW program—and adapted by second-generation programs like DTU's—needs to be integrated with a more politically conscious perspective, which social constructionist thought and critical pedagogy help provide.[12]

---

10. For example, California's controversial Proposition 187, which denies social services to illegal aliens.

---

11. I do not mean to imply here that any consensus of opinion or single ideological perspective exists in composition studies, nor that the convergent theories here delineated represent all of composition's theoretical influences, e.g., cognitive psychology; rather, I hope to suggest a sociohistorical process—often uneven and slow—of social change that has permeated all sectors of society, including higher education. The political and cultural perspectives that emerged in the 1960s and 1970s, while failing to lead to the revolutionary changes some predicted, have had widespread institutional effects that ultimately may produce more humane, progressive policies and practices in education and other social arenas. On the other hand, as can be seen in recent attacks on the arts and humanities, entitlement programs in education, and social services across the board, the sociocultural terrain remains contested and, for the time being, reactionary forces have the upper hand.

---

12. For the most part, I discuss primary theorists through the literature in composition and rhetoric. Also, due to the interrelatedness of the material, there is considerable overlap between the four categories.

Social Constructionism

In the wake of the so-called "paradigm shift"[13] in composition pedagogy from product to process and the cognitive and expressivist rhetorics that accompanied it, a significant development in composition scholarship has been the widespread adoption of social constructionist thought. But this "social turn" in composition has resulted in two versions of social constructionism: a weak version that reinforces social conformity through collaboration in a monolithic view of discourse communities based on the philosopher Richard Rorty's notion of a "conversation of mankind"; and a strong version based in Marxist thought that critically challenges the status quo. Insofar as the sociology of knowledge stems from Marxism, what Kenneth Bruffee welcomed into the field as "social construction" in 1986 had already informed the work of leftwing scholars. But it was Bruffee, more than anyone else, relying on Rorty's neopragmatic philosophy and a weak version of social constructionism, who introduced the term to composition.

Thus across the ideological spectrum, critics have characterized social constructionism as Orwellian "group think" (Johnson, 1986); an accommodation to the "workings of normal discourse" (Trimbur, 1989); another totalizing "metanarrative" (Vitanza, 1991); and relativistic (Kent, 1991). But despite its contested status, social constructionism, in various forms, has made its mark in composition (Hull et al., 1991; Lefevre, 1987; Cooper and Holzman, 1989). Thus Marilyn Cooper proposes "an ecological model of writing, whose fundamental tenet is that writing is an activity through which a person is continually engaged with a variety of socially constituted systems" (p. 6). And among John Mayher's (1990) "keystones" in his call for uncommonsense teaching are the notions of "humans as meaning-makers in a social context; interpretation as a constructive and reconstructive activity. . ." (p. 3)

In the history of composition studies, social constructionism has helped create an awareness of writing as both social act and social construct, and encouraged new classroom strategies like collaborative learning, peer group response, and process writing with an emphasis on dialogue and revision. To his credit, Bruffee's 1986 bibliographic essay on social construction, intended to guide teachers through "the relevant scholarly literature," can rightly be seen as the inauguration of the theory's impact on composition. Nevertheless, as Michael Apple (1990) points out:

---

13. See Hairston (1982).

[t]he general principle of the social construction of reality does not explain why certain social and cultural meanings and not others are distributed through schools; nor does it explain how the control of the knowledge preserving and producing institutions may be linked to the ideological dominance of powerful groups in a social collectivity. (p. 27)[14]

In other words, critical consciousness depends on the ability to analyze specific historical constructions of social reality through uncovering their assumptions, aims, and effects. Along the same lines, leftwing composition theorists have articulated a broader perspective of writing pedagogy that places the institution of composition instruction within the larger context of oppressive, unequal sociocultural relations. According to John Trimbur (1989),

Without a critique of the dominant power relations that organize the production of knowledge . . . the social constructionist rationale for collaborative learning may, unwittingly or not, accommodate its practices to the authority of knowledge it believes it is demystifying. (p. 603)

Feminists in composition have likewise viewed writing instruction in the context of sexism, revealing "internalized patriarchal structures" that affect colleagues as well as students who "seem often quite unambiguously committed to 'the system'" (Bauer, 1990). Rather than "normal discourse," Dale Bauer proposes we (feminists) "teach ethics as a kind of counter-indoctrination, a debriefing, to privatizing personal ethics" (p. 387).

Of particular interest here is the impact of social construction theories on basic writing. Early research in basic writing tended to focus on the writing processes and cognitive strategies of adult learners (Perl, 1978; Sommers, 1980). As the "social turn" deepened, this research gave way to interest in the social contexts of writing (Bizzell, 1990; Hull et al., 1991). But a social theory of writing need not preclude cognitive research (Berkenkotter, 1991; Cooper and Holzman, 1989); indeed, sociocognitive research helps explain the complex relationship between individuals and society in a dialectic that fosters a more useful theory and practice of basic writing instruction. This dialectic illuminates such questions as why basic writing emerged as a category in the first place and why some students are labeled basic writers. Lacking such an analysis, neither the socioeconomic forces that shape human consciousness nor the individual agency that shapes social realities can be fully understood. We place the onus on individuals within the system to

---

14. See also, Bowles and Gintis (1976), Freire (1988), Aronowitz and Giroux (1985), and Belenky et al. (1986).

explain their failures (and successes), *or* we see social systems as vast power structures beyond our control. This dichotomy has particularly serious consequences for basic writers, whose sense of agency is often weak and whose situation in the academy is created by oppressive and asymmetrical power relations.

The Marxist Tradition

In *The Social Construction of Reality*, Berger and Luckmann (1967) situate the sociology of knowledge in Marx's founding statement that "man's consciousness is determined by his social being" (pp. 5–6). They explore the social construction of reality based on positions articulated, respectively, by Durkheim and Weber: society possesses objective facticity; and society is constructed through activity that expresses subjective meaning (p. 18). These postulates are based on a theory of social production and reproduction through the externalization, objectivation, internalization, and legitimation of reality. Compared with Rorty's (1979) static view of knowledge as "socially justified belief," a sociological analysis shows how knowledge is dynamically created through a dialectic between individual consciousness and social structures.

Through social activity, human beings produce and so externalize an institutional world that attains an objective, given status. This objectivized world, perceived as given rather than produced, is then internalized by individuals and legitimated, justified, in cultural customs and laws. But the process is not seamless, uncontested, a simple straightforward appropriation by individuals of cultural norms; within this framework, subjective and objective forces interact:

> Every individual is born into an objective social structure within which he encounters the significant others who are in charge of his socialization. . . . This is not a one-sided, mechanistic process. It entails a dialectic between identification by others and self-identification, between objectively assigned and subjectively appropriated identity. (Berger and Luckmann, 1967, pp. 131–32)

Thus, human existence is dialectical; knowledge is constructed rather than given or unalterable; and language mediates rather than conveys thoughts, which originate in social life.

Viewing social constructionist pedagogy solely as a model for collaboration, as Bruffee does, prepares students to adapt to the dominant culture rather than analyze and critique it. Unless the microcosm of the classroom is understood in a larger social context that reflects the power relations between students and teachers, men and women, nonwhites and whites, poor and rich, collaborative learning serves to reproduce the status quo. Instead of rooting knowledge in a dialectic between "objectively assigned and subjectively appropriated identity," Bruffee's pedagogy appropriates knowledge (or writing) without questioning the process by which it is legitimated. It upholds Rorty's new pragmatist notion of a "conversation of mankind" that edifies, regardless of content, as opposed to the view of social critics—foundationalists, according to Rorty— who believe that the substance of what speakers say matters.

The Metaphor of Conversation

Based on Thomas Kuhn's theory of scientific discourse, Bruffee (1986) states that the social constructionist position "assumes that entities we normally call reality, knowledge, thought, facts, texts, selves, and so on are constructs generated by communities of like-minded peers" (p. 774). Along with Kuhn, Bruffee cites Geertz, Bakhtin, and Vygotsky, among others; but it is Rorty's philosophy—and his appropriation of Kuhn's terms—that most strongly informs Bruffee's definition of social constructionism. Ironically, Bruffee's assumption of a common ground with Rorty is contradicted in an interview conducted by Gary Olsen (1991) with Rorty in the *Journal of Advanced Composition*, in which the following exchange occurs.

> Olsen: Do you consider yourself a social constructionist?
> Rorty: What's a social constructionist? (p. 229)

For Bruffee, the key phrase in Rorty's revisionist discussion of Kuhn equates knowledge with "socially justified belief," that is, as Bruffee explains: knowledge is nonfoundational, thinking is internalized conversation, and "the matrix of thought is not the individual self but some community of knowledgeable peers and the vernacular knowledge of that community" (p. 777). Underlying this definition of knowledge is Rorty's metaphor of a "conversation" that rejects or justifies beliefs. The composition class, then, for Bruffee, becomes a community that determines the writer's language:

> . . . social constructionist work in composition is based on the assumption that writing is primarily a social act. A writer's language originates with the community to which he or she belongs. We use language primarily to join communities we do not yet belong to and to cement our membership in communities we already belong to. (p. 784)

Bruffee opposes this view of writing as a social act to that of writing in a social context, which he argues is based on a cognitivist, individualist rhetoric. Citing Vygotsky, he further defines the social constructionist basis of composition instruction in terms of how "writing re-externalizes the language of internalized conversation" (p. 785). This perspective, however, leaves little room for oppositional discourses or difference within communities; nor does it account for how material conditions, within and outside a discourse community, permeate the "conversation."

In *Philosophy and the Mirror of Nature*, Rorty (1979) argues that "edifying philosophy aims at continuing a conversation rather than at discovering truth" in order to "help us avoid the self-deception which comes from believing that we know ourselves by knowing a set of objective facts" (p. 373). This promotion of a self-perpetuating conversation that decries "the very notion of having a view" (p. 371) is problematic for critics like Nancy Hartsock (1987), who points out that people who have been historically marginalized as "others" cannot afford such disengagement. She writes, "The overall result is that the Others constructed by the Enlightenment are once again silenced, but this time in the name of a rejection of the methods, if not the values, of the Enlightenment" (p. 205).

Similarly, Trimbur (1989) criticizes Rorty's conversation as "the only truly free market, an ideal discursive space where exchange without domination is possible, where social differences are converted into abstract equalities at the level of speech acts" (p. 606). Collaborative learning modeled on a conversation based in "edifying philosophy," which practitioners like Harvey Weiner (1986) imagine as a continual widening of consensus from small group to full class discussions, assumes that agreement is both possible and desirable. But the increasing diversity of American society makes such agreement unlikely. Indeed, Bruffee's interest in collaborative learning stemmed from the reality of heterogeneous classrooms marked by difference rather than consensus, and as Trimbur points out, was "part of a wider response to political pressures from below to extend literacy and access to higher education to black, Hispanic, and working-class people who had formerly been excluded" (p. 605). Their participation in the "conversation of mankind," as defined by Bruffee, at best redrew the boundary lines that continued to define the social and academic margins.

A Rhetoric of Dissensus

Concerned that Bruffee's view of collaborative learning as "normal discourse" promotes "business as usual," Trimbur argues for a rhetoric of dissensus, "a critical term to describe the conflict among discourses and collective wills in the heterogeneous conversation in contemporary public life" (p. 609). Repudiating the goal of acculturation, Trimbur urges us to see collaborative learning as an oppositional discourse that not only demystifies "the authority of knowledge by revealing its social character" but actually transforms "the productive apparatus" (p. 612). What this entails for Trimbur is recasting consensus as a utopian project:

> . . . I want to displace consensus to a horizon which may never be reached. We need to see consensus, I think, not as an agreement that reconciles differences through an ideal conversation but rather as the desire of humans to live and work together with differences. . . . [S]tudents can learn to agree to disagree, not because 'everyone has their own opinion,' but because justice demands that we recognize the inexhaustibility of difference and that we organize the conditions in which we live and work accordingly. (p. 615)

Basic writing, by its very nature, reveals cultural and linguistic differences in students who have been historically excluded from higher education. Acknowledgement of this legacy of exclusion and oppression can help counteract normative assumptions about the "other" as inferior and expose the brutality of the dominant culture against so-called minorities. A rhetoric of dissensus, like Freirean liberatory pedagogy, could enable students to give voice to conflict and to resist as well as appropriate academic culture.

As Suzanne Clark and Lisa Ede (1990) argue in their article, "Collaboration, Resistance, and the Teaching of Writing":

> The devalued term in the discourse of teaching is *ignorance*. The failure to know exists in an apparent opposition to knowledge and so can be deconstructed. If education values knowledge, it also assumes, as the other part of a binary construction, that ignorance is bad. . . . Then the final step after the deconstructive reversal needs to be taken—that is, to see that the knowledge-ignorance opposition covers up the struggle of multiple differences that cannot be reduced to either alternative. (p. 282)

For Clark and Ede, "resistance to what is already known marks the starting point for collaboration" (p. 283). Insofar as they view effective collaboration as "a work in progress," they believe that "by conflating the knowledge imposed by education with the ignorance exposed in the struggle of collaboration, social-constructivist theories of knowledge have overlooked the significance of resistance" (p. 284). Collaborative learning, on the other hand, that appreciated resistance and the struggle of multiple differences, would value the knowledge basic writing students from subordinate communities bring to the classroom—knowledge mainstream America has often distorted and denied.

Bakhtinian Dialogics

Over the last decade, the rediscovery and publication of works by the Russian philosopher of language Mikhail Bakhtin have infused writing pedagogy with concepts like dialogism, heteroglossia, and multivoicedness (Bruffee, 1984; Schuster, 1985; Zebroski, 1989; Goleman, 1986; Bialostosky, 1991). Bakhtin, along with his compatriot Lev Vygotsky in psychology and members of his own intellectual circle like V.N. Volosinov,[15] developed a theory of discourse as dialogic, based partly on a literary analysis of the novel as a sociohistorical genre. According to Bakhtin, the novel emerges at a point in history of urbanization and industrialization that sparked dialogic rather than monologic forms of literature. On the level of everyday life, however, language for Bakhtin is inherently dialogical, social, and ideological, the site of struggle over multiple, competing meanings. Thus Bakhtin provides a framework for a writing pedagogy based on polyvocality and the relationship of external and internal forms of dialogue.

Bakhtin's theoretical contribution is best understood in the context of his response to the assertion by Ferdinand de Saussure, the founding father of modern linguistics, of a fundamental opposition between *langue* and *parole*, the system of language and its performance. In the development of structural linguistics and related disciplines, this insight was crucial in establishing the relational basis of all sign systems. Saussure argued that meaning derives not from the relationship of the symbol to the thing but from the arbitrary relationship between signs. Thus identity is based not on reference but symbolic difference—the central premise of semiotics, the science of signs.[16] However, in privileging the structural term over its historical, performative counterpart, Saussure omitted the human subject, the producer of language, from his theoretical model. In so doing, he focused on the signifier (the word, symbol, or other material form of the sign) rather than the signified (its content or meaning).

---

15. Some critics have claimed that Bakhtin is the author of several texts signed by V. N. Volosinov. For a discussion of the dispute over authorship, see Katerina Clark and Michael Holquist's *Mikhail Bakhtin* and *Rethinking Bakhtin: Extensions and Challenges*, edited by Gary Saul Morson and Cary Emerson.

16. See Terence Hawkes, *Structuralism and Semiotics*, for a more thorough discussion of semiotics. See also Kaja Silverman, *The Subject of Semiotics*, and Robert Hodge and Gunther Kress, *Social Semiotics*.

It is this separation of form and function, structure and history, that theorists like Bakhtin criticized, offering in place of the Saussurean oppositions a triadic theory of the sign that restores human agency to the process of signification.[17] Bakhtin proposes a sociological poetics composed of three terms: the speaker/writer, the "hero" or subject of the writing, and the listener/reader. These three elements of discourse are "coparticipants" in the text wherein their distinct voices can be discerned and analyzed. The writer then faces two ways, toward the "hero" and toward the reader. "Individual emotions," argues Volosinov (1976), "play only as *overtones* accompanying the *basic tone of social evaluation*. 'I' can realize itself verbally only on the basis of 'we'" (p. 100). It is this interanimation of voices in discourse that Bakhtin sought to understand.

For Bakhtin the process of the interanimation of social languages is multivoiced and ideologically accented. Language is driven by centripetal forces toward a centralized, unitary discourse and by centrifugal forces toward *heteroglossia*, the profusion of social languages that Bakhtin (1981) describes as follows:

> . . . at any given moment of its historical existence, language is heteroglot from top to bottom: it represents the co-existence of socio-ideological contradictions between the present and the past, between differing epochs of the past, between different socio-ideological groups in the present, between tendencies, schools, circles and so forth, all given a bodily form. These 'languages' of heteroglossia intersect each other in a variety of ways, forming new socially typifying 'languages.'" (p. 291)

Bakhtin called the interaction of these social voices *dialogism*. That this social flux is shot through with ideological content and conflict is a given for Volosinov (1986), who writes, "The domain of ideology coincides with the domain of signs. They equate with one another. Wherever a sign is present, ideology is present, too. *Everything ideological possesses semiotic value*" (p. 10).

This notion of conflict and tension is central to Bakhtin's concept of dialogism. Like Vygotsky, his definition of mind assumes an interaction between self and other. A fundamental condition of human existence for Bakhtin is "addressivity," or as it is sometimes translated, "answerability." By this he means that the very fact of human existence constitutes a response to the environment, and every response is historically, culturally, and ethically situated. As Michael Holquist (1990) explains:

---

17. See also C. S. Perice's triadic theories of communication (1958).

> If we imagine self and other in painterly terms, the former would be non-figurative and the latter extremely hard-edged. And yet I must have some way of forming myself into a subject having something like the particularity of the other. My "I" must have contours that are specific enough to provide a meaningful addressee: for if existence is shared, it will manifest itself as the condition of being addressed . . . The event of existence has the nature of dialogue in this sense; there is no word directed to no one. (p. 27)

In terms of language, then, the prototype of addressivity can be found in everyday life, an important concept for language educators. Bakhtin's interest in the novel stems from its capacity to represent diverse social languages. In "Discourse in the Novel," he explains that language "lies on the borderline between oneself and the other" (p. 293), mediating between social interaction and individual consciousness in a process of appropriation that is always ideologically accented. Thus social dialogue permeates and shapes consciousness, in everyday life as well as artistic expression, in the form of internalized dialogue that Vygotsky called "inner speech."

Bakhtin defined two types of speech that interact in the ideological process by which we become individuals: externally authoritative and internally persuasive speech. Explicitly identifying the former as the language of the father, the teacher, or other socially designated authority figures, he understood this process as a matter of "selectively assimilating the words of others." The outcome of the struggle between these categories of discourse is never certain, according to Bakhtin; their dialogic interrelationship determines the degree to which others' words become our own. Two points are important here: first, the dialogic process occurs internally and textually as well as in oral conversation or exchange; and second, the interanimation of languages results in what Bakhtin called "double-voicedness."[18] That is, as Volosinov (1986) puts it, a *"word is a two-sided act.* It is determined equally by *whose* word it is and *for whom* it is meant . . . I give myself verbal shape from another's point of view, ultimately, from the point of view of the community to which I belong" (p. 86).

Finally, Bakhtin addresses the question of how form and content are related. As I have already argued, a persistent problem in composition studies—and theory building generally—has been our failure to overcome Cartesian dualism and grasp the dialectic of binary pairs such as process/product, content/form, and individual/social. The tension between these binary opposites, Bakhtin tells us, permeates existence as a contradiction between

---

18. W. E. B. DuBois's concept of double consciousness of racial realities within the African American community is another expression of Bakhtin's term "double-voiced," in that it describes the internalization and interanimation of social voices.

individual consciousness and social structures. Volosinov argues there are two trends of thought in the philosophy of language: individual subjectivism and abstract objectivism. The one recognizes the value of inner thought but refuses to see language as social; the other sees language as a social system but denies its individuality. Volosinov's solution is dialectical: "the utterance is a social phenomenon."

Discourse Communities and the Politics of Identity

In initial formulations about discourse communities, composition scholars and literary critics imagined groups as more or less static entities that assumed homogeneity and consensus (Bruffee, 1986; Fish, 1980). Academic discourse communities were also viewed as monologic and unitary by a second phase of writing-across-the-curriculum (WAC) theorists who shifted WAC's early emphasis on "writing to learn" strategies to discursive practices across the disciplines (Russell, 1990). Often, in these theories of discourse communities, academic and nonacademic groups have appeared to function in isolation from impinging ideological and historical influences, as if the group alone determined meaning, immune to external forces and intergroup and intragroup conflict.

Fish argues, for example, that "communication occurs only *within* such a system (or context, or situation, or interpretive community) and the understanding achieved by two or more persons is specific to that system and determinate only within its confines" (p. 304). Despite the limits of this definition of discourse communities, Fish's 1980 essay "Is There a Text in This Class?" provides a cogent argument for multiple, context-bound interpretations. In response to attacks against deconstruction by neoconservative critics Meyer Abrams and E. D. Hirsch, Fish relates a story about a literature professor's initial misunderstanding of a student who asks on the first day of the semester, "Is there a text in this class?" At first the professor thinks she is asking if there is a required text. With her clarification—"I mean in this class do we believe in poems and things, or is it just us?"—he understands she is referring to literary theory and says to himself, according to Fish, "Ah, there's one of Fish's victims!" Fish then analyzes the production of meaning in the exchange, pointing out that both interpretations are constrained by the institutional context in which the question is posed, and that "[a]n infinite plurality of meanings would be a fear only if sentences existed in a state in which they were not already embedded in, and had come into view as a function of, some situation or other" (p. 307). In what has become a familiar and widely accepted position, Fish argues that meanings come already calculated, not because of norms embedded in language but because language is always perceived, from the very first, within a structure of norms. That structure, however, is not abstract and independent but social; and therefore it is not a single structure with a privileged relationship to the process of communication as it occurs in any situation but a structure that changes when one situation, with its assumed background of practices, purposes, and goals, has given way to another. (p. 318)

Thus in answer to charges of relativism and solipsism, Fish makes clear that postmodern theories such as deconstruction do not lead to an infinite regress of meanings but rather to the structural and political underpinnings of context-specific acts of communication. The problem with this perspective is that it may be misconstrued to imply that meaning is produced within monologic homogeneous groups. Such a view has led some theorists to see collaboration and peer critique, for example, as cozy classroom activities that foster a sense of community and decenter authority—which indeed they may—rather than sites of conflict and difference. As Clark and Ede (1990) suggest, such versions of discourse communities may ignore "powerful cultural, political, and ideological realities" (p. 277). In particular, they avoid the social tensions and conflicts of race, class, and gender differences that, especially in urban basic writing classes, are manifold. Similarly, Harris (1989) questions the underlying assumptions in much of the literature on academic discourse communities of their "organic unity" and shared goals.

Marilyn Cooper (1989) points out that the concept of discourse communities is not in itself liberatory, but rather may be used to serve different interests. In contrast to her "ideal type of discourse community," which "is concerned about each of its members, their goals, their needs and what they have to offer," Cooper explains:

A discourse community need not be thought of as an ongoing project, as something continually being made by its members. It can just as easily be thought of as an accomplished fact, a social structure that exists separately from the individuals who are its members. When it is thought of in this way, features such as shared values, conventions of language, and norms of behavior . . . become static standards that are used to determine who is and who is not a member of the community. Thought of in this way, a discourse community is a way of labeling individuals as insiders or outsiders, as people who either have the requisite values, knowledge, and skills to belong, or lack these necessary qualifications. (p. 204)

Cooper believes a hermeneutical—or interpretive—perspective supports a fluid, self-defining process of community formation, and that a foundational view of truth as objective, universal, and external to social interaction leads to a static, exclusionary sense of community. With this distinction, she hopes to defend students against the repressive effects of academic practices that "assume that valid evaluation must rely on standards that are prior to and external to the discourse of the class itself" (p. 219).

Cooper critiques foundationalism as "an ideology whose primary assumption is that truth is not a judgment made in an immediate social situation but is rather grounded in external standards" (p. 202). Thomas Kent's (1991) version of anti-foundationalism goes a step further in replacing the concept of discourse communities altogether with a communication model based on Donald Davidson's notion of "externalism" as "a hermeneutic act that brings us in unmediated touch with the world and with the minds of others" (p. 427). For Kent, social-constructionist descriptions of discourse communities lead to relativistic, ethnocentric thinking, and despair that we can ever know the world. He argues that externalism is the answer to the problem of "internalism," in which individual perception is mediated by a "conceptual scheme" (p. 425). To avoid replicating the mind–body duality in an insider–outsider theory of discourse, Kent urges the adoption of an externalist notion of "triangulation" between "someone who thinks, other sentient beings, and a world they know they share," a process in which "knowing our own minds means simultaneously knowing the minds of others existing within a world of objects we all agree exist" (pp. 431–32).

If Cooper, Bruffee, and Fish underestimate the hegemony of the dominant culture and its various symbol systems in their definitions of discourse communities, Kent's emphasis on externalism suggests a view of reality that virtually expunges contradictions from the world. His argument that "externalists want to drop altogether the Cartesian notion of a split between the subjective and the objective" (p. 436) is wishful thinking in that human consciousness, specifically language, is never commensurate with objects. Rather than a dialectic, Kent wants to get rid of "all the baggage" of discourse communities. As Edward Schiappa (1992) argues in response to Kent, "our [social constructionist] account of language and knowledge transcends strictly ephemeral interpersonal communication in order to note the significance of shared interpretation, habituated discourse practices, and the power of socialization" (p. 523).

Similarly, Bizzell (1990) argues that anti-foundationalists lend support to a sort of social atomism in which people merely "speak up for their own and everyone else's autonomy," and thus risk "tacitly supporting the political and cultural status quo" (p. 667). Bizzell describes the academic discourse community as "fraught with contradiction . . . polyvocal" and suggests "that this instability is a sign of its health, its ability to adapt to changing historical circumstances" (pp. 662–63). Although she repudiates E. D. Hirsch's neoconservative agenda of establishing a national standard for common knowledge, she accepts his call for a shared national discourse that would invigorate American education, politics, and intellectual debate.

Far from Kent's grudging admission that to "write at some historical moment means, in large part, that we talk much like our past and present neighbors talk" (p. 443), Bizzell argues that despite the inherent subjective dimension, "positional identity obviously entails group membership. Group interests hence shape individual choices for action" (p. 674). Bizzell borrows the term "positionality" from Linda Alcoff's discussion of feminist theory and a dialectic between individual identity and social constraints: "When the concept 'woman' is defined not by a particular set of attributes but by a particular position, the internal characteristics of the person thus identified are not denoted so much as the external context within which that person is situated" (quoted in Bizzell, p. 673). The notion of positionality has also been called "a politics of location" (Rich, 1986), "situated knowledge" (Belenky et al., 1986), and "standpoint theory" (Bauer and McKinstry, 1991).

If the academic discourse community is polyvocal, then to teach the rhetoric of dissensus, as Trimbur suggests, would permit not only a multiplicity of actual voices but a theoretical basis for analyzing their production. In addition to enabling teachers and students to recognize the complex weave of subject positions in any classroom, particularly nontraditional ones, a rhetoric of dissensus—what Gerald Graff has called "teaching the conflicts"—can elucidate the debates themselves. Just as the contemporary political scene requires us to bear in mind what Gayatri Spivak (1987) calls strategic essentialism—acknowledging the need for group identification—the writing class can enable students, especially those historically constituted as "other," including basic writers, to claim the authority of their own experience. At the same time, the writing class can promote critical investigations of the social forces—the competing claims of the communities to which we belong—that authorize or prohibit discourse and action.

Critical Pedagogy

Freire's Liberatory Pedagogy

In *Pedagogy of the Oppressed*, Paulo Freire (1988) states the fundamental premise of critical pedagogy:

> . . . while both humanization and dehumanization are real alter-
> natives, only the first is man's vocation. This vocation is con-
> stantly negated, yet it is affirmed by that very negation. It is
> thwarted by injustice, exploitation, oppression, and the violence
> of the oppressors; it is affirmed by the yearning of the oppressed
> for freedom and justice, and by their struggle to recover their lost
> humanity. (p. 28)

Freire's liberatory pedagogy is based on dialectical materialism and
rooted in his work with impoverished Brazilian laborers. Refuting a
long, still-entrenched tradition of Western dualism, this Marxist
dialectic stems from the relationship between human consciousness
and material realities. As Freire puts it, "one cannot conceive of
objectivity without subjectivity. Neither can exist without the other,
nor can they be dichotomized" (p. 35). He goes on to say, "World
and men do not exist apart from each other, they exist in constant
interaction. . . . If men produce social reality . . . , then transforming
that reality is an historical task, a task for men" (pp. 35–36). Once
such critical consciousness is experienced, as Freire argues, it can
set the stage for social change.

Compositionists have been drawn to Freirean pedagogy for two
reasons: first, the heterogeneity of college composition classes and
their gatekeeper role have sensitized teachers to issues of social
diversity and inequality; and second, theoretical insights into the
dialectic between language and culture, and reading and writing,
have encouraged a student-centered, interactive philosophy of
teaching that frequently utilizes critical pedagogy. As Freire makes
clear, critical pedagogy "must be forged *with*, not *for*, the oppressed
. . . [it] makes oppression and its causes objects of reflection by the
oppressed, and from that reflection will come their necessary
engagement in the struggle for their liberation" (p. 33).[19] This
reflection is a key aspect of education in a postmodern world
marked by fragmentation of cultural groups whose self-authorizing,
often essentializing claims may inadvertently reinforce the very
oppressive conditions they seek to overcome.

Critical pedagogy has also enabled a critique of transmission
models of education—in Freire's words, the "banking" concept.
Rather than receptacles for knowledge, students in Freirean pedagogy
are agents of learning who actively engage in "critical thinking and

---

19. According to the politics of difference, the identities of oppressed and oppressor become more complex and multiply constructed. Arguably, in American society, with the exception of the very rich, the vast majority of middle- and working-
class students experience "oppressor" and "oppressed" roles that coexist and over-
lap within themselves and between themselves and others.

the quest for mutual humanization" (p. 62). Problem-posing and dialogue are key elements of this pedagogy. Problem-posing, says Freire,

> rejects communiques and embodies communication. It epitomizes the special characteristic of consciousness: being conscious of, not only as intent on objects but as turned in upon itself in a Jasperian "split"—consciousness as consciousness of consciousness. (pp. 66–67)

Dialogue is not possible unless the contradiction between teacher and student is resolved so they become "teacher-student with students-teachers," a new term, a synthesis, that renders authority moot unless it is "*on the side of* freedom, not *against* it.*" This means "no one teaches another, nor is anyone self-taught. Men teach each other, mediated by the world, by the cognizable objects which in banking education are 'owned' by the teacher" (p. 67).

A pivotal difference between Freirean literacy education and more traditional programs is the use of "generative themes" that emerge out of everyday life and have revolutionary potential, insofar as one accepts Freire's argument that "the fundamental theme of our epoch [is] *domination*—which implies its opposite, the theme of *liberation* as the objective to be achieved" (p. 93). Michael Holzman (1988) points out that, like mainstream adult literacy programs, even revolutionary literacy campaigns have emphasized individual values and self-help. The Cuban literacy campaign, Holzman explains,

> reflected the actual mixed conditions of the country at the time, emphasizing, on the one hand, individualist values, and, on the other, the dependence of individuals on the state or the revolutionary group. (p. 181)

Breaking from this tradition in the 1960s, Freirean pedagogy not only provides a method for literacy instruction, but also "facilitates the organization of otherwise powerless groups of people by raising to consciousness their desires and needs and giving them tools for achieving some improvement in their lives" (p. 181). In contrast to mainstream literacy programs that "have the educational purpose of achieving basic literacy skills and the social purpose of emphasizing individual—rather than community—values" (p. 181), Freirean pedagogy is grounded in social values and has explicit political goals. In his study of adult literacy programs, Holzman reports "an emerging awareness that often the first priority of people in the Third World is not literacy itself, but the organization of local communities for their own betterment" (p. 187).

Ira Shor (1987), one of Freire's most visible American followers, outlines the relevance of critical pedagogy for teachers in the U.S. in a series of questions that introduce his and Freire's book-length dialogue entitled *A Pedagogy for Liberation*:

> What is liberatory learning? How do teachers transform themselves into liberatory educators? How do they begin the transformation of the students? What are the fears, risks and rewards of transformation? What is 'dialogical' teaching? How should teachers speak in liberatory classrooms? Does a liberating course have rigor, authority and structure? Are teachers and students equal in a liberatory program? How does liberatory education relate to political transformation in the larger society? . . . What do we mean by 'empowerment'? Can we apply a pedagogy from the Third World to the First World? How do themes of race, sex, and class fit into the liberatory process?" (pp. 1–2)

In *Education Under Siege*, Stanley Aronowitz and Henry Giroux (1985) explore the failure of the U.S. left to address these questions. One problem, they suggest, is that the traditional Marxist critique of culture is overdetermined by theories of social reproduction that downplay "the importance of human agency and the notion of resistance" and "offer little hope for challenging and changing the repressive features of schooling" (p. 71).

Aronowitz and Giroux criticize theories of economic, cultural, and hegemonic-state reproduction, which have contributed to an understanding of structural inequalities, the relationship between power and knowledge, and the function of state intervention in producing and legitimizing capitalist society, yet failed to provide the basis for an adequate theory of resistance to the logic of domination. Attempting to forge a "language of possibility," Aronowitz and Giroux argue that "the concept of resistance must have a revealing function that contains a critique of domination and provides theoretical opportunities for self-reflection and struggle in the interest of social and self-emancipation" (p. 105). In this light, theories of agency and intentionality can restore a sense of hopefulness—a discourse of possibility—to critical pedagogy and counteract the pessimism of much radical analysis. Understanding that resistance can "both challenge and confirm capitalist hegemony," the authors state:

> What is most important is the willingness of radical educators to search for the emancipatory interests that underlie such resistance and to make them visible to students and others so that they can become the object of debate and political analysis. (p. 108)

A Bahamian Idyll

Two narratives of critical pedagogy in the classroom demonstrate its liberatory and repressive potential. In Nan Elsasser and Kyle Fiore's (1988) account of teaching a college preparatory language skills class to Bahamian women, their liberatory curriculum results in a "perfect Freirean synthesis" (p. 286). Combining Freirean pedagogy with Lev Vygotsky's theory of inner speech, Elsasser and Fiore replace a traditional skills-drills course with an "experimental approach" that investigates the movement from inner speech to written product and utilizes generative themes. The women choose the theme of marriage, which they subdivide into housework, divorce, sexuality, and domestic violence, spending a week reading related articles and writing on each subtopic. Elsasser describes three phases in the students' development: more skillful elaboration of their experience linked to a wider social context; pursuit of knowledge outside their experience; and increased critical consciousness that enables them to use writing as a means of social intervention (p. 291).

The semester concludes with the publication in local newspapers of a collective "Letter to Bahamian Men" about which the women "argue over punctuation, style, and semantics. They debate whether to separate the list of men's inconsiderate actions with colons, semicolons, or full stops . . ." (p. 297). All the women pass the college entrance writing exam, and continue "to read about women in other countries, broaden their understandings, and write a resource book for Bahamian women" (p. 299).

Ellsworth's "Pedagogy of the Unknowable"

Elsasser and Fiore's island idyll sharply contrasts with Elizabeth Ellsworth's (1989) story of a special topics course, "Media and Anti-Racist Pedagogies," which she taught at the University of Wisconsin at Madison in 1988. Using the language of critical pedagogy, Ellsworth designed the course to investigate and intervene against recent incidents of campus racism. Her experience, however, revealed contradictions that lead her to argue

> that key assumptions, goals, and pedagogical practices fundamental to the literature on critical pedagogy—namely, "empowerment," "student voice," "dialogue," and even the term "critical"—are repressive myths that perpetuate relations of domination. (p. 298)

The key question she raises is: "What diversity do we silence in the name of 'liberatory' pedagogy?" (p. 299) More problematic than the abstract, decontextualized language that permeates critical pedagogy, according to Ellsworth, are the "rational assumptions" underlying its educational goals, which she says Aronowitz and Giroux see as "the teaching of analytic and critical skills for judging the truth and merit of propositions, and the interrogation and selective appropriation of potentially transformative moments in the dominant culture" (pp. 303–4). This appeal to reason is untenable, according to Ellsworth, in light of the "extent to which the myths of the ideal rational person and the 'universality' of propositions have been oppressive to those who are not European, White, male, middle class; Christian, able-bodied, thin, and heterosexual" (p. 304). Of particular interest here are Ellsworth's comments on student voice, specifically in educational settings in which students are from socially oppressed groups. In contrast to the glowing description of Elsasser's involvement with Bahamian women, Ellsworth questions the unequal relations between teachers and students who have been silenced:

> As an Anglo, middle-class professor . . . I could not unproblematically "help" a student of color to find her/his authentic voice as a student of color. I could not unproblematically "affiliate" with the social groups my students represent and interpret their experience to them. (p. 309)

Rather than a safe space, Ellsworth's classroom was fraught with tensions and conflicts that eventually led students to form unofficial affinity groups that gave them support and prepared them to participate in class discussions. Ultimately, class members and Ellsworth saw their task "not as one of building democratic dialogue between free and equal individuals, but of building a coalition among the multiple, shifting, intersecting, and sometimes contradictory groups carrying unequal weights of legitimacy within the culture and the classroom" (p. 317). Thus Ellsworth rejects the rationalism of critical pedagogy, affirming instead a "pedagogy of the unknowable" that assumes all narratives are partial, beyond knowing—to some degree, even to oneself—and potentially oppressive.

A Language of Critique and Possibility

Acknowledging the influence of postmodernist and feminist theory, Henry Giroux and Peter McLaren (1991) echo Ellsworth's concerns—though perhaps not to the extent she would wish—asserting that "[c]ritical pedagogy commits itself to *forms of learning and action that are undertaken in solidarity with subordinated and marginalized groups*" (p. 155). They seem to agree with her critique of critical pedagogy when they declare that "critical pedagogy can be accused of purveying either a mechanical and deterministic view of the social order or a liberal, humanist, and Cartesian view of human agency" (p. 157). They also admit that critical pedagogy has emphasized individual subjectivity rather than collective struggle, and accept the need to challenge claims of unitary and universal experiences based on race, class, and/or gender. However, in delineating a cultural politics, a language of critique and possibility, and a pedagogy rooted in student experience, Giroux and McLaren build an argument for educational reform in which the affirmation of students' voices is accompanied by criticism of expressions of racist, sexist, and other oppressive ideologies.

It is important to recall Ellsworth's concern that critical educators fail to address the complexity of actual classroom discourse in which oppression is often multilayered and ambiguously framed; however, it seems equally important to heed Giroux and McLaren's warning that "Without a shared vision of democratic community we risk endorsing struggles in which the politics of difference collapses into new forms of separatism" (p. 182). Finally, they seem to be answering Ellsworth's critique directly when they conclude:

> To reject the language of possibility as idealistic abstractions or impractical utopian longings is to fail to comprehend it as expressing those elements of a critical praxis that have not yet been realized and that must be dialectically appropriated and grounded in a critical theory of culture and politics of representation. (p. 182)

In their argument against anti-utopianism, Giroux and McLaren conclude with a set of terms that acknowledges the provisionality, partialness, and incompleteness of a pedagogy that for Ellsworth, as we have seen, is unknowable. Although they articulate different positions on critical pedagogy, both Ellsworth and Giroux and McLaren show how postmodern and feminist discourses, to which I turn in the next chapter, have sensitized us to universal claims and given us theoretical perspectives that intersect with and deepen an understanding of the construction of social reality.

Chapter Seven

A Multiplicity of Voices
Postmodern and Feminist Pedagogies

What is emerging in feminist writings is, instead, the concept of a multiple, shifting, and often self-contradictory identity, a subject that is not divided in, but rather at odds with, language; an identity made up of heterogeneous and heteronomous representations of gender, race, and class, and often indeed across languages and cultures; an identity that one decides to reclaim from a history of multiple assimilations, and that one insists on as a strategy. (1986, p. 9)

Teresa de Lauretis

Postmodern Pedagogy

The influence of postmodern theory on writing instruction, already evident in the discussion of social constructionism and critical pedagogy in the previous chapter, is at once extensive and hard to pin down. In addition to the penetration of postmodern language into cultural spheres like education, where it spreads as if by osmosis, the welter of theories called postmodern complicates an analysis of their impact. As Teresa Ebert (1991) points out, a distinction can be made between *resistant* postmodernism and *ludic* postmodernism: the first, an overtly political stance that uses postmodern theories of discourse, knowledge and power, and subject positions strategically to challenge existing social structures; the second, a playful, anarchistic stance that eschews any system in favor of an endless deconstructive impulse. For Linda Hutcheon (1989), the two contradictory terms of postmodernism are the inner-directed world of art (parody) and the outer-directed realm of "real life" (worldliness). Arguing "these two qualities co-exist in an uneasy and problematizing tension that provokes an investigation of how we make meaning in culture" (p. 18), she defines postmodernism as follows:

> . . . the postmodern's initial concern is to de-naturalize some of the dominant features of our way of life; to point out that those entities that we unthinkingly experience as 'natural' (they might even include capitalism, patriarchy, liberal humanism) are in fact 'cultural'; made by, not given to us. Even nature, postmodernism might point out, doesn't grow on trees. (p. 2)

At a 1990 conference on cultural studies, Cornel West (1992) hailed the importance of postmodernism along distinctly political lines, attributing despair in American society to "the collapsing of structures of meaning, and the collapsing of structures of feeling such that hopelessness becomes the conclusion and walking nihilism becomes the enactment of it" (p. 691). Given its interrogative capacity, postmodernism creates a lens through which to see history unfold. As West puts it, "The term postmodern becomes useful . . . precisely because it helps us situate a new kind of culture being created in the midst of the restructuring of the capitalist international order" (p. 690). Thus, we can understand

> postmodernism not just as a set of styles and forms but as a cultural dominant of a restructured international capitalist order with its automation, robotization, computerization, its de-skilling of the working class, its re-skilling of the working class, and creating space for people like us: an expanding professional managerial strata. We must situate the academy within the context of the postmodern crisis, given this restructuring of capitalism as we understand it. (p. 690)

Both ludic and resistant, parodic and worldly strands of postmodernism can be seen in composition studies, producing a new a set of questions about the writing class that focus on difference, power, knowledge, resistance, and play. To understand how postmodern thought has influenced composition, it will be useful to review composition scholars' expositions of key theorists: Derrida, Foucault, Lacan, and Lyotard.[20]

Derrida and Deconstructive Pedagogy

Sharon Crowley (1989) suggests that the implications of deconstruction for writing pedagogy both undermine conventional wisdom and affirm some recent teaching practices, in particular, the widespread adoption of a process-writing approach. The assumptions that deconstruction calls into question include the notion of a unitary, originating author and the belief "that language is a transparent representation of the world and/or of the minds which populate it" (p. 31). According to a deconstructive analysis, Western metaphysics has privileged the first term and devalued the second term of binary opposites like mind–body, presence–absence, inside–outside, and thought–language. Knowledge is thus predicated on "self-identity, presence, sameness" rather than on difference and absence. Structural linguistics establishes the relational basis of language in that meanings emerge not as essential or given, but as relative to—different from—other meanings. Identity is established not in relation to itself but to that which it is not; the process of semiosis thus yields multiple interpretations from inherently unstable texts and contexts in which the relational basis of meaning is constantly in flux.

The illusion of authorial sovereignty is maintained, Crowley suggests, by the power it authorizes in spite of the prior and multiple "voices" that pervade writing. Even process writing pedagogy, which challenges a linear model of composing, reasserts the notion that thought precedes writing in its "prewriting" stage. Such techniques, Crowley explains, "no matter how intricate, nevertheless presume that writers first engage in some activity that is not necessarily linguistic before they begin to write" (p. 40). Finally, Crowley outlines a deconstructive writing pedagogy that would: "reject the traditional model of authority" of the teacher's knowledge and the writer's sovereignty; reinforce the idea that writing is a process, but one of "differentiation and not repetition of the same"; necessitate that a syllabus for a writing course always be in revision; and demonstrate the need for continued interrogation of writing pedagogy itself.

---

20. Postmodern feminist theory is treated in both this section and the following section on feminist pedagogy. Rather than attempt a comprehensive review of postmodern literature, my aim in this chapter is to suggest its major points of connection to composition theory. Additionally, although Bakhtin is discussed in the section on social constructionism, he has been viewed as an early postmodernist by some critics (e.g., Clark and Holquist, Morson and Emerson).

Setting out to liberate composition studies from the tradition of Western philosophy, Jasper Neel (1988) advocates what he calls "strong discourse"—sophistic rhetoric—-in defiance of both Plato and Derrida. Neel writes:

> Plato lays a curse on rhetoric and writing by requiring the rhetor to know the truth before attempting persuasion and by claiming that truth, by definition, cannot occur in writing. Derrida lays a curse on the entire tradition of Western metaphysics since Plato by showing that philosophy never for one minute escapes writing or rhetoric. (pp. 202–3)

These philosophical positions, according to Neel, are "two moments of the same maneuver" in that one seeks the truth the other deconstructs. Rhetoricians juggle both balls in the air, distinguishing between persuasion and deceit, making public, ethical choices, compensating for the "unknowability of truth," and generating beliefs that are never impermeable to analysis. Like Crowley, Neel celebrates the turn in contemporary composition pedagogy toward contextualized writing; only Neel defines this rhetoric as sophistic rather than Derridean or deconstructive.

If strong discourse permits debate and tolerates uncertainty, then weak discourse depends on tyranny and rigid controls as exhibited by what Neel calls "antiwriting." As the negation of Platonic writing, antiwriting might assume the shape of the five-paragraph essay, the student's confession, which Neel translates as: "I am not writing. I hold no position. I have nothing at all to do with discovery, communication, or persuasion. I care nothing about the truth. What I *am* is an essay" (p. 85). Describing the "pre-Platonic internal certainty" students experience prior to writing, Neel explains that once students begin to write, they confront their own insufficiency, the "cure" for their "'disease' of internal certainty" (p. 83), a dialectic that approaches but never attains the truth. Interestingly, this deferral of the truth resembles John Trimbur's rhetoric of dissensus as the deferral of consensus, which might then be redefined "as a utopian project, a dream of difference without domination" (p. 615), as well as the "language of possibility" imagined by critical educators.

Foucault: Discourse, Knowledge, and Power in the Composition Class

The production of power and the propagation of knowledge through discourse are Foucault's themes in his histories of knowledge, madness, sexuality, and the penal system. In *The History of Sexuality*

(1990), he asks: "Why has sexuality been so widely discussed, and what has been said about it? What were the effects of power generated by what was said? . . . What knowledge . . . was formed as a result of this linkage?" (p. 11) As Foucault explains in terms of sexuality, "we are dealing less with *a* discourse on sex than with a multiplicity of discourses produced by a whole series of mechanisms operating in different institutions" (p. 33). In composition theory, Foucault's investigation of systems of knowledge and social organization in relation to discursive practices has provided a means of analyzing the relationship between the "I" who writes and the institutional contexts that permit or prohibit such writing. Summing up Foucault's argument in conjunction with writing pedagogy, Linda Brodkey (1992) states:

> we are at once constituted and unified as subjects in language and discourse. The discursive subject is of particular interest to those of us who teach writing because language and discourse are understood to be complicit in the representation of self and others, rather than the neutral or arbitrary tools of thought and expression that they are in other modern theories . . . (p. 97)

Brodkey's Foucauldian analysis of letters exchanged between middle-class teachers and working-class adult basic education students demonstrates how such discursive acts always bear a social and political dimension, bound up with the production of knowledge and power. Echoing Neel's treatment of Plato and Derrida, Bruce Herzberg (1991) relies on Foucault in arguing for the restoration of sophistic rhetoric to examine the sociohistorical production of truth, "treating discourse as a practice, a form of action, and not a reflection of the world" (p. 73). Kurt Spellmeyer (1989), meanwhile, examines the tendency among compositionists to bifurcate the individual and social, the subjective and objective forces Foucault places in constant tension with one another.

All three composition theorists refer to Foucault's lecture-essay, "The Discourse on Language" (1972), in which he describes the anxiety of beginning to speak, entering a preexisting discourse, and navigating its perils. Not surprisingly, a key passage for writing teachers is the internal dialogue that Foucault enacts between "Inclination" and "Institutions":

> Inclination speaks out: 'I don't want to have to enter this risky world of discourse; I want nothing to do with it insofar as it is decisive and final; I would like to feel it all around me, calm and transparent, profound, infinitely open, with others responding to my expectations, and truth emerging, one by one. All I want is to allow myself to be borne along, within it, and by it, a happy wreck'. Institutions reply: 'But you have nothing to fear from launching

out; we're here to show you discourse is within the established order of things, that we've waited a long time for its arrival, that a place has been set aside for it—a place which both honours and disarms it; and if it should happen to have a certain power, then it is we, and we alone, who give it that power'. (pp. 215–16)

In Brodkey's research on the correspondence between teachers enrolled in her course on basic writing instruction and students in an adult basic education course, she examines the institutional forces—in this case, class and gender—that appear unexpectedly in what she describes as the teachers' "occasional moments of linguistic as well as discursive awkwardness . . . intermittent improprieties . . . [and] unexpected errors." The teachers' responses lead her to conclude that only "the power of a discourse over even its fluent writers . . . could begin to explain the errors of these otherwise literate individuals" (p. 101)—errors that ranged from spelling mistakes such as "thier" to a "refusal to acknowledge the content of their correspondents' narratives" (p. 102). The teachers' indifference to the working-class issues raised by the basic education students, such as neighborhood violence, created a disjuncture in their correspondence that alienated the students and reproduced existing social inequalities, or as Foucault puts it, "the established order of things."

Both Herzberg and Spellmeyer enlist Foucauldian theory to support the tendency within composition toward an open-ended, critical rhetoric, the impetus for which Spellmeyer calls "eventful inquiry" (p. 727), and Herzberg describes as "a desire to oppose negative and oppressive power, a desire to mend the world" (p. 80). Rather than closure, resolution, the goal of teaching writing would be, as Spellmeyer comments in his account of a student's paper, "to prolong discursive tension still further and to encourage critical reflection on the knowledge she has produced" (p. 727). The tension between "inclination" and "institution" is inescapable, even for so masterful a rhetorician as Foucault, who invokes his teacher's name, Jean Hyppolite, at the end of "The Discourse on Language." Foucault admits he "borrowed both the meaning and the possibility" of his own work from Hyppolite, concluding, "I now know which voice it was I would have wished for, preceding me, supporting me, inviting me to speak and lodging within my own speech . . ." (p. 237). For less experienced writers, like the students in Brodkey's study, the tension may be so overwhelming that silence is the only response. What Foucault insists on asking is *who is authorized to speak*, recognizing that

[e]ducation may well be, as of right, the instrument whereby every individual, in a society like our own, can gain access to any kind

of discourse. But we well know that in its distribution, in what it permits and in what it prevents, it follows the well-trodden battle lines of social conflict. Every educational system is a political means of maintaining or modifying the appropriation of discourse with the knowledge and the powers it carries with it. (p. 227)

"Just Drift": Lyotard's Counterpedagogy

True to the anti-totalizing spirit of ludic postmodernism, Victor Vitanza (1991) declares that "the subject of this paper (de)centers on three countertheses that will be stated, elaborated, and celebrated as perverse comedy" (p. 140). Vitanza wonders why compositionists have not embraced this "French Freudian-Lacanian psychoanalysis-cum-Deleuzian-Guattarian postpsychoanalysis" (p. 141). The central theorist on whom Vitanza builds his "perverse comedy" (he dedicates his paper to Lenny Bruce, "the most perverse of all comics" (p. 139)) is Jean-Francois Lyotard. It is Lyotard's deep suspicion of all hegemonic discourses or metanarratives, Marxist as well as capitalist, that Vitanza uses to launch his "countertheses" or "counterresponses" to composition's

> will *to control* (this) language (specifically, its modes of representation) for the general ends of both traditional and modern rhetoric(s) and, hence, for a (homogeneous) community. These ends, as commonly accepted, are noble. And yet, I irrepressibly ask, are they? I would think other(wise): These rhetorics—their modes of representation—are insidious and invidious. While they appear to be informed by a set of assumptions that (democratically-capitalistically) value heterogeneity (in the name of the "individual"), they are, instead, only a reactionary devaluing of heterogeneity through the homogenization of heterogeneity (as mass society). While they allow, they simultaneously disallow and disenable. (p. 141)

Thus the problem with composition pedagogy, including progressive versions of it, lies in its rationalist presuppositions. Critical educators like Aronowitz and Giroux fail to go far enough in their critiques of American schooling; indeed, Vitanza points to "social epistemic" composition theorists (Berlin, Trimbur) as the "wave of the nineties" that "must be resisted strongly and, if necessary, comedically-perversely" (p. 143).

According to Vitanza, rationalist, universalizing theories can best be resisted paralogically—by invoking "that which does not logically follow" (p. 164)—a means of disrupting the naturalized flow of discourse through a kind of "gaming, moving from one language game to the next, or drifting or just linking . . ." (p. 147). Indeed, at one point in his paper, Vitanza exclaims, "Just drift! Just be pagan!" (p. 151). What Vitanza means by this is evident, more or less, in his discussion of David Bartholomae's article on basic writers, "Inventing the University." Vitanza refers to the often quoted passage in which Bartholomae says "that all writers, in order to write, must imagine themselves the privilege of being 'insiders' . . ." (p. 143). In reply, Vitanza points out that "Lyotard is against privilege and all that it entails; he is diametrically opposed to writing from such a position, within academic discourse, because it does, indeed, finally exclude others (that is, both people and ideas) from being 'expressed within that discourse'" (p. 159). He goes on to explain that Lyotard—and presumably, Vitanza as well—"tries to write from inside but as an outsider" in order to introduce ideas into a given discourse even if the textual difficulty means excluding some readers from his audience. On the one hand, he argues that "ideas make the audience"; on the other hand, "[a]kademia and (the exchange of) its discourse, its symbolic kapital, no doubt, foster a private club" (159).

Although Vitanza's ultraleft, anti-state politics lead him to criticize composition pedagogy's universalizing, totalizing tendencies, his "plague on both your houses" political position is ahistorical. The left, though deeply imperfect, has worked for peace and socioeconomic justice, seeking with admittedly mixed results to liberate human potential and redistribute material resources, knowledge, and power more equitably, while the right has sought to preserve systemically unfair, unequal conditions that serve the interests of an elite class. However, insofar as Vitanza invites us to question our own metanarratives, his "perverse comedy" is a worthwhile endeavor.

Lacan: The Pedagogical Unconscious

Robert Con Davis's 1987 double issue of *College English* outlines the relevance of psychoanalytic theory to composition instruction. Although Freud understood the close connection between language and consciousness, it was Lacan, in the postmodern era, who grounded psychoanalysis in speech and language. Influenced by semiotics, Lacan rereads Freud to state "the unconscious is structured like a language." Linking psychoanalysis to pedagogy, Gregory Jay argues that "the systematic bringing to discourse of unconscious thoughts (or resistances to thought) is the teacher's primary task" (p. 789). A key term here is *resistance*. As Patrick McGee explains, Freud "discovered the real object of analysis in the speech of his patients and in their resistance to speech—a resistance that, from the Lacanian viewpoint, could be read as a resistance to language as a system and to everything that is structured like a language" (p. 668).

The "pedagogical unconscious," says Jay, is just such "a structure of investments—an ideological discourse . . . which both enables and restricts verbal or written expression" (p. 790). He makes the cogent point that within the field of education there has historically been resistance to the effects of race, class, and gender on who and what gets taught. This resistance to knowledge is exactly what prevents learning from taking place; instead, it establishes the teacher as the "subject who is supposed to know" and reinforces traditional social relations and practices. Since one point of view supplants another, Jay persuasively argues, the goal of pedagogy should be to disclose the range of critical stances, or perspectives, available to us. Rather than teach literature per se, which is impossible because reading is experiential, we should be teaching literary criticism as a means of eliciting a range of possible responses to literature.

A second key term in psychoanalytic theory is *transference*, "a dynamic structure located partly within a person and partly between people" that takes place, according to Lacan, "as soon as there is the Subject Supposed to Know" (Brooke, p. 681). The Subject Supposed to Know, in Lacanian psychoanalysis, is the analyst—or any other authority figure, particularly, in this case, the teacher—who serves as a kind of screen for the analysand or student. The patient, striving to understand some aspect of baffling behavior, turns to the analyst, the Subject Supposed to Know, and interprets herself on the basis of knowledge projected onto the analyst. Robert Brooke states that the key relationship

> is largely *within* the divided person, since it involves a relationship between her conscious self and her projection or current understanding of the knowledge and purpose of the knowing authority. The real dialogue between people is less important for psychic growth than the internal dialogue with the person who supposedly knows. (p. 681)

In "Lacan, Transference, and Writing Instruction," Brooke focuses on the similarity between Lacanian psychoanalysis and what he calls "response teaching" practiced by writing teachers like Donald Murray and Peter Elbow.

Based on Murray's accounts of his success with conferencing, Brooke imagines a five-minute conference between Murray and a student in which Murray nods sagaciously, asks open-ended questions, and nods again as the student exits "refreshed and eager to write" (p. 679). Brooke asks why this method, or those popularized by Peter Elbow like freewriting, should help students become better writers? According to the theory of transference, just as the analysand learns to tolerate incoherence, incompleteness, a self that is divided, plural, and in flux, the student writer learns to accept the messiness and instability of the writing process and products. As Brooke puts it, "The process is messy and the product is endlessly postponed" (p. 690). While this notion of teaching is appealing, especially its implicit redistribution of classroom authority, it reproduces the same individualist, expressionistic ethos that James Berlin has criticized in Elbow's work. In arguing that "internal dialogue" is more important for psychic growth than "real dialogue," Brooke assumes a subjectivist stance that fails to explain the dialectic between the two forms of speech.

In a more recent article, Laurie Finke (1993) makes explicit the connections between psychoanalytic theory, critical pedagogy, and feminist pedagogy. Claiming that each of these discourses is potentially transforming, Finke links the idea of the pedagogical unconscious to feminist and critical pedagogies which, in explaining oppression in sociopolitical terms, have often overlooked the effects of unconscious forces on human behavior. She gives an example of a classroom scene in Shakespeare's *Henry V*, in which the French princess Katherine has a language lesson with her lady-in-waiting prior to her marriage to Henry and the "dynastic merger" between the French and the English. The English lesson, Finke points out, focuses exclusively on parts of the body. Although elements of resistance to English hegemony can be seen in puns—for example, "the English 'elbow' for the French 'bilbow,' or sword" (p. 11)— Katherine submits to social pressures and remains in a position marked by gender and national interests.

Finke uses this scene to render problematic the notion of "voice" that has been central to both feminist and process-writing pedagogy. Beyond the physical, embodied voice, she argues that "all of these terms—self, voice, experience—have been placed under erasure by poststructuralist semiotics and Lacanian psychoanalysis, which define these concepts in terms of their radical discursivity" (p. 13). The self is not given, it is made *through* language; feminist pedagogy seeks to describe "not the student's *discovering* a voice that is already there, but her *fashioning* one from the discursive environment through and in which the feminist subject emerges" (p. 14). Accordingly, not only students but teachers, too, are "constituted by the dominant discourse and practices they oppose and seek to demystify" (p. 9). In her attempt to integrate critical, feminist, and psychoanalytic thought, she questions the impulse to locate oppression either in individual consciousness or in social and historical forces. The former approach "calls for a psychoanalytic pedagogy; the latter, a political one. The task of a feminist pedagogy seems to demand some integration of both approaches" (p. 9).

Feminist Writing Pedagogy[21]

In her essay, "Me and My Shadow," Jane Tompkins (1988) states that she now "tend[s] to think that theory itself, at least as it is usually practiced, may be one of the patriarchal gestures women *and* men ought to avoid" (p. 122). Responding to an article by Ellen Messer-Davidow, entitled "The Philosophical Bases of Feminist Literary Criticisms," Tompkins describes an internal split between the *critic*, who disagrees on epistemological grounds with Messer-Davidow, and the *person* "who wants to write about her feelings" (p. 122). This private-public dichotomy, "which is to say, the public-private *hierarchy*, is a founding condition of female oppression" (p. 123). The assumption in academic discourse that "emotion should be excluded from the process of attaining knowledge" upholds a paradigmatically "male" discourse of reason and forbids a "female" discourse of personal experience. Thus Tompkins argues that "an epistemology which excludes emotions from the process of attaining knowledge radically undercuts women's epistemic authority" (p. 124). Consequently, women hide the unsanctioned, private, emotional part of themselves in public discourse. Tompkins goes on to quote Ursula Le Guin's commencement address at Bryn Mawr College, in which Le Guin distinguishes between the "father tongue" and the "mother tongue," the voice of reason and objectivity achieved through acts of distancing, and the voice of conversation and connectedness whose power is "not in dividing but in binding" (p. 127).

Tompkins concedes that ultimately what counts as "personal" depends on the person; for example, Felix Guattari would be excited by "an article whose first sentence has the words 'machine', 'structure', and 'determination'" . . . (p. 134). She theorizes (and I would call this theorizing, despite her polemic against theory):

> What is personal is completely a function of what is perceived as personal. What is perceived as personal by men, or rather, what is

21. There is now an emerging area of composition studies influenced by gay and lesbian studies that should be included in any future reviews of literature of this sort, but that I omit here, in part because it is so new and in part because the ground I have staked out is already vast (e.g., see Harriet Malinowitz, 1995).

gripping, significant, 'juicy', is different from what is felt to be that way by women. For what we are really talking about is not the personal as such, what we are talking about is what is important, answers one's needs, strikes one as immediately *interesting*. For women, the personal is such a category. (p. 134)

Tompkins' essay raises many of the key issues feminist compositionists have grappled with, not the least of which is the relationship between personal and public discourse in writing instruction. Another issue that Tompkins frames is the debate between essentialist and social constructionist perspectives, articulated here as a challenge to prevailing academic mores made by injecting the personal (the situated "voice," the view from her window, the sunny North Carolina day after the grueling summer, the suicide of her friend, her father's illness) into the scholarly critique of Messer-Davidow's definition of epistemology.

When Tompkins suggests a difference between what women and men find "gripping, significant, 'juicy,'" and that "the personal is such a category" for women, she essentializes gender in ways that reduce identity to a single dimension. However, her anger at "the way women are used as extensions of men, mirrors of men, devices for showing men off—"so much so that she finally exclaims, "Sometimes I think *the world* contains no women" (p. 137)—underscores painful historical and emotional realities that have excluded women from public discourse and relegated them to private, domestic spaces on the margins of society. As Teresa de Lauretis (1986) puts it, "The relation of experience to discourse, finally, is what is at issue in the definition of feminism" (p. 5). For de Lauretis,

> feminism defines itself as a political instance, not merely a sexual politics but a politics of experience, of everyday life, which later then in turn enters the public sphere of expression and creative practice, displacing aesthetic hierarchies and generic categories, and which thus establishes the semiotic ground for a different production of reference and meaning. (p. 10)

In this light, Tompkins' exploration of "subjective" discourse as an alternative to the "objective" discourse of the academy can be seen as indicative of the politics of experience, rather than as an essentializing gesture signifying women's greater appreciation of the personal. That gender difference is historically contingent upon women's and men's social experience is precisely the point: rather than any intrinsic female predisposition for the personal, it is Tompkin's anger at having been silenced as a woman, and the *particular* experience of the "personal" that such conditions produce, that compel her to disrupt—or try to disrupt—the normal flow of academic discourse.

Berenice Fisher (1987) provides another view of the personal—what she calls the "emotional"—in an article entitled, "The Heart Has Its Reasons: Feeling, Thinking, and Community-Building in Feminist Education." Relating the emphasis on the emotions in feminist pedagogy to its roots in consciousness-raising (CR) groups, Fisher delineates three assumptions upon which CR groups rested: emotions are socially conditioned; they form an *active* rather than a passive dimension of experience; and they "have a decidedly rational content" (p. 48). Thus, Fisher maintains that

> [N]ot just our experience of oppression but the particular feelings that emerge as we deal with that oppression become the object of collective inquiry. This is easier said than done, of course, but I see it as the core of feminist pedagogy. (p. 49)

Women's Ways of Writing

Not ten years ago, Elizabeth Flynn (1988) argued that "the fields of feminist studies and composition studies have not engaged each other in a serious or systematic way" (p. 425). Since then, national conferences and journals of composition reflect the growth in feminist scholarship and debate in composition and rhetoric. Three views have predominated in these discussions, one based on gender identity that assumes "women's ways of knowing" are different from men's; another based on postmodernist theory that seeks to invent a "new language" with "truly radical potential" (Worsham, 1991, 84–85); and a third based on a social theory perspective that sees female consciousness in a dialectical relationship to social structures (Weedon, 1991; Weiler, 1991). What unites all three feminist explorations of composition is the political objective of challenging patriarchal structures that have silenced and oppressed women.

Flynn bases her analysis of student writing on the theoretical groundwork laid by Nancy Chodorow's (1978) *The Reproduction of Mothering*, Carol Gilligan's (1982) *In a Different Voice*, and Mary Belenky, Blythe Clinchy, Nancy Goldberger, and Jill Tarule's (1986) *Women's Ways of Knowing*. Each of these works has been influential in feminist studies, providing a lens through which to examine women's experience. According to Chorodow, women's primary parenting role produces a fundamental difference between female and male children. Challenging the Freudian account of women's development in relation to the Oedipal complex, Chodorow theorizes that girls remain connected to the mother, the primary love object, and that boys separate from the mother in order to identify with the father. This early process of gender identification results in deeply ingrained cultural and psychological patterns of male and female behavior.

Retheorizing early formulations of the primacy of autonomy in the child's development, Chodorow (1989) explains that "[D]iffer-entiation is not distinctness and separateness, but a particular way of being connected to others. This connection to others, based on early incorporations, in turn enables us to feel that empathy and confidence that are basic to the recognition of the other as a self" (p. 107). But at the same time, Chodorow is eager in her later work to distance herself from essentialist thinking. She writes:

> To speak of difference as a final, irreducible concept and to focus on gender differences as central is to reify them and to deny the reality of those processes which create the meaning and significance of gender. To see men and women as qualitatively dif-ferent kinds of people, rather than seeing gender as processual, reflexive, and constructed, is to reify and deny relations of gender, to see gender differences as permanent rather than as created and situated. (1989, p. 113)

Like Chodorow, Gilligan and Belenky et al. have struggled to define new territory in developmental studies that previously had depended on data collected by and from male participants. Gilligan focuses on gender differences in moral development; Belenky et al. are concerned with gender differences in intellectual development. Both studies were inspired by prior research conducted, respec-tively, by Lawrence Kohlberg and William Perry, who covered the same psychological terrain but excluded female subjects from their analyses. Gilligan found that women responded to moral problems in terms of responsibility and caring, while men responded accord-ing to notions of abstract justice, a response that Kohlberg universal-ized as superior in his spectrum of stages of moral development. In *Women's Ways of Knowing*, Belenky et al. delineate five stages of women's intellectual development: silence, received knowledge, subjective knowledge, procedural knowledge, and constructed knowledge. According to this schema, as women move through these different stages, they are confronted with male models of learning that emphasize autonomy, independence, and abstract critical thought. In contrast, Belenky et al. propose an educational system that emphasizes "connection over separation, understanding and acceptance over assessment, and collaboration over debate" (p. 229).

In "Composing as a Woman," Flynn describes recent develop-ments in composition pedagogy as "a feminization of our previous conceptions of how writers write and how writing should be taught," a framework in which the composition specialist might be seen as a "nurturing mother" rather than an "authoritative father" (p. 423). She points to female role models in composition, a turn to the private sphere represented in the work of many male theorists, and the marginality shared by both composition studies and feminist studies; despite these parallels, she argues, there remains a need to link the two fields. As a step in theorizing a feminist writing pedagogy, Flynn analyzes several student papers using Chodorow, Gilligan, and Belenky et al. as her interpretive lens.

In each of four student papers, she discerns a gender bias: the men write stories about autonomy and achievement or frustrated achievement; the women write narratives that turn on communication and connection or frustrated connection. Flynn acknowledges that the student narratives are "as often characterized by inconsistency and contradiction as by a univocality of theme and tone" (p. 431), and that rather than validate feminist scholarship, her review of the student writing underscores the relevance of feminist theory and research to composition studies. However, the underlying assumptions of "composing as a woman" rest on a binary opposition that postmodern feminist pedagogy has called into question.

Perspectives of Postmodern Feminists

In "The 'Difference' of Postmodern Feminism," Teresa L. Ebert (1991) argues for resistant postmodernism that "views the relation between the word and world, language and social reality or, in short 'difference,' not as the result of textuality but as the effect of social struggles" (p. 887). She explains that *differance*, as Derrida employs the term, means "*a difference within* a difference itself" (p. 893). This notion of difference undoes the classic binary oppositions that riddle Western thought—male/female, mind/body, public/private, etc.—by illuminating the divisions within identity.

> Male is thus not a clearly bounded identity *different from* female but is instead self-divided and traversed by its other, that is, by the female, which is its supplement, the difference on which it depends for its coherent meaning and full existence. Deconstruction is thus a critical operation that demonstrates how the binary other is always the suppressed supplement. (p. 894)[22]

---

22. The notion of supplementarity has informed an analysis of the construction of heterosexuality in queer theory and that of the construction of race in works like Toni Morrison's *Playing in the Dark: Whiteness and the Literary Imagination*. In both cases, Ebert's explanation of Derrida's concept of the supplement shows how the "difference of the primary term [in any binary opposition] is not outside but 'within' the term itself; any identity is always *divided within* by its other, which is not opposed to it but rather 'supplementary'" (p. 893).

Thus the internal difference is projected as an external dichotomy and the privileged term is maintained by devaluing the other (female) term. By comparing resistant postmodernism to ludic postmodernism, Ebert hopes to convince us that 1) postmodernism itself is not monolithic; and 2) that while ludic postmodernism, including *l'ecriture feminine*, can provide effective strategies for unraveling binary oppositions, they are not emancipatory projects but rather "formalist moves based on a textual notion of meaning and a panhistorical, transocial, purely formal notion of language and discourse" (p. 896). Instead, she proposes a "postmodern materialist feminism" that accepts the poststructuralist argument that language mediates reality but uses this knowledge politically to analyze and transform the concrete historical conditions that oppress and exploit women.

To advance this position, she must address the postmodern suspicion of totalizing narratives. In the history of feminist struggles, for example, she points out the limitations of both the Enlightenment demand for women's equality with men, which left intact oppressive social structures, and the insistence of radical and cultural feminists that there is a "fundamental difference *between* men and women" (p. 889), thus perpetuating the same binary opposition. Ludic postmodern feminism, she argues, provides a theory of "difference not as an identity but as self-divided, as always split by its other" (p. 892). While this insight can enable us to avoid reproducing oppressive conditions and to articulate a perspective that more fully accounts for the complex interrelationship between human consciousness and social structures, it cannot by itself, fueled as it is by anti-totalizing gestures, ground theory in political practice.

According to Ebert, one deleterious effect of such gestures has been unmitigated attacks on feminist theorists like Nancy Chodorow, Catherine MacKinnon, and Carol Gilligan. What Ebert proposes, alternatively, is to "rewrite" the system of patriarchy with the postmodern understanding that it is "always self-divided, different from itself and multiple; it is traversed by 'differences within,' by *differance*" (p. 899). Specifically, she argues that pluralistic strategies intended to avoid totalizing narratives may in fact overlook the global effects of patriarchy by focusing exclusively on its local manifestations. Thus, she argues, "women in postmodern patriarchal America, Islamic fundamentalist Iran, and feudal Europe share the same collective identity that results from—is an effect of—their shared position within the patriarchal structure of oppression" (p. 901).

Although Ebert's explicit political agenda is persuasive in many respects, Lynn Worsham's (1991) discussion of *ecriture feminine* illuminates another aspect of phallocentrism that can be read as a cautionary footnote to the ways in which feminists like Ebert have used postmodern theory to advance emancipatory projects. Worsham relies on Julia Kristeva's distinction between political and postmodern[23] styles of reading, the one rooted in "the desire to give meaning, to explain, to interpret" (p. 83), and the other a "new language"—*ecriture feminine*—"which arises not from the desire to give meaning but from the desire to go beyond meaning to a topos of pure invention where discourse becomes more radically political to the extent that it approaches the heterogeneous in meaning" (p. 84). This heterogeneity arises from the concept of "writing the body" that French feminism has popularized, for which female sexuality provides a metaphor of the multiplicity and diffusion of meanings as opposed to the male logic of coherency, unity, and singular purpose. Thus *ecriture feminine* becomes "a practice of resistance and an inscription of heterogeneity . . . [that] allows departures, breaks, partings, separations in meaning, the effect of which is to make meaning infinite and, like desire, nontotalizable" (p. 90).

As Worsham points out, the emphasis in composition pedagogy on discourse communities and initiation into academic discourse is antithetical to the goals of *ecriture feminine*, which are to subvert that very same discourse. Despite enthusiastic reviews of French feminism by compositionists—which, according to Worsham, have resulted in neutralizing its radical potential—*ecriture feminine* "cannot be freely imported into the writing classroom alongside academic discourse toward the goal of literacy . . . [which is] itself a regime of meaning to be interrogated regarding its power to recuperate the power of those already in a position to order and give meaning to the social world" (p. 93). Indeed, were *ecriture feminine* to exert its radical potential on writing instruction,

> [i]t would not be entirely inaccurate to say that composition would cease to exist as we know it, and by implication the university, along with its constituent discourses, would come tumbling down. (p. 94)

Rather than a pedagogical practice, a set of strategies, such as the use of experimental texts, an emphasis on voice, or decentering classroom authority, Worsham argues that *ecriture feminine* might be employed to "refashion composition as cultural criticism" (p. 101) that could enable students to "discover ways to make something of what has been made of them; they may begin to discover

---

23. Kristeva's distinctions between "political" and "postmodern" seem here to correspond roughly to Ebert's "resistant" and "ludic" and to Hutcheon's "worldliness" and "parody."

and to invent the 'flavor' of life in a society whose general tendency is toward conformity" (p. 102).

Convergences: Feminism, Postmodernism, and Critical Pedagogy

Both Chris Weedon (1991) and Kathleen Weiler (1991) articulate a politics of education that weaves together feminist and postmodernist theories with critical pedagogy. Weedon inserts postmodern theories of language and subjectivity into her critique of capitalist patriarchy. As an antidote to both liberal and radical feminist theories that essentialize female experience, reducing it to a biological or natural phenomenon, Weedon argues for a "post-structuralist feminist critical practice" that deconstructs the unified subject and the transparency of language, and asserts a connection between language and power (p. 55). Weiler questions the universal goals of both feminist and Freirean pedagogy because they "do not address the specificity of people's lives; they do not directly analyze the contradictions between conflicting oppressed groups or the way in which a single individual can experience oppression in one sphere while being privileged or oppressive in another" (p. 450).

While acknowledging the historical significance in the women's movement of consciousness raising groups, which sought in large part to validate women's experience, Weiler explains that theoretical advances emanated from critiques by women of color and postmodern feminists of "the concept of a universal 'women's experience'" (p. 467). One early expression of this position was the Combahee River Collective's (1992) "A Black Feminist Statement," describing a multilayered oppression in which

> sexual politics under patriarchy is as pervasive in Black women's lives as are the politics of class and race. We also often find it difficult to separate race from class from sex oppression because in our lives they are most often experienced simultaneously. (pp. 134–5)

Audre Lorde (1992), too, points out that "The oppression of women knows no ethnic nor racial boundaries, true, but that does not mean it is identical within those differences" (p. 139).

The convergence of feminist, postmodernist, and critical theories has both led to new insights into sociocultural realities and complicated the horizon of political action. As Michele Wallace (1992) explains in her paper, "Towards a Black Feminist Cultural Criticism," the recent warm public reception of African American women writers like Toni Morrison contrasts sharply with the unchanged "status or condition of black women in general" (p. 662). Thus Wallace recognizes that the black feminist project is "part of the same scheme as that production of knowledge that trivialized the 'silence' of women of color in the first place" and so "needs profound and multiple acts of revision" (p. 662). Concretely, Wallace argues that such revisions must question the disparity between an intellectual elite that is absorbed into the capitalist system of production and dissemination of images and information, on the one hand, and "the world of poverty and despair . . . which cannot 'speak for itself' . . ." (p. 663). The problem of representation then becomes paramount. As Wallace puts it:

> What I am calling into question is the idea that black feminism (or any program) should assume, uncritically, its ability to speak *for* black women, most of whom are poor and "silenced" by inadequate education, health care, housing, and lack of public access. Not because I think that black feminism should have nothing to do with representing the black woman who cannot speak for herself but because the problem of silence, and the shortcomings inherent in any representation of the silenced, need to be acknowledged as a central problematic in an oppositional black feminist process. (p. 663)

The same problem—of asymmetrical power relations, rooted in the politics of class, race, and gender—needs to be addressed in the basic writing class.

A Theory of Basic Writing for the 1990s

The four perspectives reviewed in Chapters 6 and 7—social constructionism, critical pedagogy, postmodernism, and feminist theories—suggest a theory of basic writing for the 1990s, reflective of the sociohistorical conditions we face globally and locally at the turn of the century: economic polarization, social injustice, large-scale immigration, and at least a temporary victory of capitalism over international movements for social change. The BRW program at the University of Pittsburgh inspired discussion and curricular reforms across the country, I believe, because it encompassed some of the most compelling theoretical advances in the field of composition. It combined a postmodern understanding of language as a signifying system with the insights of composition researchers into the writing process and those of reading theorists into the interrelationship between reading and writing. To see writing and reading as reciprocal and recursive, as part of a continual flow of meaning rather than defined by discrete skills, challenged the most basic assumptions of a type of remedial composition instruction that privileged correctness over meaning, divorced reading from writing, and concentrated on rote exercises. Instead of trying to simplify complex acts of interpretation for weak readers and writers, Pittsburgh teachers understood that for students to participate in academic discourse, they would simply have to begin—to read, write, discuss, debate, meaningfully and bravely.

However, the Pittsburgh curriculum as described in *Facts, Artifacts, and Counterfacts* overlooks serious issues of representation, power, and sociolinguistic and cultural identity within the academy. The politics of race, class, and gender remain marginal at best to the central concerns of Bartholomae and Petrosky, who tend to flatten or universalize the basic writing student, and imply that the process of accommodation to mainstream culture in BRW programs is inevitable and desirable. The underlying assumptions are that academic discourse is neutral and students rather than the academy must change. This perspective ignores the modern university's role in reproducing knowledge and the institutions, including itself, that create, use, and disseminate it. For a deeper understanding of how this happens, we can turn to social construction theory and critical pedagogy. Social construction theorists explain how knowledge (including, for example, class prejudice or racist beliefs) is produced, legitimized, internalized, and reproduced. Critical pedagogy theorists, similarly, explain the processes of social reproduction and resistance as a dialectic between individual consciousness and social systems that suggests a "language of possibility," a way to denaturalize, critique, and resist oppressive conditions.

Feminist theorists have contributed immensely to our understanding of the construction of social identity. Because of the social, political, and psychological oppression that historically defines female identity in opposition to male identity, feminists have been particularly interested in the question of difference. Coinciding with the "linguistic turn" of the French semioticians, feminist theorists of difference appropriated a postmodern view of language as a relational symbolic system to develop a theory of identity as socially constructed rather than biologically or naturally determined. This move, in turn, has produced an important debate between essentialist and constructionist thinkers, illuminating the social process by which, for example, the belief that women are connected, caring, and nurturing, while men are detached and autonomous, constructs gender in stereotypical terms and undermines liberation.

A postmodern knowledge of how language mediates reality can be used politically to analyze and transform the historical conditions that oppress women, people of color, and the working poor, and that also produced the category of basic writing instruction and large groups of students who have not developed adequate reading and writing skills. These discussions of the constructedness of identity and the problems of essentialism are important to the development of a theory of basic writing that goes beyond the Pittsburgh curriculum, takes up the politics of race, class, and gender, and reflexively critiques the institutions to which we belong.

Let me conclude by outlining some of the principles that such a theory of basic writing might include:

- *A postmodern philosophy of discourse.* Language mediates reality; it is relational, based in difference, constructed, not given or essential. Language is heteroglot, historical, decentralized, ideological; diverse social languages coexist and compete; language is inherently dialogical, doubly accented in its orientation to an "other" and a subject. As a semiotic system, invested in power and knowledge, language authorizes or prohibits speech in a process marked by struggle and conflict. The transformation of externally authoritative speech into internally persuasive speech is central to the education of all students, but particularly those who enter college as basic readers and writers.

- *A social theory that illuminates the dialectic between individual consciousness and social structures.* Like any writer, basic writers must struggle to articulate a point of view through already existing systems of language, thought, and social organization. But especially for students who have been constructed as "academic outsiders," it is imperative to root basic writing instruction in an understanding of language and other social systems as humanly produced and therefore subject to change.

- *A pedagogy for liberation that recognizes its own capacity to silence voices and advocates "dissensus" but strives, at the same time, for the clearest sociopolitical analysis possible in the struggle for human freedom.* Such a pedagogy will sometimes require what Gayatri Spivak calls "strategic essentialism," a recognition of the politics of race, class, and gender, and of the need to defend the rights of particular oppressed groups in a sociohistorical context while nonetheless continuing to see all social relations and identities as fluid, relational, and multi-voiced.

- *The creation of standards and evaluative criteria that are not viewed as fixed, eternal verities but rather arise out of the concrete social contexts in which we find ourselves.* In addition to opening a discussion with faculty and administrators about standards—a program's goals, expectations, measurements of success—a dialogue with students would ground the development of such criteria in their experience, foster their sense of themselves as agents of their own learning, and create the possibility for a more democratic pedagogy. Such a dialogue would also hopefully encourage students, faculty, and administrators to view the development of critical reading and writing skills as a lifelong intellectual project rather than merely a requirement for the baccalaureate.

Chapter Eight

Conclusion
Basic Writing and the Politics of Articulation

At home, the forecast is disquieting, at least. Some of us have looked into a future and we have seen that the future will not be white, or spoken or written in Standard English. Of course these facts imply that, finally, our domestic demographics and our domestic multihinged realities will soon become more of a micro- cosmic, accurate reflection of the global village just out- side our national boundaries. (1992, p. 94)

June Jordan

The Future of Basic Writing

Like June Jordan's forecast for the country, the future of basic writing probably "will not be white, or spoken or written in Standard English." Situated on the academic margins, basic writing students and their teachers disturb the academic center; they threaten its sta- bility and the certitude of its traditions: the sanctity of the canon, and the rites of acceptance, graduation, promotion, and tenure. More than theoretical speculation, their presence on the margins has shaken up the status quo and forced universities to change, to adapt to the new and different needs of a postmodern global population that has crossed U.S. national borders, as well as class and color lines, and demanded a slice of the proverbial pie. It is in this context of rapidly occurring global change that basic writing assumes a radical character yet reproduces the status quo as colleges reorient themselves to capitalize on emerging new markets.

There is a widespread perception, purveyed by neoconservatives, of these social transformations as the end of Western civilization and the commencement of relativistic, quota-driven, diluted education. This view is usually accompanied by nostalgia for a fictive past of shared values, common interests, and high standards that conveniently erases the legacies of slavery, racism, colonialism, and imperialism, which continue to impoverish and oppress the majority of the world's population. As Jordan puts it in regard to education:

> Higher education has meant higher than most people. The best universities have continued the worst kind of class privilege. They have enshrined tyrannical reflections of Western white male narcissism. These . . . ivory towers . . . have erected themselves stiff and imperturbable above the multimillionfold folk realities of everyday suffering and rage. They even celebrate the height of their distance from such mass disturbances as homelessness and battered wives. Instead, they commit themselves to an exorbitant and sometimes fatal mythology of "pure research" and/or "pure science." (p. 90)

Students at California community colleges, for example, outnumber their counterparts at the University of California campuses by nearly eight to one, yet receive less than half as much state funding per student, per year; moreover, only 4.5 percent of all black high school graduates qualify for admission to the University of California.[24] Since Jordan's gloomy report on these disparities, California's Proposition 187 has denied social, health, and educational services to illegal immigrants. In February of 1995, New York State Governor George Pataki proposed massive budget cuts in public schools and city and state universities, along with the elimination of Higher Education Opportunities Programs and remedial programs like SEEK. Together with massive federal cuts proposed by the Republican majority, these actions constitute a vicious war on the poor.

---

24. According to Jordan, there are 1,277,900 students at California community colleges, 355,166 students at state of California universities, and 161,522 students at University of California campuses. Community college students receive state funding per year per student in the amount of $2,899; California state students get $6,671 and University of California students get $13,260. (p. 96)

On the cultural front, meanwhile, assaults are escalating against the National Endowment for the Humanities, the National Endowment for the Arts, and public radio and television. As former NEH Chairman Lynne Cheney stated in testimony before the House subcommittee that prepares the budget for the endowments, "The humanities—like the arts—have become highly politicized. Many academics and artists now see their purpose not as revealing truth or beauty, but as achieving social and political transformation" (Burd, 1995, p. A22). Thus progressive intellectuals and artists, as well as working-class and working poor immigrants, inner city residents, and the rural and suburban poor, are casualties of the neoconservative "contract *on* America." Hardly hotbeds of radicalism, the humanities and arts organizations have consistently taken progressive stands on social and human rights issues, providing an outlet for oppositional voices in a hostile, reactionary political climate. It is no accident that the right has tried to silence the academic and cultural left at the same time it moves to dismantle entitlement programs for the poor.

Indeed, basic writing, as I have argued throughout this book, is a key site for the theory and practice of what bell hooks, after Freire, calls "education as the practice of freedom." Potentially subversive, transformative, it brings together white and nonwhite working-class students, inner-city youth, immigrants, and progressive faculty to study the "realities of everyday suffering and rage" through themes like identity, environment, work, and popular culture. At its best, basic writing fosters literacy and critical consciousness, produces intellectuals among students *and* teachers, theorizes its own marginal status, and challenges the status quo. Inherently political, it has attracted both liberal reformers with accommodationist perspectives and progressives who believe in restructuring higher education itself, including the practices of increased reliance on part-time faculty and, not too far off, distance learning. This vision of basic writing, though far from representing a consensus, is grounded in recent composition research and theory; ultimately, it enables a collective social critique—a dialogue—that is anathema to Cheney and impossible in most academic programs, where more privileged students and faculty talk mainly to themselves.

Looking Backward: The Construction of Basic Writing

The discursive structures and practices that we call "basic writing" were produced through a historical process that engendered, as most do, multiple definitions and interpretations, and has served several, sometimes conflicting purposes. With the advent of open admissions at CUNY and Mina Shaughnessy's coinage of the term "basic writing," a new dialectic, a new set of contradictions, was set into motion. The large, heterogeneous group of students who entered college under open admissions challenged assumptions about the development of linguistic competence and traditional methods of remedial instruction. As Shaughnessy created a pedagogy based on the logic of error, other SEEK teachers like Adrienne Rich (1979) recorded the intellectual and political ferment in the classroom. As these teachers learned, often for the first time, about African American and other subcultural literatures, they started to question their own assumptions about education, such as the uncritical imposition of standard English and the Western canon on diverse students. The groundwork was laid for a sweeping change in basic writing instruction, but by the mid-1970s, as Rich notes, the "tragic competition for resources" pitted students against one another as budget cuts gutted the program.

Meanwhile, basic writing was becoming institutionalized nationwide with an influx of programs, a separate category at conferences, and the publication of *The Journal of Basic Writing*. Simultaneously, partly in response to the basic writing boom and the need to staff undergraduate courses, composition and rhetoric was emerging as a legitimate field of study within English. As the first generation of composition scholars in the post-open admissions era—many of whom had been trained in literature—rethought issues of error and the relation of reading to writing, the second generation was entering new composition and rhetoric doctoral programs. Particularly with the theory explosion and the cross-disciplinary influence first of the "linguistic turn" and then the "social turn," composition studies seemed inviting: interdisciplinary, innovative, vibrant. At the same time, historically, the Conference on College Composition and Communication was seen as a refuge for teachers who cared about pedagogy. Altogether, these phenomena created a fertile ground for research and scholarship on basic writing.

Research during the 1970s and early '80s reflects the shift to a pedagogy rooted in the writing process movement. Writing protocols and quantitative analysis predominated in investigations of the composing process, often focusing on adult basic writing students. These studies—and cognitive and expressivist rhetorics generally— were later interrogated by social critics who questioned their underlying assumptions and goals. The publication in 1986 of *Facts, Artifacts, and Counterfacts* gave national prominence to the Pittsburgh program's theory and method of basic writing, which reconnects reading with writing, eschews skills-drills, places error in the context of revision and editing, and challenges basic writers

with difficult, thematically linked texts to become theorists themselves, doing the work of the academy, assuming there is no other
entry into academic discourse.

Since then, alternative theories to assimilation and accommodation have emerged based on negotiation, engagement, and transactional, dialogic models of communication. More politically oriented
teachers have connected basic writing with Freire's pedagogy of the
oppressed and Gramsci's notions of cultural hegemony and the
organic intellectual. The relationship between language and culture
has been foregrounded in several ways: the culture of the academy
itself has been scrutinized (see, for example, Villanueva, 1993); a
plethora of multicultural readers has been published that both reflect
and commodify changing perspectives; writing-across-the-curriculum and collaborative learning initiatives have focused attention on
discourse communities; and postmodern theories of the subject have
recast basic writing—once thought of in relation to cognitive
deficiencies and developmental gaps—in terms of social location,
marginality, and difference. These theories have infused the critical
discourse on basic writing, along with others like Bakhtinian dialogics and Mary Louise Pratt's (1995) contact zone. Along similar lines,
autocritical writing by authors like Gloria Anzaldúa and Guillermo
Gómez-Peña theorize cultural borders as sites of struggle and conflict
marked by hybridity and competing discourses.

Basic writing, as it has evolved over the last twenty-five years,
is a complex, multivoiced, contradictory site of education. Its
significance goes beyond the classroom, research into error analysis,
and the problem of illiteracy. Insofar as open admissions students
have also been labeled basic writers, the very presence of basic writing courses and programs on campuses across the country has contributed to changes in higher education. These changes include
challenges to the Western canon, multicultural curriculum reform,
and perhaps most important, stronger affirmative action admissions
and hiring policies. At the same time, the increased need for teachers to staff large basic writing programs has exacerbated the
exploitation of part-time adjuncts, turning them into a permanent
underclass within universities. This phenomenon has in turn abet-
ted the creation of a two-track system in higher education within
institutions between full-time and part-time faculty and between
elite and nonelite schools.

As I have tried to show, the academic margin that basic writing
students and teachers occupy has a geographical and social counterpart. Like the academic border, national and internal borders
have opened up and a process of globalization has begun. Although
it would be difficult to reseal these entry points into higher educa-

tion, they are increasingly vulnerable to attack in the reactionary political climate of the 1990s. As contradictory as basic writing may be, reinscribing the academic margins and segregating students on the basis, usually, of a single placement essay, it continues to provide access to higher education for masses of students. It is their future that is jeopardized by rightwing attacks on open admissions, financial aid, and other entitlement programs, including basic writing. Thus the phenomenon of basic writing is one small aspect of massive social changes taking place on a global scale: it functions as an opening and a barrier, a complex border where social outsiders whose language is often nonstandard threaten insiders who have enjoyed the privileges of the dominant culture and want to keep the borders closed. As Dorothy Allison (1994) puts it:

> The horror of class stratification, racism, and prejudice is that some people begin to believe that the security of their families and communities depends on the oppression of others, that for some to have good lives there must be others whose lives are truncated and brutal. It is a belief that dominates this culture. (p. 35)

Looking Forward: Redrawing the Boundary

The DTU basic reading and writing program combines the University of Pittsburgh model with a more explicitly political perspective, resulting in a theoretical fusion of the Pittsburgh program's postmodern stress on reading and writing as interrelated, reading as a "constructive act," and all readings as partial, with a critique of the dominant culture rooted in feminist and critical educational thought. As this study suggests, basic writing (including site- and student-specific cases) cannot be adequately understood outside a larger historical, sociopolitical, and economic context. Although the DTU program remains contested, as evidenced by the range of teacher perspectives presented in the study, a strong wing of new faculty believe a BRW course in an urban, socially diverse university cannot ignore the politics of race, class, and gender that account for its very existence.

As new BRW programs like DTU's emerge, however, faculty confront the same contradiction that CUNY teachers faced twenty-five years ago between a genuine desire to democratize higher education and adherence to traditional views of language and literature. The assumptions underlying this contradiction are deeply ingrained in commonsense notions about the acquisition of writing skills, specifically, an essentialist view of language in which meaning precedes linguistic form, and an often tacit belief in the superiority of the language and literature of the dominant culture. Such

beliefs conflict with the progressive theories and political perspectives[25] that shaped DTU's program: language is social, diverse, and
contested; literature cannot be understood apart from its sociohistorical contexts; and the politics of identity permeate all social
structures, including the basic writing class.

A widely held goal of basic writing instruction at DTU is to foster critical consciousness of language and society rather than merely
acculturate or accommodate students to the dominant culture. A
frequent objection to this pedagogy in the 1990s is that students
want to assimilate into mainstream culture and conform to the standards it sets. However, those who view basic writing as an imposition on students would do well to remember the role of politically
active students, particularly at CUNY in the 1960s and '70s, who
fought for open admissions. The demands and actions of students
then, and their sheer diversity today, defy both rightwing and leftwing portraits of basic writers as passive consumers of mass education who fail to become literate despite the heroic efforts of individual teachers and institutional curricular reforms.

To argue that remedial education should take place in the high
schools, the elementary schools, the community colleges, or some
other intermediate level, is meaningless without real change in
those locations. To their credit, many composition theorists and
teachers have become active in high school and community literacy
programs; they have also transformed basic writing from a course
that focused on error and deficiency to one that assumes verbal and
cognitive skills in nontraditional college students and offers them a
challenging, thematically-driven reading and writing seminar.
Although the pedagogy can and *does* "cross tracks" and disciplines,
enriching the college curriculum in general, many of the students
will not. If they do, their academic survival will be severely jeopardized by inadequate instruction and support services as well as
increased tuition and what I believe will be an increasingly hostile
environment for us all.

While some basic writing students will go on to become the next
generation of novelists, Ph.D.s, and English professors, the majority
will not produce rhetorically sophisticated, error-free academic
writing by the time they graduate, let alone in fourteen weeks. To
exclude them from higher education on the basis of weak writing
skills is to sever ties to a generation who can benefit from more
schooling in numerous ways, make substantial progress as readers
and writers, and contribute their own knowledge and experience to
universities. On the other hand, to view basic writing as simply

---

25. As I have discussed elsewhere, these views correspond closely to what various
theorists have termed "resistant postmodernism."

"different" from more skilled writing, or as a product of particular cultural experiences, is to confuse unconventionality with error and to misrepresent the struggle to make meaning *within* systems of language, a struggle that never takes place in a vacuum.

To sanction "low standards" is not the same as advocating for students located on the margins of society. Basic writing students deserve to be as skilled as their mainstream counterparts; skill and rhetorical gesture, though certainly intertwined, are not the same. A high standard need not debilitate basic writing programs nor eliminate basic writing students from the university. Merely to accept existing, tacit, often vaguely defined standards, on the other hand, is to accept the inevitability of institutional authority. That is precisely why programs like DTU's need to develop and adopt evaluative criteria based on local conditions and new assessment tools like portfolio grading. Those that do not are likely to encounter a contradiction between forms of assessment and methods of instruction; those that do begin to counter official standards with more meaningful local articulations of goals and objectives.

A commitment to a democratic decision-making process could become the basis for a university-wide discussion of standards and assessment involving both faculty and students. It would be particularly useful, though not easy, to start a dialogue with basic writing students themselves about evaluative criteria and educational objectives. Teachers may consciously and unconsciously resist student participation, while students may feel uncomfortable discussing their own performance. Nevertheless, a democratic process can be initiated by arguing that evaluation is intertwined with the politics of language and culture, not superordinate to them, and raises key questions about dialect, cultural dominance, and the relationship between power and knowledge. Such a critique of essentialist views of language could be accompanied by critiques of essentialist views of culture and the promotion of a deeper understanding of phenomena like "race" as social constructs. Although local criteria might closely resemble evaluative language already familiar to many writing teachers—say, fluency, clarity, reasonable correctness—the "standard" as diverse, heteroglot, and ideological would require us to rethink what "clarity" and "correctness" mean. In other words, standards are social constructs and evaluative criteria need to be negotiated within individual writing programs based on specific contexts and conditions.

To redraw the boundaries of basic writing in the context of current political and economic realities would mean: 1) continuing to build innovative, challenging curricula that reunite reading and writing, emphasize revision as a process of shaping content into form, and pose genuine intellectual problems; 2) restructuring basic writing courses to provide more contact hours and opportunities for extracurricular activities; 3) restructuring writing programs generally (as well as, eventually, liberal arts courses across the disciplines) from the perspective of the margins, that is, altering mainstream academic studies through a reflexive critique of thematic subject matter and the integration of writing with reading; 4) creating forms of assessment that reflect local conditions and self-consciously shift the emphasis from institutional standards to student need; 5) maintaining and expanding the opportunities for higher education provided to masses of students by open admissions and basic writing in a period of economic and political contraction; and 6) developing a politics of articulation that liberates the voices of students and teachers on the academic margins and begins to publish and circulate their points of view.

A Politics of Articulation

Like the history of basic writing in general, its construction at DTU has been a multivoiced and contradictory process. There are, however, conditions at DTU that allowed for certain types of curricular change as well as a particular kind of conversation about basic writing. DTU is a medium-sized, private, urban university, with a multicultural, working-class student population whose literacy skills reflect a deteriorating public school system, particularly in the inner city, and extremely diverse educational experiences outside the States. At the same time, DTU students reflect the cosmopolitan, savvy, sophisticated culture of urban life. They frequently lead triple lives of work, family, and school, and bring to the university extraordinarily rich experiences and observations. Although the campus was on the verge of collapse in the mid-1980s, a resurgence had occurred by 1990 under the direction of a sympathetic new provost. As enrollment increased, full-time faculty lines opened up across the disciplines, especially in English, which had implemented the BRW-1/2 program in the fall of 1990.

The new BRW-1/2 courses radically restructured the English Department by combining three credits of a developmental reading skills course that had been offered outside the department and three credits of the existing basic writing course to form a two-semester sequence of twelve credits. In addition, students who placed into BRW-1 took a four-hour workshop the first semester, followed by a two-hour workshop attached to BRW-2 the second semester, making a total of eighteen contact hours between the classes and the workshops. Consequently, the part-time adjunct population tripled, creating a three-to-two ratio of part-time to full-time faculty, while additional staff—novice teachers or graduate students who used the experience as a stepping-stone—were hired to teach workshops. By the time this study was completed, half a dozen new full-time writing specialists had been hired as well, and a greater sense of community (as well as more exploitation of part-time workers) had developed in the department as a whole.

So situated, DTU basic writing classes have the potential to engender a "politics of articulation" (Hall, 1986), a social space that gives voice to those who have been historically silenced and authorizes them to speak for themselves. Their testimony—what Pratt calls "autoethnography"—is important not only as part of an effort to diversify the curriculum or recognize the multicultural mix of the classroom, but also as new knowledge, with liberatory potential, counternarratives to the dominant culture's account of life at the turn of the century. Such students might become what Antonio Gramsci termed "organic intellectuals" who "could bridge the gap between academic institutions and the specific issues and workings of everyday life" (Giroux, 1988, p. 159). Teachers and students on the borders of the academy might then begin to generate a "language of possibility," reflective of their needs and interests.

This process of articulation could be seen in an evening class I taught in the spring of 1994, in which students bonded together in a testament to the importance of BRW-1's ten hours a week of contact. Mostly Caribbean, older, several with children in college, they exuded a warmth that made me feel, as their teacher, a privileged outsider welcomed into the community they created. The spirit of collective good will and caring for each other was epitomized by the response to one student who was repeating the course and had entered the class with a smug attitude, affected diction, and contentious but unfocused opinions. In her previous class, students had made fun of her, but in this one, they interpreted her behavior as defensive rather than hostile. Through their acceptance—-by no means uncritical—she became more integrated into the class, focused in her observations, and receptive to other points of view.

The theme of identity had been defined by bicultural stories like Judith Cofer's *Silent Dancing* and Michelle Cliff's account of her experience as a light-skinned, upper-class Jamaican lesbian alienated from her own language and culture by her U.S. and British education. Both pieces of writing became touchstones for students who identified with the authors. A male student from Jamaica, for example, with strong nationalist sentiments spoke stiffly, if at all, early in the semester. Tense, moody, apparently irritated by class discussions, he would occasionally smile skeptically to himself, as if noting the futility of a verbal response. His writing had depth and sophistication, and after he began leaving margins, his sentences cohered instead of literally spilling off the page. As he gained confidence in communicating his point of view in writing, he became more relaxed in class. Cliff's essay provoked a series of reflections about skin color in Jamaica and the U.S. that led him to question some of his assumptions about racism, privilege, and their origins. Eventually he explained he had believed it impossible to discuss cultural differences or social inequality because he saw them as predetermined, locking us intractably into positions based on race, class, and other cultural markers.

In the spring of 1995, four of the students—Esmie, Veronica, Sherina, and Selwyn—agreed to participate in a conference on basic writing at the University of Pittsburgh. Together we read David Bartholomae's article, "The Tidy House," and discussed the current debates about basic writing. We met every few weeks to talk about ideas for papers and, as the conference date approached, we regularly shut down the building on Thursday nights. In her paper, "The Fear of Speaking Out," Esmie describes her struggle to overcome her silence, learned as a girl in Jamaica, where women were supposed to be seen, not heard. A returning student who had always been busy taking care of others, including her now teenaged children, Esmie had never had the opportunity to attend college and almost had to drop out her first semester for financial reasons. She was both intimidated and captivated by her courses, eager to learn, excited by the books and ideas she encountered, and increasingly frustrated by her inability to participate in class discussions. What had changed was her consciousness of her need to speak and the reasons for her silence; the conference paper became a means of transforming herself through articulating her desire.

Sherina writes about how important it was to her to learn grammar in BRW-1, having grown up in Trinidad where she spoke "broken English" at home and proper English at school. At first, her paper uncritically stressed the value of grammar instruction in BRW-1, but, as the group discussed it, another dimension emerged: at home in Trinidad, students' writing was judged by its content rather than grammatical correctness and her diction was unremarkable; but in the States, coworkers criticized how she spoke and she felt degraded by her accent. In "The Extractive Student: Mining the University," Selwyn recounts that he did not pass the island-wide exhibition exam in Trinidad at age eleven. Rather than attend secondary school, he went to the library where he read Shakespeare, James Baldwin, Erich Fromm, and Dr. Eric Williams. As he writes, "My interests and curiosity provided my syllabus." Alluding to Freire, whom Selwyn had read in a freshman composition class in the fall, he compares his experience as "the extractive student" to that of his peers, who were "victims of the 'banking concept of education.'" As for himself, he notes, "the slots the qualifieds were headed for all seemed to have conformity and deference as their foremost requirement."

Although Esmie's topic was fear of speaking, it was Veronica whose face turned pale and lips quivered as she read her first draft aloud to our small group. She confessed she had "pins and needles and butterflies sticking out all over" and could not sleep at night she was so nervous. So it was especially gratifying when she came up with half her title, "People as Ants." After we had tossed around some ideas based on what she had written so far, Selwyn suggested the subtitle, "The Intellectual Basic Writer." Having drawn a distinction between "basic writers" who simplify language and "intellectual writers" who use language complexly, Veronica struggled to put into words her desire to be an intellectual writer like Annie Dillard, whom she had just struggled to read in BRW-2. After she finished reading her revised paper aloud, the rest of us applauded. But it was only after a larger group of faculty and students met in preparation for the conference that Veronica felt truly motivated—empowered—to read her paper as a response to one person's view, with which she sharply disagreed, of basic writing as "coddling" students and giving them false hopes.

Toward Cultural Studies

As may be obvious to some readers, my account of the history, theory, practice, and politics of basic writing is congruent with many aspects of the burgeoning field of cultural studies. Like Bakhtinian dialogics, the perspectives of cultural studies enable a deeper analysis of the social and discursive structures and practices through which basic writers and their teachers are constituted. Cultural studies, according to Stuart Hall, is itself "a discursive formation" composed of "multiple discourses" and "different histories." Its roots in the early British adult education movement and the New Left make it particularly appealing to those of us trying to work out similar pedagogical and political problems today. James Berlin and Michael Vivion's (1992) *Cultural Studies in the English Classroom* indicates the widespread influence cultural studies has already had on teachers of literature and composition. My purpose here is to outline its relevance for basic writing and raise some questions for further research and curricular reform.

Providing a useful narrative of the evolution of cultural studies, Hall's (1992a) review of its theoretical legacies starts with the New Left's response to Marxism at the historical juncture of 1956 and the Soviet invasion of Hungary. It was out of this conjuncture and a critique of Marxism that the Birmingham Centre for Cultural Studies emerged. While Hall and his colleagues criticized Marxism, they were profoundly influenced by the questions it "put on the agenda: the power, the global reach and history-making capacities of capital; the question of class; [and] the complex relationships between power . . . and exploitation . . ." (p. 279). Their critique was of the reductionism, economism, and Eurocentrism of Marxist thought. Filling this theoretical void, Gramsci's theories of hegemony and the organic intellectual "displaced" Marxism to provide a more complex analysis of social relations. Most crucial to cultural studies was the idea that organic intellectuals had both to be at the forefront of intellectual work, competing with traditional intellectuals who represented the interests of the dominant culture, and to transmit knowledge to those outside the intelligentsia who could represent the interests of their (subordinate) class.[26]

The other two major turns in cultural studies, according to Hall, were feminism and the politics of race. Feminist theory raised questions about subjectivity, power, gender and sexuality, and the relationship between social theory and psychoanalysis. Questions of race and cultural politics probed the impact of the decolonization of the third world and the civil rights and black struggles of the black diaspora. Finally, the "linguistic turn" and the explosion of semiotic, structuralist, and poststructuralist theories created a new set of questions about discursivity, textuality, and the problem of representation. These four strands of cultural studies—social theory, feminist theory, questions of race, and semiotics—have strongly influenced the direction of a progressive movement within composition studies.

Berlin and Vivion acknowledge the influence of the Birmingham Centre and suggest the role of cultural studies in the classroom:

> The classroom is a proving ground for a reformulation of the relationship between theory and practice, the two interacting dialecti-

---

26. As Hall cautions, the project of producing organic intellectuals can be misconstrued as a vulgar reduction of complex pedagogical and political issues: "The problem about the concept of an organic intellectual is that it appears to align intellectuals with an emerging historic movement and we couldn't tell then, and can hardly tell now, where that emerging movement was to be found. We were organic intellectuals without any organic point of reference" (281). Thus I do not mean to imply that basic writing provides such a point of reference; but I do believe that conceiving of basic writing along these lines creates a discursive opening for students and teachers.

cally in constant revision of each other. This relationship, furthermore, is inherently political. It is in the texts of culture, as broadly
conceived here, that the ideological battles of the historical
moment are fought. . . . English teachers are engaged in a cultural
politics in which the power of students as citizens in the democratic public sphere is at stake. The aim is to make them subjects
rather than the objects of historical change. Both teachers and students then will engage in critique, in a critical examination of the
economic, social, and political conditions within which the signifying practices of culture take place. (p. xii)

A general impulse in recent composition pedagogy has been to
revalue student writing and call attention to the composing process,
a tendency that lends itself to cultural studies' interest in the production and reception of texts and discourses. In the basic writing
class, where superficial aspects of the written code like punctuation
and spelling often violate the rules of standard written English, the
social contexts of writing are obvious, bound up in the meaning of
the surface structures themselves, which signify error, dialect—
often Black English—a second language, a restricted linguistic code,
and so on. In mainstream writing classes, on the other hand, student
writing can seem transparent, unmarked, and so tends more easily
to reproduce the ideology of the dominant culture. Cultural studies
in basic writing would do two things: make available a critique of
the dominant culture and mass education, and open a space for critical writing, autoethnography, and testimony of students from subordinate social groups.

Cultural studies offers a basis for what Sandra Bennett called a
"two-way flow" between student and teacher, and it creates the
"bridge" between theory and everyday life that Anna Tremont
needed as a graduate student to understand deconstruction. In its
embrace of semiotics, cultural studies recognizes the multiplicity
and diffusion of meanings, the struggle for control of language and
representation, and the conflict between theoretical and political
questions. As Hall suggests, the conflict between the intellectual
work of cultural studies and its political interventions is "what
defines cultural studies as a project" in that it "holds theoretical and
political questions in an ever irresolvable but permanent tension . . .
without insisting on some final theoretical closure" (p. 284). In basic
writing classes, it would enable a critical analysis of texts and contexts and provide teachers and students a means of reading the cultural discourses in which texts are embedded as well as the texts
themselves. This type of reading would facilitate a response to student texts as traces of discourses, linked to complex social structures
and practices, rather than isolated products of individual writers.

Cultural studies enables an alternative view of culture, neither as the province of the elite and a body of canonical works, nor as mass consumerism and commodification, but as a contest, often evasively waged, between subordinate and dominant cultures. For basic writing students and teachers, it would introduce a theoretical framework for understanding the dialectic between social structures and individual consciousness. The metaphor of reading would enable students to grasp the different subject positions available to them of accommodation, negotiation, and resistance. Situated on the academic margins, basic writing students and teachers could challenge dominant cultural assumptions of hierarchy, mastery, and class mobility. Rather than view the margin as a site of deprivation, it could become a site of resistance to oppressive conditions like high-interest government loans, part-time employment, racism, class prejudice, linguistic chauvinism, and other forms of discrimination. As Hall says, "we cannot forget how cultural life, above all in the West, but elsewhere as well, has been transformed in our lifetimes by the voicing of the margins" (1992b, p. 23).

Whatever else can be said about basic writing, it seems safe to predict it will not be a permanent fixture of education, at least by name. However, the role it has played in the transformation of higher education over the last twenty-five years cannot be underestimated. At this moment of reactionary attacks on entitlement programs, basic writing's strategic value seems to outweigh legitimate objections to its complicity in sorting students out according to class, race, and language background. As part of an effort to reconfigure higher education on a more egalitarian basis within and between institutions, it may be advantageous for several reasons to *choose* to locate ourselves on the margins as basic writing teachers and researchers.

For one, the borders between inner-city and immigrant communities and universities, multilingual and heterogeneous, are key sites for the sort of pedagogical project imagined by cultural studies, as well as the most interesting work in basic writing and composition. Second, the margin will not vanish simply because we evacuate. A worst-case scenario would be the elimination of entitlement programs and basic writing courses, which would close universities to students who failed to meet admissions requirements and vastly reduce the number of part-time teachers. While the latter would be welcome under other circumstances, the very dependence of basic writing on adjunct labor underscores the contradiction of a system that gives low priority to nonelite students. Third, the problem of illiteracy remains deeply embedded in social structures that admittedly cannot be changed in the realm of schooling alone but nonetheless need to be addressed within institutions of higher learning. Finally, it seems to me that basic writing gave rise to a progressive pedagogy of reading and writing, relatively free of the stigma of remediation, which has opened the academic border to diverse students who are reshaping American universities.

Appendix A:
Teacher Interview Questions

I. Intertextual dialogue.
   1. Please choose three of the student's papers on the basis of which ones interest, satisfy, or trouble you the most. (If teacher fails to choose at least one of the same papers selected by the student, I will ask her/him to choose from the student's selections.)
   2. Read each paper aloud. As you read, please stop and comment on the writing.
   3. Please tell me why you chose these three papers.

II. Perceptions of the student.
   1. What did you notice about the experience of commenting aloud on the student's writing?
   2. How would you describe the student's class?
   3. How would you describe the student as a writer? A reader?
   4. How would you describe her/his writing?
   5. Can you account for the quality of the student's writing?
   6. What grades did she/he receive? Did she/he pass the exit exam?
   7. What were your goals with this student? What are your goals generally with your students?

III. Role as a writing teacher.
   1. What is your experience as a writing teacher?
   2. How would you describe your theory of teaching writing? [follow-up: Are there any theorists with whom you identify?]
   3. What is your experience teaching basic writing?
   4. How would you describe your theory of teaching basic writing? [follow-up: Are there any theorists with whom you identify?]

IV. Authority relationships and communication system.
  1. What is the relationship between you and the students you teach?
  2. What power do teachers have in shaping students' writing?
  3. What is the relationship between you and the college where you teach?
  4. What power does the college have in shaping students' writing?

V. Role as a writer.
  1. Please describe your family background.
  2. As a child, what did you want to be, at various ages, when you grew up?
  3. What is your own reading/writing experience starting with early childhood?
  4. Please describe your educational experience through high school.
  5. Please describe your post-high school educational experience.
  6. Do you identify yourself as a writer? If so, at what point did you begin to do so? If not, why not?
  7. What does "being a writer" mean to you?
  8. What does "learning to write" mean to you?
  9. Do you identify yourself as a [writing] teacher? If so, at what point did you begin to do so? If not, why not?
  10. What does "being a [writing] teacher" mean to you?

Appendix B:
Student Interview Questions

I. Intertextual dialogue.
1. Please choose three of your papers on the basis of which ones interest, satisfy, or trouble you the most.
2. Read each paper aloud. As you read, please stop and comment on the writing.
3. Please tell me why you chose these three papers.

II. Family background.
1. What can you tell me about your family's history? [follow-up: parents' level of education; occupations; number of children in family]
2. How would you describe your family's values and beliefs? [follow-up: Give examples such as: Was your family religious? Were family members involved in politics?]

III. Educational experience.
1. What are your earliest memories of reading/writing/talking/listening?
2. Please describe your educational experience through high school. What was your attitude toward school?
3. Please describe your educational experience since high school. What is your attitude now toward school?

IV. Work experience and goals.
1. What type(s) of work have you done? Are you currently employed? If so, doing what?
2. What are your goals? What obstacles have you encountered? Outside of work, what do you want to do with your life?
3. At various stages as a child, what did you want to be when you grew up?

V. Role as student and writer.
1. How would you describe yourself as a student?
2. How would you describe yourself as a writer?
3. How would you describe your writing?
4. What were your goals in BRW-1/2? To what extent did you accomplish them?
5. What do the words "being a writer" mean to you?
6. What do the words "learning to write" mean to you?
7. What do the words "basic writer" mean to you?

References

Allison, D. 1994. *Skin: Talking about Sex, Class & Literature*. Ithaca, NY: Firebrand Books.

Apple, M. 1990. *Ideology and Curriculum*. 2nd ed. New York: Routledge.

Aronowitz, S. and H. Giroux. 1985. *Education Under Siege*. South Hadley, MA: Bergin and Garvey.

Atlas, J. 1995. "The Counterculture." *New York Times Magazine*. Feb. 12: 32–65.

Bakhtin, M. 1984. *Problems of Dostoevsky's Poetics*. Ed. and trans. C. Emerson. Minneapolis: University of Minnesota Press.

———. 1981. *The Dialogic Imagination*. Ed. M. Holquist. Trans. C. Emerson. Austin: University of Texas Press.

Barthes, R. 1972. *Mythologies*. Trans. A. Lavers. 2nd ed. New York: Hill and Wang.

Bartholomae, D. 1993. "The Tidy House: Basic Writing in the American Curriculum." *Journal of Basic Writing* 12 (1): 4–21.

———. 1988a. "Inventing the University." In *Perspectives on Literacy*, eds. E.R. Kintgen, B.M. Kroll, and M. Rose, 273–85. Carbondale: Southern Illinois University Press.

———. 1988b. "The Study of Error." In *The Writing Teacher's Sourcebook*, eds. G. Tate and E.P.J. Corbett, 303–17. 2nd ed. New York: Oxford University Press.

———. 1987. "Writing on the Margins: The Concept of Literacy in Higher Education." In *A Sourcebook for Basic Writing Teachers*, ed. T. Enos, 66–83. New York: Random House.

Bartholomae, D. and A. Petrosky. 1986. *Facts, Artifacts, and Counterfacts: Theory and Method for a Reading and Writing Course*. Portsmouth, NH: Boynton/Cook.

Bauer, D. 1990. "The Other 'F' Word: The Feminist in the Classroom." *College English* 52 (April): 385–96.

———. 1988. *Feminist Dialogics: A Theory of Failed Community*. Albany: State University of New York Press.

Bauer, D.M. and S.J. McKinstry. 1991. *Feminism, Bakhtin, and the Dialogic*. Albany: State University of New York Press.

Belenky, M.F., B.M. Clinchy, et al. 1986. *Women's Ways of Knowing: The Development of Self, Voice, and Mind*. New York: Basic Books.

Berger, P.L. and T. Luckmann. 1967. *The Social Construction of Reality: A Treatise in the Sociology of Knowledge.* New York: Doubleday and Company.

Berkenkotter, C. 1991. "Paradigm Debates, Turf Wars, and the Conduct of Sociocognitive Inquiry into the Classroom." *College Composition and Communication* 42 (May): 151–69.

Berlin, J. 1988. "Rhetoric and Ideology in the Writing Class." *College English* 50 (Sept.): 477–94.

———. 1987. *Rhetoric and Reality: Writing Instruction in American Colleges, 1900–1985.* Carbondale: Southern Illinois University Press.

Berlin, J. and M.J. Vivion. 1992. *Cultural Studies in the English Classroom.* Portsmouth, NH: Boynton/Cook.

Bialostosky, D.H. 1991. "Liberal Education, Writing, and the Dialogic Self." In *Contending with Words: Composition and Rhetoric in a Postmodern Age*, eds. P. Harkin and J. Schilb, 11–22. New York: The Modern Language Association of America.

Bizzell, P. 1990. "Beyond Anti-Foundationalism to Rhetorical Authority: Problems Defining 'Cultural Literacy.'" *College English* 52 (Oct.): 661–75.

———. 1986. "What Happens When Basic Writers Come to College." *College Composition and Communication* 37 (Oct.): 294–301.

Bogdan, R.C. and S. Knopp Biklen. 1982. *Qualitative Research for Education: An Introduction to Theory and Methods.* Boston: Allyn and Bacon.

Bowles, S. and H. Gintis. 1976. *Schooling in Capitalist America: Educational Reform and the Contradictions of Economic Life.* New York: Basic Books.

Britton, J. 1970. *Language and Learning.* London: Penguin Books.

Brodkey, L. 1992. "On the Subjects of Class and Gender in 'The Literacy Letters.'" In *Becoming Political: Readings and Writings in the Politics of Literacy Education*, ed. P. Shannon, 97–112. Portsmouth, NH: Heinemann.

Brooke, R. 1987. "Lacan, Transference, and Writing Instruction." *College English* 49 (Oct.): 679–91.

———. 1986. "Social Construction, Language, and the Authority of Knowledge: A Bibliographic Essay. *College English* 48 (Dec.): 773–90.

Bruffee, K. 1984. "Peer Tutoring and the 'Conversation of Mankind.'" In *Writing Centers: Theory and Administration*, ed. G.A. Olson. Illinois: NCTE.

Burd, S. 1995. "Cultural Crossfire: Federal Programs for the Arts and Humanities Assaulted in Congress." *The Chronicle of Higher Education.* Feb. 3: A22–3.

Cayton, M.K. 1991. "Writing as Outsiders: Academic Discourse and Marginalized Faculty." *College English* 53 (Oct.): 647–60.

Chodorow, N.J. 1989. *Feminism and Psychoanalytic Theory.* New Haven, CT: Yale University Press.

——. 1978. *The Reproduction of Mothering: Psychoanalysis and the Sociology of Gender.* Berkeley: University of California Press.

Clark, K. and M. Holquist. 1984. *Mikhail Bakhtin.* Cambridge, MA: The Belknap Press of Harvard University Press.

Clark, S. and L. Ede. 1990. "Collaboration, Resistance, and the Teaching of Writing." In *The Right to Literacy*, eds. A.A. Lunsford, H. Moglen, and J. Slevin, 276–85. New York: Modern Language Association of America.

Coles, N. and S.V. Wall. 1987. "Conflict and Power in the Reader-Responses of Adult Basic Writers." *College English* 49 (March): 298–314.

Combahee River Collective. 1992. "A Black Feminist Statement." In *Modern Feminisms: Political, Literary, Cultural*, ed. M. Humm, 133–36. New York: Columbia University Press.

Cooper, M.M. 1989. "Why Are We Talking About Discourse Communities? Or, Foundationalism Rears Its Ugly Head Once More." In *Writing as Social Action*, eds. M.M. Cooper and M. Holzman. Portsmouth, NH: Boynton/Cook.

Cooper, M.M. and M. Holzman. 1989. *Writing as Social Action.* Portsmouth, NH: Boynton/Cook.

Crawford, C. 1993. *Toward a Curriculum of Ancient Egyptian Art for High School Students in Multicultural Studies.* Ann Arbor, MI: University Microfilms.

Crowley, S. 1989. *A Teacher's Introduction to Deconstruction.* Urbana, IL: NCTE.

Davis, R.C. 1987. "Freud's Resistance to Reading and Teaching." *College English* 49 (Oct.): 621–27.

De Lauretis, T., ed. 1986. *Feminist Studies, Critical Studies.* Bloomington: Indiana University Press.

DiPardo, A. 1993. *A Kind of Passport: A Basic Writing Adjunct Program and the Challenge of Diversity.* Urbana, IL: NCTE.

Eagleton, T. 1983. *Literary Theory: An Introduction.* Minneapolis: University of Minnesota Press.

Ebert, T. 1991. "The 'Difference' of Postmodern Feminism." *College English* 53 (Dec.): 886-904.

Elbow, P. 1973. *Writing Without Teachers.* London: Oxford University Press.

Ellison, R. [1947] 1972. *Invisible Man.* New York: Vintage.

Ellsworth, E. 1989. "Why Doesn't This Feel Empowering? Working Through the Repressive Myths of Critical Pedagogy." *Harvard Educational Review* 59 (Aug.): 297–324.

Elsasser, N. and K. Fiore. 1988. "'Strangers No More': A Liberatory Literacy Curriculum." In *Perspectives on Literacy*, eds. E.R. Kintgen, B.M. Kroll and M. Rose, 286–99. Carbondale: Southern Illinois University Press.

Enos, T., ed. 1987. *A Sourcebook for Basic Writing Teachers*. New York: Random House.

Finke, L. 1993. "Knowledge as Bait: Feminism, Voice, and the Pedagogical Unconscious." *College English* 55 (Jan.): 7–27.

Fish, S. 1980. *Is There a Text in This Class? The Authority of Interpretive Communities*. Cambridge, MA: Harvard University Press.

Fisher, B. 1987. "The Heart Has Its Reasons: Feeling, Thinking, and Community-Building in Feminist Education." *Women's Studies Quarterly* XV (3 and 4): 47–57.

Flynn, E.A. 1988. "Composing as a Woman." *College Composition and Communication* 39 (Dec.): 423–35.

Fogarty, J. and S. Robins. 1990. "Beyond Bartholomae and Petrosky: Will It Work for the Rest of Us?" CCCC Workshop Paper.

Foucault, M. 1990. *The History of Sexuality, an Introduction*. Vol. 1. 2nd ed. New York: Vintage.

———. 1979. *Discipline and Punish: The Birth of the Prison*. New York: Vintage.

———. 1972. *The Archaeology of Knowledge and the Discourse on Language*. New York: Pantheon Books.

Freire, P. 1988. *Pedagogy of the Oppressed*. Trans. M. Bergman Ramos. New York: Continuum.

Freire, P. and I. Shor. 1987. *A Pedagogy for Liberation: Dialogues on Transforming Education*. South Hadley, MA: Bergin and Garvey.

Fuss, D., ed. 1991. *Inside/Out: Lesbian Theories, Gay Theories*. New York: Routledge.

Galeano, E. 1988. "In Defense of the Word: Leaving Buenos Aires, June 1976." In *The Graywolf Annual Five: MultiCultural Literacy: Opening the American Mind*, eds. R. Simonson and S. Walker, 113–25. St. Paul, MN: Graywolf Press.

Gilligan, C. 1982. *In a Different Voice: Psychological Theory and Women's Development*. Cambridge, MA: Harvard University Press.

Gilyard, K. 1991. *Voices of the Self: A Study of Language Competence*. Detroit: Wayne State University Press.

Giroux, H. 1988. *Teachers as Intellectuals: Toward a Critical Pedagogy of Learning*. New York: Bergin and Garvey.

Giroux, H.A. and P.L. McLaren. 1991. "Radical Pedagogy as Cultural Politics: Beyond the Discourse of Critique and Anti-Utopianism." In *Theory/ Pedagogy/Politics: Texts for Change*, eds. D. Morton and M. Zavarzadeh, 152–86. Urbana: University of Illinois Press.

Goleman, J. 1986. "The Dialogic Imagination: More Than We've Been Taught." In *Only Connect: Uniting Reading and Writing*, ed. T. Newkirk, 131–42. Upper Montclair, NJ: Boynton/Cook.

Gramsci, A. 1971. *Selections from the Prison Notebooks*. Ed. and trans. Q. Hoare and G.N. Smith. New York: International Publishers.

Grene, M. 1974. *The Knower and the Known*. Berkeley: University of California Press.

Hairston, M. 1982. "The Winds of Change: Thomas Kuhn and the Revolution in the Teaching of Writing." *College Composition and Communication* 33: 272–82.

Hall, S. 1992a. "Cultural Studies and Its Theoretical Legacies." In *Cultural Studies*, eds. L. Grossberg, C. Nelson, and P. Treichler, 277–94. New York: Routledge.

———. 1992b. "What Is This 'Black' in Black Popular Culture?" In *Black Popular Culture*, ed. M. Wallace, 21–33. Seattle: Bay Press.

———. 1986. "On Postmodernism and Articulation: An Interview with Stuart Hall." Ed. L. Grossberg. *Journal of Communication Inquiry* 10: 45–60.

Halsted, I. 1975. "Putting Error in Its Place." *Journal of Basic Writing* 1 (1): 72–86.

Haraway, D. 1992. "The Promises of Monsters: A Regenerative Politics for Inappropriate/d Others." In *Cultural Studies*, eds. L. Grossberg, C. Nelson, and P. Treichler, 295–337. New York: Routledge.

Harrington, M. [1962] 1981. *The Other America: Poverty in the United States*. Reprinted. New York: Penguin Books.

Harris, J. 1989. "The Idea of Community in the Study of Writing." *College Composition and Communication* 40 (Feb.): 11–22.

Hartsock, N. 1987. "Rethinking Modernism: Minority vs. Majority Theories." *Cultural Critique* (Fall): 187–206.

Hawkes, T. 1977. *Structuralism and Semiotics*. Berkeley: University of California Press.

Heath, S.B. 1983. *Ways with Words: Language, Life, and Work in Communities and Classrooms*. Cambridge, MA: Cambridge University Press.

Henning, B. 1991. "The World Was Stone Cold: Basic Writing in an Urban University." *College English* 53 (Oct.): 674–85.

Herzberg, B. 1991. "Michel Foucault's Rhetorical Theory." In *Contending with Words: Composition and Rhetoric in a Postmodern Age*, eds. P.

Harkin and J. Schilb, 69–81. New York: The Modern Language Association of America.

Hirsch, E.D., Jr. 1988. *Cultural Literacy: What Every American Needs to Know*. New York: Vintage Books.

Hodge, R. and G. Kress. 1988. *Social Semiotics*. Ithaca, NY: Cornell University.

Holquist, M. 1990. *Dialogism: Bakhtin and His World*. London: Routledge.

Holzman, M. 1988. "A Post-Freirean Model for Adult Literacy Education." *College English* 50 (2): 177–89.

hooks, b. 1990. *Yearning: Race, Gender, and Cultural Politics*. Boston, MA: South End Press.

Horning, A.S. 1987. *Teaching Writing as a Second Language*. Carbondale: Southern Illinois University Press.

Hull, G., M. Rose, K.L. Fraser, and M. Castellano. 1991. "Remediation as Social Construct: Perspectives from an Analysis of Classroom Discourse." *College Composition and Communication* 42 (3): 299–329.

Hunter, P. 1992. "'Waiting for Aristotle' in the Basic Writing Movement." *College English* 54 (Dec.): 914–27.

Hutcheon, L. 1989. *The Politics of Postmodernism*. London: Routledge.

Jay, G.S. 1987. "The Subject of Pedagogy: Lessons in Psychoanalysis and Politics." *College English* 49 (Nov.): 785–800.

Johnson, T.S. 1986. Comment. *College English* 48 (Jan.): 76.

Jordan, J. 1992. *Technical Difficulties: African-American Notes on the State of the Union*. New York: Pantheon Books.

Kent, T. 1991. "On the Very Idea of a Discourse Community." *College Composition and Communication* 42 (Dec.): 425–45.

Kozol, J. 1991. *Savage Inequalities: Children in America's Schools*. New York: Crown Publishers.

Labov, W. 1972. *Language in the Inner City: Studies in the Black English Vernacular*. Philadelphia: University of Pennsylvania Press.

Lakoff, G. and M. Johnson. 1980. *Metaphors We Live By*. Chicago: The University of Chicago Press.

Lauter, P. 1991. *Canons and Contexts*. New York: Oxford University Press.

Lazere, D. 1992. "Back to Basics: A Force for Oppression or Liberation?" *College English* 54 (Jan.): 7–21.

Lefevre, K.B. 1987. *Invention as a Social Act*. Carbondale: Southern Illinois University Press.

Lorde, A. 1992. "An Open Letter to Mary Daly." In *Modern Feminisms: Political, Literary, Cultural*, ed. Maggie Humm, 137–39. New York: Columbia University Press.

Lu, M. 1993. "The Role of Conflict in Basic Writing." Conference on College Composition and Communication paper.

———. 1992. "Conflict and Struggle in Basic Writing." *College English* 54 (Dec.): 887–913.

———. 1991. "Redefining the Legacy of Mina Shaughnessy: A Critique of the Politics of Linguistic Innocence." *Journal of Basic Writing* 10.1 (Spring): 26–40.

Lubiano, W. 1992. "Multiculturalism: Negotiating Politics and Knowledge." *Concerns*: 11–21.

Lunsford, A. 1978. "What We Know—and Don't Know—about Remedial Writing." *College Composition and Communication* 29 (Feb.): 47–52.

Malinowitz, H. 1995. *Textual Orientations: Lesbian and Gay Students and the Making of Discourse Communities*. Portsmouth, NH: Boynton/Cook.

Mayher, J. 1990. *Uncommon Sense: Theoretical Practice in Language Education*. Portsmouth, NH: Boynton/Cook.

McGee, P. 1987. "Truth and Resistance: Teaching as a Form of Analysis." *College English* 49 (Oct.): 667–78.

Miller, S. 1991. *Textual Carnivals: The Politics of Composition*. Carbondale: Southern Illinois University Press.

———. 1989. *Rescuing the Subject: A Critical Introduction to Rhetoric and the Writer*. Carbondale: Southern Illinois University Press.

Morrison, T. 1992. *Playing in the Dark: Whiteness and the Literary Imagination*. Cambridge, MA: Harvard University Press.

Morson, G.S. and C. Emerson. 1989. *Rethinking Bakhtin: Extensions and Challenges*. Evanston, IL: Northwestern University Press.

Neel, J. 1988. *Plato, Derrida, and Writing*. Carbondale: Southern Illinois University Press.

Neil, A.S. 1960. *Summerhill: A Radical Approach to Education*. New York: Hart.

Nespor, J. and L. Barber. 1991. "The Rhetorical Construction of 'the Teacher.'" *Harvard Educational Review* 61 (Nov.): 417–33.

Ohmann, R. 1993. "English After the USSR." *Radical Teacher* 44 (Winter): 41–46.

———. 1988. "Use Definite, Specific, Concrete Language." In *The Writing Teacher's Sourcebook*, 2nd. ed., eds. G. Tate and E.P.J. Corbett, 353–60. New York: Oxford University Press.

———. 1976. *English in America: A Radical View of the Profession*. New York: Oxford University Press.

Olsen, G.A. and I. Gale, eds. 1991. *(Inter)views: Cross-Disciplinary Perspectives on Rhetoric and Literacy*. Carbondale: Southern Illinois University Press.

Peirce, C.S. 1958. *Charles S. Peirce: Selected Writings.* Ed. P.P. Wiener. New York: Dover Publications.

Perl, S. 1978. "The Composing Processes of Unskilled College Writers." *Research in the Teaching of English* 13: 317–36.

Pratt, M.L. 1995. "Arts of the Contact Zone." In *Reading the Lives of Others: A Sequence for Writers,* eds. D. Bartholomae and A. Petrosky, 179–94. Boston: Bedford Books.

Rich, A. 1986. *Blood, Bread, and Poetry: Selected Prose 1979–1985.* New York: W.W. Norton.

———. 1979. "Teaching Language in Open Admissions." *On Lies, Secrets, and Silence: Selected Prose 1966–1978.* New York: W.W. Norton.

Rodriguez, R. 1983. *Hunger of Memory: The Education of Richard Rodriguez.* New York: Bantam.

Rorty, R. 1979. *Philosophy and the Mirror of Nature.* Princeton, NJ: Princeton University Press.

Rose, M. 1985. "The Language of Exclusion: Writing Instruction at the University." *College English* 47 (April): 341–59.

———. 1989. *Lives on the Boundary.* New York: Penguin Books.

———. 1988. "Remedial Writing Courses: A Critique and a Proposal." In *The Writing Teacher's Sourcebook,* 2nd ed., eds. G. Tate and E.P.J. Corbett, 318–36. New York: Oxford University Press.

Rouse, J. 1979. "The Politics of Composition." *College English* 41 (Sept.): 1–12.

Russell, D.R. 1990. "Writing Across the Curriculum in Historical Perspective: Toward a Social Interpretation." *College English* 52 (Jan.): 52–73.

Salvatori, M. 1987. "Reading and Writing a Text: Correlations Between Reading and Writing Patterns." In *A Sourcebook for Basic Writing Teachers,* ed. T. Enos, 176–86. New York: Random House.

Schiappa, E. 1992. "Response to Thomas Kent, 'On the Very Nature of a Discourse Community.'" *College Composition and Communication* 43 (Dec.): 522–23.

Schuster, C.I. 1985. "Mikhail Bakhtin as Rhetorical Theorist." *College English* 47 (Oct.): 594–607.

Scribner, S. and M. Cole. 1988. "Unpackaging Literacy." In *Perspectives on Literacy,* eds. E.R. Kintgen, B.M. Kroll, and M. Rose, 57–70. Carbondale: Southern Illinois University Press.

Shaughnessy, M. 1988. "Diving In: An Introduction to Basic Writing." *The Writing Teacher's Sourcebook,* 2nd ed., eds. G. Tate and E.P.J. Corbett, 297–302. New York: Oxford University Press.

———. 1977. *Errors and Expectations: A Guide for the Teacher of Basic Writing.* New York: Oxford University Press.

Silverman, K. 1983. *The Subject of Semiotics.* New York: Oxford University Press.

Smitherman, G. 1987. "Toward a National Public Policy on Language." *College English* 49 (Jan.): 29–36.

Sommers, N. 1980. "Revision Strategies of Student Writers and Experienced Adult Writers." *College Composition and Communication* 31 (Dec.): 378–88.

Spellmeyer, K. 1989. "Foucault and the Freshman Writer: Considering the Self in Discourse." *College English* 51 (Nov.): 715–29.

Spivak, G.C. 1987. *In Other Worlds: Essays in Cultural Politics.* New York: Methuen.

Steiner, G. 1975. *After Babel.* New York: Oxford University Press.

Tompkins, J. 1988. "Me and My Shadow." In *Gender and Theory: Dialogues on Feminist Criticism*, ed. Linda Kaufman. Oxford: Blackwell Publications.

Traub. J. 1994. *City on a Hill: Testing the American Dream at City College.* Reading, PA: Addison-Wesley.

Trimbur, John. 1989. "Consensus and Difference in Collaborative Learning." *College English* 51 (Oct.): 602–616.

Villanueva, V. 1993. *Bootstraps: From an American Academic of Color.* Urbana, IL: NCTE.

Vitanza, V.J. 1991. "Three Countertheses: Or, A Critical In(ter)vention into Composition Theories and Pedagogies." In *Contending with Words: Composition and Rhetoric in a Postmodern Age*, eds. P. Harkin and J. Schilb, 139–72. New York: The Modern Language Association of America.

Volosinov, V.N. 1986. *Marxism and the Philosophy of Language.* Cambridge, MA: Harvard University Press.

———. 1976. *Freudianism: A Critical Sketch.* Bloomington: Indiana University Press.

Vygotsky, L. 1978. *Mind in Society: The Development of Higher Psychological Processes.* Eds. M. Cole, et al. Cambridge, MA: Harvard University Press.

Wallace, M. 1992. "Towards a Black Feminist Cultural Criticism." In *Cultural Studies*, eds. L. Grossberg, C. Nelson, and P. Treichler, 654–71. New York: Routledge.

———. 1988. "Invisibility Blues." In *The Graywolf Annual Five: MultiCultural Literacy: Opening the American Mind*, eds. R. Simonson and S. Walker, 161–72. St. Paul, MN: Graywolf Press.

Weedon, C. 1991. "Post-Structuralist Feminist Practice." In *Theory/Pedagogy/ Politics: Texts for Change*, eds. D. Morton and M. Zavarzadeh, 47–63. Urbana: University of Illinois Press.

Weiler, K. 1991. "Freire and a Feminist Pedagogy of Difference." *Harvard Educational Review* 61 (Nov.): 449–74.

———. 1988. *Women Teaching for Change: Gender, Class, and Power.* New York: Bergin and Garvey.

Weiner, H.S. 1986. "Collaborative Learning in the Classroom: A Guide to Evaluation." *College English* 48: 52–61.

West, C. 1992. "The Postmodern Crisis of the Black Intellectuals." In *Cultural Studies*, eds. L. Grossberg, C. Nelson and P. Treichler, 689–705. New York: Routledge.

Williams, P.J. 1991. *The Alchemy of Race and Rights: Diary of a Law Professor.* Cambridge, MA: Harvard University Press.

Worsham, L. 1991. "Writing against Writing: The Predicament of *Ecriture Feminine* in Composition Studies." In *Contending with Words: Composition and Rhetoric in a Postmodern Age*, eds. P. Harkin and J. Schilb, 82–104. New York: The Modern Language Association of America.

Zebroski, J.T. 1989. "A Hero in the Classroom." In *Encountering Student Texts: Interpretive Issues in Reading Student Writing*, eds. B. Lawson, S. Sterr Ryan, and W.R. Winterowd, 35–47. Urbana, IL: NCTE.

Index

Abrams, Meyer, 150
abuse, as theme in student writing, 50–51, 52, 62
academic community. *See also* discourse communities
    dominant culture and, 41–46
    nature of, 150
    outsider status for basic writers in, 39–46
academic language
    acquisition of, 37
    as preferred, 38
academic margins. *See* marginality
academic writing, by marginalized teachers, 30–31
accommodation, education as, 8, 94, 188
acculturation, education as, 8, 188
addressivity, 148, 149
adjunct teachers, xv, 186
adult literacy campaigns, 155. *See also* literacy
African Americans, *See also* minorities; race; racism
    Black English, 28, 99, 195
    black feminism, 177–78
    loss of traditional culture by, 102
    omission of in science fiction, 80, 83–88, 101–02
Alchemy of Race and Rights, The (Williams), 45
Alcoff, Linda, 153
Allison, Dorothy, 10–11, 187
alternate realities, 101–05
answerability, 148
anti-foundationalism, 152
anti-Semitism, as theme in student writing, 113–14
antiwriting, 62, 63, 163
Anzaldúa, Gloria, 8, 186
Apple, Michael, 141–42
Aristotle, 99
Aronowitz, Stanley, 156, 158, 166
articulation, politics of, 191–93
artifacts, 12

arts, funding cuts, 184
authorization for writing, 111, 131–35
autobiographical narratives, 16, 51–64
autoethnography, 191
autonomy, development of, 173

back-to-basics movement, 24–25
Bakhtin, Mikhail, xvii, xviii, xxii–xxiii, 17, 70, 78, 111, 131, 139, 147–50, 162
Bakhtinian dialogics, 147–50, 186, 193
Baldwin, James, 103
banking concept of education, 94, 154–55
Barthes, Roland, xxii
Bartholomae, David, xiv, xix, 12, 13–14, 16, 17, 30, 36, 38–41, 44–45, 46, 130, 167, 179, 192
basic reading courses
    curriculum design, 13–18
    politicizing/historicizing course content, 14
basic writers, *See also* students; writers
    vs. intellectual writers, 193
    outsider status of, 39–46
    in the university, 99–100
basic writing, *See also* writing
    construction of, 184–87
    context of, 82–91, 187, 189–90, 195
    criteria for placement in, 91–92
    cultural studies and, 193–97
    development of, xix–xxi, 186
    funding cuts, 183–84, 187
    future of, x–xii, 182–90
    initiation of, 185
    institutionalization of, 185
    mainstream writing vs., 44–45
    minority group realities in, 8–9
    model programs, 12–13, 187–90
    opposition to, 23
    politics of marginalization and, 10–12
    as practice of freedom, 184
    restructuring, 189–90

213